# Britain's
# Best**Hotels**

**AA**

Advertising Sales:
advertisementsales@theAA.com

Editorial:
lifestyleguides@theAA.com

Assessments of AA inspected establishments are based on the experience of the hotel and restaurant inspectors on the occasion of their visit(s) and therefore descriptions given in this guide necessarily dictate an element of subjective opinion which may not reflect or dictate a reader's own opinion on another occasion. We have tried to ensure accuracy in this guide but things do change and we would be grateful if readers would advise us of any inaccuracies they may encounter.

Typeset by AA Lifestyle Guides

Printed and bound by Graficas Estella, Spain

Editorial contributors: Phil Bryant, Chris Cooper, Penny Phenix and Pam Stagg

Cover credits
Front cover: Headland Hotel, Newquay
Back cover: Royal Garden Hotel, London

A CIP catalogue record for this book is available from the British Library

ISBN-10: 0-7495-5176-6
ISBN-13: 978-0-7495-5176-3

Published by AA Publishing, which is a trading name of Automobile Association Developments Limited, whose registered office is:
Fanum House, Basing View
Basingstoke
Hampshire RG21 4EA
www.theAA.com

Registered number 1878835

A03094

# Britain's
# Best**Hotels**

# Contents

# Welcome

Britain's Best Hotels is a brand new and highly authoritative addition to the Britain's Best series and covers a selection of the very best hotels in England, Scotland, Wales and the Channel Islands.

## A Place to Stay

This guide covers more than 260 town and country houses, small and metro hotels. Every establishment has received a star rating and percentage merit score following a visit by an AA inspector. This will help ensure that you will have a friendly welcome, comfortable surroundings, excellent food and a good service. Further details about the AA scheme, inspections and awards and rating system can be found on pages 10–11 of this guide.

## Before You Travel

Some places may offer special breaks and facilities not available at the time of going to press. If in doubt, it's always worth calling the hotel before you book. See also the useful information provided on pages 8–9.

# Using the guide

Britain's Best Hotels has been designed to enable you to find an establishment quickly and efficiently. Each entry provides clear information about the type of accommodation, the facilities available and the local area.

Use the contents (page 3) to browse the main gazetteer section by county and the index to find either a location (page 304) or a specific hotel (page 309) by name.

**Finding Your Way**

The main section of the guide is divided into four main parts covering England, Channel Islands,

Scotland and Wales. The counties within each of these sections are ordered alphabetically as are the town or village locations (shown in capital letters as part of the address) within each county. Finally, the establishments are listed alphabetically under each location name. Town names featured in the guide can also be located in the map section (page 289).

## The Old Rectory

**★★★  86% ®® HOTEL**

| | |
|---|---|
| **Address:** | Ash Lane, WHITCHURCH, |
| | Salisbury, SA38 2PP |
| **Tel:** | 01963 300123 |
| **Email:** | rectory@hotelgroup.co.uk |
| **Website:** | www.hotelgroup.co.uk/oldroctory |
| **Map ref:** | 3, SZ32 |
| **Directions:** | Next to church at S end of Whitchurch |
| **Rooms:** | 24, S £85–£120, D £95–£120 |

**Facilities:** Gardens Children welcome Outdoor seating
**Parking:** 22 **Notes:** ⌖ ⊕ Free House ♥ 7

Formerly a rectory and now a stylish and sophisticated retreat, perfect for relaxing and recharging your batteries. Beautifully restored, with its character carefully preserved, it features contemporary furnishings that cleverly complements the spacious internal architecture. The award-winning spa has a range of luxurious facilities including a state-of-the-art gym with hydrotherapy pool, sauna, steam room, solarium and a beauty treatment centre. The bedrooms are a treat, comfortably furnished and with stunning views of the Downs. In the restaurant, chef, Andrew Capon, makes good use of local organic produce in a delicious health-conscious menu that will satisfify the heartiest appetite.
**Recommended in the area**
Salisbury Cathedral, New Forest National Park; Stonehenge and Salisbury Plain

**❶ Stars and symbols**

All entries in the guide have been inspected by the AA and, at the time of going to press, belong to the AA hotel scheme. Every establishment in the scheme is classified for quality with a rating of one to five stars (★). Every establishment in Britain's Best Hotels has three, four or five stars and a high merit score (%). The very best hotels in each of these categories have been given red

stars (★). The majority of the establishments in this guide have been rated using the new system of common quality standards which also provides one of six descriptive categories for each hotel: HOTEL, TOWN HOUSE HOTEL, COUNTRY HOUSE HOTEL, SMALL HOTEL, METRO HOTEL and BUDGET HOTEL.

See pages 8–10 for more information on the AA ratings and awards scheme.

**Rosette Awards** ◉**:** This is the AA's food award (see page 11 for further details).

## ➋ Contact Details

The establishment address includes a locator or place name in capitals (e.g. NORWICH). Within each county, entries are ordered alphabetically first by this place name and then by the name of the establishment.

Telephone and fax numbers, and e-mail and website addresses are given where available. See page 8 for information about booking online. The telephone and fax numbers are believed correct at the time of going to press but changes may occur. The latest establishment details are on the Hotel pages at www.theAA.com.

Website addresses have been supplied by the establishments and lead you to websites that are not under the control of Automobile Association Developments Ltd. AADL has no control over and accepts no responsibility or liability in respect of the material on any such websites. By including the addresses of third-party websites AADL does not intend to solicit business.

## ➌ Map reference

The map reference is composed of two parts. The first number shows the atlas map number (from 1–13) at the back of the guide (see page 290 onwards). The second part is a National Grid reference. To find the town or village location one of the maps, locate the lettered square and read the first figure across and the second figure vertically using the gridlines to help guide you. For example, a map reference of '3, TQ28' refers to map 3 in the atlas section, grid square TQ on the map and a location of two across the grid square, running east-west and eight in a north-south direction. The map section of this guide also provides road and county information.

Maps locating each establishment and a route planner are available at www.theAA.com.

## ➍ Directions

Where possible, directions have been given from the nearest motorway or A road. Distances are provided in miles (m) and yards (yds).

## ➎ Room Information

The entries show the number of en suite letting bedrooms available. Bedrooms that have a private bathroom adjacent may be included as en suite. Further details of facilities provided in the rooms are listed in the main entry description (see ➒). Always phone in advance to ensure that the hotel has the facilities you require.

**Prices:** Prices are per room per night (unless otherwise specified) and are provided by the hoteliers in good faith. These prices are indications and not firm quotations. Always check before booking.

## ➏ Facilities

This section lists a selection of facilities offered by the hotel. It includes sports facilities such as indoor and outdoor swimming pools, golf, tennis and gym, options for relaxation such as spa, jacuzzi and solarium, and services such as satellite TV and Wi-fi and Internet accessibility. Use the key to the symbols on page 7 to help identify what's available at a particular hotel.

Additional facilities, such as access for disabled people, or notes about other services may be listed here and it is by no means exhaustive. Some hotels have restricted service during quieter months, and at this time some of the listed facilities will not be available. If unsure, contact the hotel before your visit.

## Payment

As most hotels now accept credit or debit cards we only indicate if an establishment does not accept any cards for payment. Credit cards may be subject to a surcharge – check when booking if this is how you intend to pay. Not all hotels accept travellers' cheques.

## ➐ Parking

This shows the number of parking spaces available. Other types of parking (on road or Park and Ride) may also be possible; check the descriptions for further information. Phone the establishment in advance of your arrival to check.

**➑ Notes**

This section provides details specific details relating to:

**Smoking Policy:** The no smoking symbol by itself indicates a ban on smoking throughout the premises. If the establishment is only partly no smoking, the areas where smoking is not permitted are shown alongside the no smoking symbol.

The Smoking, Health and Social Care (Scotland) Act came into force in March 2006 (clearingtheairscotland.com). The law bans smoking in no-smoking premises in Scotland, which includes guest houses and inns with two or more guest bedrooms. The proprietor can designate one or more bedrooms with ventilation systems where the occupants can smoke, but communal areas must be smoke-free. Communal areas include the interior bars and restaurants in pubs and inns.

Similar laws covering England, Wales and Northern Ireland are due to come into effect during 2007. If the freedom to smoke or to be in a non-smoking atmosphere is important to you, we recommend that you check with the establishment when you book.

**Dogs:** Establishments that state no dogs may accept assist/guide dogs. Some places that do accept dogs may restrict the size and breed of dog and the rooms into which they can be taken.

Always check the conditions of the hotel when making a booking.

**Children:** No children means children cannot be accommodated, or a minimum age may be specified, e.g. No children under 4 means no children under four years old. The main description may also provide details about other facilities available.

Establishments with special facilities for children may include a babysitting service or baby-intercom system, playroom or playground, laundry facilities, drying and ironing facilities, cots, high chairs and special meals. If you have very young children, check before booking.

**Other notes:** Additional facilities, such as access for disabled people, or notes about other services. See the specific entries for details. Always contact the hotel beforehand if you are unsure.

**➒ Description**

This may include specific information about the various facilities offered in the rooms, a brief history of the establishment, notes about special features and descriptions of the food where an award has been given (see ➊ above).

**➓ Recommended in the Area**

This listings gives places of interest, local sights to visit and potential day trips and activities.

# Key to symbols

| | | | | |
|---|---|---|---|---|
| | | Triple | Triple room | |
| | | Family | Family room | |
| ★ | Black stars (see page 10) | ⊗ | No smoking in area indicated | |
| ★ | Red stars (see page 11) | ⊗ | No dogs allowed in area indicated | |
| % | Merit score | ⚲ | Dogs allowed in area indicated | |
| ◎ | AA Rosette (see page 11) | Wi-fi | Wireless network available where | |
| 3, TQ28 | Map reference (see pages 471-485) | | indicated | |
| S | Single room | STV | Satellite television | |
| D | Double room | ⊡ | Indoor swimming pool | |
| T | Twin room | ⌐ | Outdoor swimming pool | |

# Useful Information

If you're unsure about any of the facilities offered, always check with the establishment before you visit or book accommodation. Up-to-date information on contacting all hotels in this guide can be found in the travel section of the www.theAA.com

## Hints on booking your stay

It's always worth booking as early as possible, particularly for the peak holiday period from the beginning of June to the end of September. Bear in mind that Easter and other public holidays may be busy too, and in some parts of Scotland, the ski season is a peak holiday period.

Some hotels will ask for a deposit or full payment in advance, especially for one-night bookings. And some hotels charge half-board (bed, breakfast and dinner) whether you require the meals or not, while others may only accept full-board bookings. Not all hotels will accept advance bookings for bed and breakfast, overnight or short stays. Some will not take reservations from mid week.

Once a booking is confirmed, let the hotel know at once if you are unable to keep your reservation. If the hotel cannot re-let your room you may be liable to pay about two-thirds of the room price (a deposit will count towards this payment). In Britain a legally binding contract is made when you accept an offer of accommodation, either in writing or by telephone, and illness is not accepted as a release from this contract. You are advised to take out insurance against possible cancellation, for example AA Single Trip Insurance or visit www.theAA.com.

## Booking online

Booking a place to stay can be a very time-consuming process, but you can search quickly and easily online for a place that best suits your needs. Simply visit www.theAA.com/hotels to search from around 8,000 quality rated hotels and B&Bs in Great Britain and Ireland. Then either check availability and book online by clicking on the 'Booking' button, or contact the establishment for further information.

## Prices

The AA encourages the use of the Hotel Industry Voluntary Code of Booking Practice, which aims to ensure that guests know how much they will have to pay and what services and facilities are included, before entering a financially binding agreement. If the price has not previously been confirmed in writing, guests should be given a card stipulating the total obligatory charge when they register at reception.

The Tourism (Sleeping Accommodation Price Display) Order of 1977 compels hotels, travel accommodation, guest houses, farmhouses, inns and self-catering accommodation with four or more letting bedrooms, to display in entrance halls the minimum and maximum price for one or two persons but they may vary without warning.

## Facilities for disabled guests

The final stage (Part III) of the Disability Discrimination Act (access to Goods and Services) came into force in October 2004. This means that service providers may have to make permanent adjustments to their premises. For further information, see the government website www.disability.gov.uk/dda.

Please note: AA inspectors are not accredited to make inspections under the National Accessibility Scheme. We indicate in the descriptions if an establishment has ground floor rooms; and if a hotel tells us that they have disabled facilities this is also included in the text.

The establishments in this guide should all be aware of their responsibilities under the Act. We recommend that you always telephone in advance to ensure that the establishment you have chosen has appropriate facilities.

Other useful websites to visit include:
www.holidaycare.org.uk
www.dptac.gov.uk/door-to-door

## Licensing Laws

Licensing laws differ in England, Wales, Scotland, the Republic of Ireland, the Isle of Man, the Isles of Scilly and the Channel Islands. Public houses are generally open from mid morning to early afternoon, and from about 6 or 7pm until 11pm, although closing times may be earlier or later and some pubs are open all afternoon. Unless otherwise stated, establishments listed are licensed. Hotel residents can obtain alcoholic drinks at all times, if the licensee is prepared to serve them. Non-residents eating at the hotel restaurant can have drinks with meals. Children under 14 may be excluded from bars where no food is served. Those under 18 may not purchase or consume alcoholic drinks. Club license means that drinks are served to club members only, 48 hours must lapse between joining and ordering.

## Fire Safety

The Fire Precautions Act does not apply to the Channel Islands, Republic of Ireland, or the Isle of Man, which have their own rules. As far as we are aware, all hotels listed have applied for and not been refused a fire certificate.

### Bank and Public Holidays 2007

| | |
|---|---|
| New Year's Day | 1st January |
| New Year's Holiday | 2nd January (Scotland) |
| Good Friday | 6th April |
| Easter Monday | 9th April |
| May Day Bank Holiday | 7th May |
| Spring Bank Holiday | 28th May |
| August Holiday | 1st August (Scotland) |
| Late Summer Holiday | 27th August |
| Christmas Day | 25th December |
| Boxing Day | 26th December |

# www.theAA.com

Go to www.theAA.com to find more AA listed guest houses, hotels, pubs and restaurants – some 12,000 establishments.

Routes & Traffic on the home page leads to a route planner. Simply enter your postcode and the establishment postcode given in this guide and click Confirm. Check your details and then click GET MY ROUTE and you will have a detailed route plan to take you from door-to-door.

Use the Travel section to search for Hotels & B&Bs or Restaurants & Pubs by location or establishment name. Scroll down the list of finds for the interactive map and local routes.

Postcode searches can also be done on www.ordnancesurvey.co.uk and www.multimap.com, which will also provide useful aerial views of your destination.

# Best Quality

All entries in Britain's Best Hotels have excelled in several categories set by the AA inspection team. Red stars are awarded to the very best establishments in each star category.

**High Standards**

Hotels recognised by the AA should:

- have high standards of cleanliness
- keep proper records of booking
- give prompt and professional service to guests, assist with luggage on request, accept and deliver messages
- provide a designated area for breakfast and dinner, with drinks available in a bar or lounge
- provide an early morning call on request
- have good quality furniture and fittings
- provide adequate heating and lighting
- undertake proper maintenance

The hotels in Britain's Best Hotels all have a three, four or five black or red star rating. The following is brief guide to some of the general expectations for each star classification:

### ★★★ Three Star

- Management and staff smartly and professionally presented and usually wearing a recognisable uniform
- A dedicated receptionist on duty at peak times
- At least one restaurant or dining room open to residents and non-residents for breakfast and dinner whenever the hotel is open
- Last orders for dinner no earlier than 8pm
- Remote-control television, direct-dial phone
- En suite bath or shower and WC

### ★★★★ Four Star

- A formal, professional staffing structure with smartly presented, uniformed staff anticipating and responding to your needs or requests
- Usually spacious, well-appointed public areas
- Reception staffed 24 hours by well-trained staff
- Express checkout facilities where appropriate

- Porterage available on request
- Night porter available
- At least one restaurant open to residents and non-residents for breakfast and dinner seven days per week, and lunch to be available in a designated eating area
- Last orders for dinner no earlier than 9pm
- En suite bath with fixed overhead shower and WC

### ★★★★★ Five Star

- Luxurious accommodation and public areas with a range of extra facilities. First time guests shown to their bedroom
- Multilingual service
- Guest accounts well explained and clearly presented
- Porterage offered
- Guests greeted at hotel entrance, full concierge service provided

- At least one restaurant open to residents and non-residents for all meals seven days per week
- Last orders for dinner no earlier than 10pm
- High-quality menu and wine list
- Evening service to turn down the beds.
- Remote-control television, direct-dial telephone at bedside and desk, a range of luxury toiletries, bath sheets and robes.
- En suite bathroom incorporating fixed overhead shower and WC

★ **Inspectors' Choice**
Each year the AA selects the best hotels in each rating. These hotels stand out as the very best in the British Isles, regardless of style. The selected Inspectors' Choice hotels in the main section of this guide are identified by red stars.

**Types of hotel**
The majority of establishments in this guide come under the category of Hotel; other categories are listed below:

**Town House Hotel:** A small, individual city or town centre property, which provides a high degree or personal service and privacy.

**Country House Hotel:** These are quietly located in a rural area

**Small Hotel:** Has less than 20 bedrooms and is managed by the owner

**Metro Hotel:** A hotel in an urban location that does not offer an evening meal

**Budget Hotel:** These are usually purpose built modern properties offering inexpensive accommodation. Often located near motorways and in town or city centres

A small number of hotels in the guide are not rated because their star classification was not confirmed at the time of going to press. Check the AA website www.theAA.com for current information and ratings.

# AA Rosette Awards

Out of the many thousands of restaurants in the UK, the AA identifies some 1,800 as the best. The following is an outline of what to expect from restaurants with AA Rosette Awards. For a more detailed explanation of Rosette criteria please see www.theAA.com

◉ Excellent local restaurants serving food prepared with care, understanding and skill, using good quality ingredients.

◉ ◉ The best local restaurants, which aim for and achieve higher standards, better consistency and where a greater precision is apparent in the cooking. There will be obvious attention to the selection of quality ingredients.

◉ ◉ ◉ Outstanding restaurants that demand recognition well beyond their local area.

◉ ◉ ◉ ◉ Amongst the very best restaurants in the British Isles, where the cooking demands national recognition.

◉ ◉ ◉ ◉ ◉ The finest restaurants in the British Isles, where the cooking stands comparison with the best in the world.

# Inspectors' Choice
# Red Star Hotels

Assessed and announced annually, the AA's Inspectors' Choice Awards recognise the very best hotels in Britain. These hotels offer consistently outstanding levels of quality, comfort, cleanliness and customer care. Hotels are listed in county order, showing their star classification, rosettes and telephone number.

## ENGLAND

### BERKSHIRE

Maidenhead — **Fredrick's Hotel**
★★★★  ◉◉◉  ☎ 01628 581000

Newbury — **The Vineyard at Stockcross**
★★★★★  ◉◉◉◉  ☎ 01635 528770

### BUCKINGHAMSHIRE

Aylesbury — **Hartwell House**
★★★★  ◉◉◉  ☎ 01296 747444

Taplow — **Cliveden**
★★★★★  ◉◉◉  ☎ 01628 668561

### CHESHIRE

Chester — **The Chester Grosvenor & Spa**
★★★★★  ◉◉◉  ☎ 01244 324024

Sandiway — **Nunsmere Hall**
★★★★  ◉◉  ☎ 01606 889100

### CORNWALL & ISLES OF SCILLY

Bryher — **Hell Bay Hotel**
★★★  ◉◉  ☎ 01720 422947

Fowey — **Marina Hotel**
★★  ◉◉  ☎ 01726 833315

Portscatho — **Driftwood**
★★★  ◉◉◉  ☎ 01872 580644

St Martin's — **St Martin's on the Isle**
★★★  ◉◉◉  ☎ 01720 422090

Tresco — **The Island Hotel**
★★★  ◉◉  ☎ 01720 422883

### CUMBRIA

Brampton — **Farlam Hall Hotel**
★★★  ◉◉  ☎ 016977 46234

Grange-over-Sands — **Clare House**
★  ◉  ☎ 015395 33026

Grasmere — **White Moss House**
★★  ◉  ☎ 015394 35295

Howtown — **Sharrow Bay Country House Hotel**
★★★  ◉◉  ☎ 017684 86301

Keswick — **Swinside Lodge**
★★  ◉◉  ☎ 017687 72948

Watermillock — **Rampsbeck Country House Hotel**
★★★  ◉◉◉  ☎ 017684 86442

Windermere — **Gilpin Lodge Country House Hotel**
★★★★  ◉◉◉  ☎ 015394 88818

Windermere — **Holbeck Ghyll Country House Hotel**
★★★★  ◉◉◉  ☎ 015394 32375

Windermere — **Lindeth Fell Country House Hotel**
★★  ◉  ☎ 015394 43286

Windermere — **Linthwaite House Hotel**
★★★  ◉◉◉  ☎ 015394 88600

Windermere — **Miller Howe***
★★★  ☎ 015394 42536

Windermere — **The Samling**
★★★  ◉◉◉  ☎ 015394 31922

### DERBYSHIRE

Baslow — **Fischer's Baslow Hall**
★★★  ◉◉◉◉  ☎ 01246 583259

## DEVON

| Ashwater | | **Blagdon Manor Hotel &** |
|---|---|---|
| | | **Restaurant** |
| ★★★ | ◉◉ | ☎ 01409 211224 |
| Burrington | | **Northcote Manor** |
| ★★★ | ◉◉ | ☎ 01769 560501 |
| Chagford | | **Gidleigh Park** |
| ★★★ | ◉◉◉◉ | ☎ 01647 432367 |
| Chagford | | **Mill End Hotel** |
| ★★ | ◉◉ | ☎ 01647 432282 |
| Honiton | | **Combe House Hotel &** |
| | | **Restaurant - Gittisham** |
| ★★★ | ◉◉ | ☎ 01404 540400 |
| Kingsbridge | | **Buckland-Tout-Saints** |
| ★★★ | ◉◉ | ☎ 01548 853055 |
| Lewdown | | **Lewtrenchard Manor** |
| ★★★ | ◉◉◉ | ☎ 01566 783256 |
| Torquay | | **Orestone Manor Hotel** |
| ★★★ | ◉◉ | ☎ 01803 328098 |

## DORSET

| Evershot | | **Summer Lodge Country** |
|---|---|---|
| | | **House Hotel** |
| ★★★★ | ◉◉◉ | ☎ 01935 482000 |
| Gillingham | | **Stock Hill Country House** |
| ★★★ | ◉◉◉ | ☎ 01747 823626 |
| Poole | | **Best Western** |
| | | **Mansion House Hotel** |
| ★★★ | ◉◉ | ☎ 01202 685666 |

## CO DURHAM

| Romaldkirk | | **Rose & Crown Hotel** |
|---|---|---|
| ★★ | ◉◉ | ☎ 01833 650213 |
| Seaham | | **Seaham Hall Hotel** |
| ★★★★★ | ◉◉◉ | ☎ 0191 516 1400 |

## ESSEX

| Dedham | | **Maison Talbooth** |
|---|---|---|
| ★★★ | ◉◉ | ☎ 01206 322367 |

## GLOUCESTERSHIRE

| Buckland | | **Buckland Manor** |
|---|---|---|
| ★★★ | ◉◉◉ | ☎ 01386 852626 |
| Cheltenham | | **Hotel on the Park** |
| ★★★ | ◉◉ | ☎ 01242 518898 |
| Chipping Campden | | **Cotswold House** |
| ★★★★ | ◉◉◉ | ☎ 01386 840330 |
| Corse Lawn | | **Corse Lawn House Hotel** |
| ★★★ | ◉◉ | ☎ 01452 780479 |
| Lower Slaughter | | **Lower Slaughter Manor** |
| ★★★ | ◉◉ | ☎ 01451 820456 |

| Tetbury | | **Calcot Manor** |
|---|---|---|
| ★★★★ | ◉◉ | ☎ 01666 890391 |
| Thornbury | | **Thornbury Castle** |
| ★★★ | ◉◉ | ☎ 01454 281182 |
| Upper Slaughter | **Lords of the Manor** | |
| ★★★ | ◉◉◉ | ☎ 01451 820243 |

## HAMPSHIRE

| Beaulieu | | **Montagu Arms Hotel** |
|---|---|---|
| ★★★ | ◉◉ | ☎ 01590 612324 |
| Brockenhurst | | **Rhinefield House** |
| ★★★★ | ◉◉ | ☎ 01590 622922 |
| New Milton | | **Chewton Glen Hotel** |
| ★★★★★ | ◉◉◉ | ☎ 01425 275341 |
| Rotherwick | | **Tylney Hall Hotel** |
| ★★★★ | ◉ | ☎ 01256 764881 |
| Winchester | | **Lainston House Hotel** |
| ★★★★ | ◉◉◉ | ☎ 01962 863588 |

## HEREFORDSHIRE

| Hereford | | **Castle House Hotel** |
|---|---|---|
| ★★★ | ◉◉◉ | ☎ 01432 356321 |

## ISLE OF WIGHT

| Yarmouth | | **George Hotel** |
|---|---|---|
| ★★★ | ◉◉◉ | ☎ 01983 760331 |

## KENT

| Ashford | | **Eastwell Manor** |
|---|---|---|
| ★★★★ | ◉◉ | ☎ 01233 213000 |
| Lenham | | **Chilston Park** |
| ★★★★ | ◉◉ | ☎ 01622 859803 |

## LEICESTERSHIRE

| Melton Mowbray | | **Stapleford Park** |
|---|---|---|
| ★★★★ | ◉◉ | ☎ 01572 787522 |

## LINCOLNSHIRE

| Winteringham | | **Winteringham Fields** |
|---|---|---|
| ★★★ | | ☎ 01724 733096 |

## LONDON

| London E14 | | **Four Seasons Hotel** |
|---|---|---|
| | | **Canary Wharf** |
| ★★★★★ | ◉ | ☎ 020 7510 1999 |
| London NW1 | | **The Landmark London** |
| ★★★★★ | ◉◉ | ☎ 020 7631 8000 |
| London SW1 | | **The Berkeley** |
| ★★★★★ | ◉◉◉◉◉ | ☎ 020 7235 6000 |
| London SW1 | | **The Goring** |
| ★★★★★ | ◉◉ | ☎ 020 7396 9000 |

**13**

London SW1 ★★★★★ ◎◎◎ ☎ 020 7333 1000 **The Halkin Hotel**

London SW1 ★★★★★ ◎◎ ☎ 020 7235 1234 **Jumeirah Carlton Tower Hotel**

London SW1 ★★★★★ ◎◎ ☎ 020 7259 5599 **The Lanesborough**

London SW1 ★★★★★ ◎◎◎◎◎ ☎ 020 7235 2000 **Mandarin Oriental Hyde Park**

London SW1 ★★★★★ ☎ 020 7300 0041 **No 41**

London SW1 ★★★★ ◎◎ ☎ 020 7493 0111 **The Stafford**

London SW3 ★★★★★ ◎◎◎◎ ☎ 020 7589 5171 **The Capital**

London SW7 ★★★★★ ◎◎ ☎ 020 7368 5700 **Baglioni Hotel**

London W1 ★★★★★ ◎ ☎ 020 7499 3464 **Athenaeum**

London W1 ★★★★★ ◎◎◎ ☎ 020 7629 8860 **Claridge's**

London W1 ★★★★★ ◎◎◎ ☎ 020 7499 7070 **The Connaught**

London W1 ★★★★★ ◎◎ ☎ 020 7629 8888 **The Dorchester**

London W1 ★★★★★ ◎ ☎ 020 7499 0888 **Four Seasons Hotel London**

London W1 ★★★★★ ◎◎ ☎ 020 7493 8181 **The Ritz**

London W8 ★★★★★ ◎◎◎ ☎ 020 7937 8000 **Royal Garden Hotel**

London W8 ★★★★★ ◎ ☎ 020 7917 1000 **Milestone Hotel**

London WC2 ★★★★★ ◎◎ ☎ 020 7300 1000 **One Aldwych**

## NORFOLK

Blakeney ★★★ ◎◎◎ ☎ 01263 741041 **Morston Hall**

Grimston ★★★ ◎◎ ☎ 01485 600250 **Congham Hall Country House Hotel**

North Walsham ★★★ ◎◎ ☎ 01692 403231 **Beechwood Hotel**

Norwich ★★ ◎◎ ☎ 01603 700772 **The Old Rectory**

## NORTHAMPTONSHIRE

Daventry ★★★★ ◎◎◎ ☎ 01327 892000 **Fawsley Hall**

## NOTTINGHAMSHIRE

Nottingham ★★★ ◎◎◎◎ ☎ 0115 986 6566 **Restaurant Sat Bains with Rooms**

## OXFORDSHIRE

Great Milton ★★★★★ ◎◎◎◎◎ ☎ 01844 278881 **Le Manoir Aux Quat' Saisons**

## RUTLAND

Oakham ★★★★ ◎◎◎◎ ☎ 01572 756991 **Hambleton Hall**

## SHROPSHIRE

Worfield ★★★ ◎◎◎ ☎ 01746 716497 **Old Vicarage Hotel**

## SOMERSET

Bath ★★★★ ◎◎◎ ☎ 01225 331922 **The Bath Priory Hotel**

Bath ★★★ ◎◎ ☎ 01225 447928 **The Queensberry Hotel**

Porlock ★★★ ◎ ☎ 01643 862265 **The Oaks Hotel**

Shepton Mallet ★★★★ ☎ 01749 342008 **Charlton House\***

Wellington ★★★ ◎◎ ☎ 01823 400070 **Bindon Country House Hotel & Restaurant**

## STAFFORDSHIRE

Lichfield ★★★★ ◎◎ ☎ 01543 481494 **Swinfen Hall Hotel**

## SUFFOLK

Hintlesham ★★★★ ◎◎◎ ☎ 01473 652334 **Hintlesham Hall Hotel**

## SURREY

Bagshot ★★★★★ ◎◎◎ ☎ 01276 471774 **Pennyhill Park Hotel & The Spa**

## EAST SUSSEX

Forest Row ★★★★ ◎◎ ☎ 01342 824988 **Ashdown Park Hotel and Country Club**

Newick ★★★ ◎◎ ☎ 01825 723633 **Newick Park Hotel & Country Estate**

Uckfield ★★★ ◎◎ ☎ 01825 750581 **Horsted Place**

| WEST SUSSEX | | |
|---|---|---|
| Cuckfield | | **Ockenden Manor** |
| ★★★ | ◉◉◉ | ☎ 01444 416111 |
| East Grinstead | | **Gravetye Manor Hotel** |
| ★★★ | ◉◉◉ | ☎ 01342 810567 |
| Gatwick Airport | | **Langshott Manor** |
| ★★★ | ◉◉ | ☎ 01293 786680 |
| Lower Beeding | | **South Lodge Hotel** |
| ★★★★ | ◉◉◉ | ☎ 01403 891711 |
| Turners Hill | | **Alexander House Hotel** |
| ★★★★ | ◉◉ | ☎ 01342 714914 |

| WARWICKSHIRE | | |
|---|---|---|
| Alderminster | | **Ettington Park Hotel** |
| ★★★★ | ◉◉ | ☎ 01789 450123 |
| Royal Leamington Spa | | **Mallory Court Hotel** |
| ★★★ | ◉◉◉ | ☎ 01926 330214 |

| WILTSHIRE | | |
|---|---|---|
| Castle Combe | | **Manor House Hotel & Golf Club** |
| ★★★★ | ◉◉◉ | ☎ 01249 782206 |
| Colerne | | **Lucknam Park** |
| ★★★★★ | ◉◉◉ | ☎ 01225 742777 |
| Malmesbury | | **Whatley Manor** |
| ★★★★★ | ◉◉◉ | ☎ 01666 822888 |

| WORCESTERSHIRE | | |
|---|---|---|
| Chaddesley Corbett | | **Brockencote Hall Country House Hotel** |
| ★★★ | ◉◉ | ☎ 01562 777876 |

| YORKSHIRE, NORTH | | |
|---|---|---|
| Bolton Abbey | | **The Devonshire Arms Country House Hotel** |
| ★★★★ | ◉◉◉◉ | ☎ 01756 710441 |
| Crathorne | | **Crathorne Hall Hotel** |
| ★★★★ | ◉◉ | ☎ 01642 700398 |
| Harrogate | | **Rudding Park Hotel & Golf** |
| ★★★★ | ◉◉ | ☎ 01423 871350 |
| Masham | | **Swinton Park** |
| ★★★★ | ◉◉◉ | ☎ 01765 680900 |
| Yarm | | **Judges Country House Hotel** |
| ★★★ | ◉◉ | ☎ 01642 789000 |
| York | | **The Grange Hotel** |
| ★★★ | ◉◉ | ☎ 01904 644744 |
| York | | **Middlethorpe Hall & Spa** |
| ★★★★ | ◉◉◉ | ☎ 01904 641241 |

| YORKSHIRE, WEST | | |
|---|---|---|
| Wetherby | | **Wood Hall Hotel** |
| ★★★★ | ◉◉ | ☎ 01937 587271 |

# CHANNEL ISLANDS

| JERSEY | | |
|---|---|---|
| Rozel | | **Château la Chaire** |
| ★★★ | ◉◉ | ☎ 01534 863354 |
| St Brelade | | **The Atlantic Hotel** |
| ★★★★ | ◉◉◉ | ☎ 01534 744101 |
| St Helier | | **The Club Hotel & Spa** |
| ★★★★ | ◉◉◉◉ | ☎ 01534 876500 |
| St Saviour | | **Longueville Manor Hotel** |
| ★★★★ | ◉◉◉ | ☎ 01534 725501 |

# SCOTLAND

| ABERDEENSHIRE | | |
|---|---|---|
| Ballater | | **Darroch Learg Hotel** |
| ★★★ | ◉◉◉ | ☎ 013397 55443 |

| ANGUS | | |
|---|---|---|
| Glamis | | **Castleton House Hotel** |
| ★★★ | ◉◉◉ | ☎ 01307 840340 |

| ARGYLL & BUTE | | |
|---|---|---|
| Eriska | | **Isle of Eriska** |
| ★★★★★ | ◉◉◉ | ☎ 01631 720371 |
| Port Appin | | **Airds Hotel** |
| ★★★★ | ◉◉◉ | ☎ 01631 730236 |
| Tobermory (Isle of Mull) | | **Highland Cottage** |
| ★★★ | ◉◉ | ☎ 01688 302030 |

| CITY OF EDINBURGH | | |
|---|---|---|
| Edinburgh | | **Channings** |
| ★★★★ | ◉◉ | ☎ 0131 332 3232 |
| Edinburgh | | **The Howard Hotel** |
| ★★★★ | ◉ | ☎ 0131 557 3500 |
| Edinburgh | | **Prestonfield** |
| ★★★★★ | ◉◉ | ☎ 0131 225 7800 |

| DUMFRIES & GALLOWAY | | |
|---|---|---|
| Newton Stewart | | **Kirroughtree House** |
| ★★★ | ◉◉ | ☎ 01671 402141 |

| Portpatrick | **Knockinaam Lodge** |
| ★★★ ◉◉◉ | ☎ 01776 810471 |

**EAST LOTHIAN**

| Gullane | **Greywalls Hotel** |
| ★★★ ◉◉◉ | ☎ 01620 842144 |

**FIFE**

| Markinch | **Balbirnie House** |
| ★★★★ ◉◉ | ☎ 01592 610066 |
| St Andrews | **The Old Course Hotel, Golf Resort & Spa** |
| ★★★★★ ◉◉◉ | ☎ 01334 474371 |
| St Andrews | **Rufflets Country House & Garden Restaurant** |
| ★★★★ ◉◉ | ☎ 01334 472594 |
| St Andrews | **St Andrews Golf Hotel** |
| ★★★ ◉◉ | ☎ 01334 472611 |

**CITY OF GLASGOW**

| Glasgow | **One Devonshire Gardens** |
| ★★★★ ◉◉ | ☎ 0141 339 2001 |

**HIGHLAND**

| Fort William | **Inverlochy Castle Hotel** |
| ★★★★★ ◉◉◉ | ☎ 01397 702177 |
| Lochinver | **Inver Lodge Hotel** |
| ★★★★ ◉ | ☎ 01571 844496 |
| Nairn | **Boath House** |
| ★★★ ◉◉◉◉ | ☎ 01667 454896 |
| Poolewe | **Pool House Hotel** |
| ★★★ ◉◉ | ☎ 01445 781272 |
| Strontian | **Kilcamb Lodge Hotel** |
| ★★★ ◉◉ | ☎ 01967 402257 |

| Tain | **The Glenmorangie Highland Home at Cadboll** |
| ★★ ◉◉ | ☎ 01862 871671 |
| Torridon | **The Torridon** |
| ★★★ ◉◉ | ☎ 01445 791242 |

**NORTH AYRSHIRE**

| Brodick (Isle of Arran) | **Kilmichael Country House Hotel** |
| ★★★ ◉◉ | ☎ 01770 302219 |

**PERTH & KINROSS**

| Auchterarder | **The Gleneagles Hotel** |
| ★★★★★ ◉◉◉◉ | ☎ 01764 662231 |
| Dunkeld | **Kinnaird** |
| ★★★★ ◉◉◉ | ☎ 01796 482440 |
| Kinclaven | **Ballathie House Hotel** |
| ★★★ ◉◉ | ☎ 01250 883268 |

**SCOTTISH BORDERS**

| Peebles | **Cringletie House** |
| ★★★★ ◉◉ | ☎ 01721 725750 |

**SOUTH AYRSHIRE**

| Ballantrae | **Glenapp Castle** |
| ★★★★ ◉◉◉ | ☎ 01465 831212 |
| Maybole | **Ladyburn** |
| ★★ ◉ | ☎ 01655 740585 |
| Troon | **Lochgreen House Hotel** |
| ★★★★ ◉◉◉ | ☎ 01292 313343 |
| Turnberry | **The Westin Turnberry Resort** |
| ★★★★★ ◉◉ | ☎ 01655 331000 |

# WALES

**CEREDIGION**

| Eglwysfach | **Ynyshir Hall** |
| ★★★ ◉◉◉◉ | ☎ 01654 781209 |

**CONWY**

| Llandudno | **Bodysgallen Hall & Spa** |
| ★★★★ ◉◉◉ | ☎ 01492 584466 |
| Llandudno | **Osborne House** |
| ★★★★ ◉ | ☎ 01492 860330 |
| Llandudno | **St Tudno Hotel and Restaurant** |
| ★★ ◉◉ | ☎ 01492 874411 |

**GWYNEDD**

| Caernarfon | **Seiont Manor** |
| ★★★ ◉◉ | ☎ 01286 673366 |

**POWYS**

| Llangammarch Wells | **Lake Country House Hotel** |
| ★★★ ◉◉ | ☎ 01591 620202 |

**SWANSEA**

| Reynoldston | **Fairyhill** |
| ★★★ ◉◉ | ☎ 01792 390139 |

Hotels marked with an asterisk * have not had their Rosette rating confirmed at the time of going to press.
See the AA website www.theAA.com for current information.

# ENGLAND

North Cornish coast.

# BERKSHIRE

Windsor Castle.

# Regency Park Hotel

★★★★  79% ◉ HOTEL

| | |
|---|---|
| Address: | Bowling Green Road, Thatcham, NEWBURY RG18 3RP |
| Tel: | 01635 871555 |
| Fax: | 01635 871571 |
| Email: | info@regencyparkhotel.co.uk |
| Website: | www.regencyparkhotel.co.uk |
| Map ref: | 3, SU56 |
| Directions: | From M4 junct 12 take A4 to Thatcham |

Rooms: 109, S and D £95–£175 Facilities: ⊙ Sauna Jacuzzi Solarium Gym STV Wi-fi in bedrooms
Parking: 160 Notes: ⊗ in bedrooms ⊘ in restaurant

Each bedroom of this contemporary hotel features a seriously large bed. The menus of the award-winning Watermark Restaurant specialise in contemporary British food with classical influences and use local produce. The Escape leisure club and Revive health and beauty salon are free to guests.

**Recommended in the area**

Newbury Racecourse; Highclere Castle; Oracle Shopping Centre

# Millennium Madejski Hotel Reading

★★★★  75% ◉◉  HOTEL

| | |
|---|---|
| Address: | Madejski Stadium, READING RG2 0FL |
| Tel: | 0118 925 3500 |
| Fax: | 0118 925 3501 |
| Email: | sales.reading@mill-cop.com |
| Website: | www.millenniumhotels.com |
| Map ref: | 3, SU77 |
| Directions: | M4 junct 11 onto A33, follow signs |

Rooms: 140, S £75–£200 D £95–£200 Facilities: ⊙ Sauna Jacuzzi Solarium Gym STV Wi-fi Parking: 150

Forming part of the impressive Madejski Stadium Complex, the Millennium's de luxe bedrooms are all well-equipped. The ground floor features the award-winning Cilantro Restaurant serving international cuisine, complemented by an extensive wine collection while Le Café offers more informal dining.

**Recommended in the area**

Windsor Castle; Legoland; Henley-on-Thames

# Sir Christopher Wren's House Hotel & Spa

★★★★ 75% ◎◎ HOTEL

| | |
|---|---|
| Address: | Thames Street, WINDSOR SL4 1PX |
| Tel: | 01753 861354 |
| Fax: | 01753 860172 |
| Email: | reservations@wrensgroup.com |
| Website: | www.sirchristopherwren.co.uk |
| Map ref: | 3, SU97 |

Directions: M4 junct 6, 1st exit from relief road, follow signs to Windsor, 1st major exit on left, turn left at lights
Rooms: 90, S £165 D £220 Facilities: Sauna Jacuzzi Solarium Gym STV Parking: 15 Notes: ⊗ in bedrooms ⊘ in restaurant

This hotel occupies a 17th-century town house, listed as Grade II for its architectural importance. It has all the elegance to be expected of a home designed and lived in by Sir Christopher Wren, England's greatest architect. It enjoys a beautiful location beside the River Thames, between Eton Bridge and Windsor Castle. There are reception and meeting rooms for functions of all kinds, including business conferences, wedding parties and other celebrations. Much of the interior decor, with its rich wood panelling and plasterwork, was designed by Wren. The modern furnishings are in an equally rich style, and chrome and marble adorn bathrooms. Radio, television, tea-and coffee-making facilities and a trouser press are standard. Serviced apartments, with kitchens and lounge/study areas, are available for longer-term guests. At the award-winning Strok's Restaurant diners can enjoy outstanding cuisine on the riverside champagne terrace. Wren's Club, a luxurious health centre, offers a choice of pampering treatment packages for both beauty and fitness. The hotel is also well placed for easy access to Heathrow Airport and the West End of London.

**Recommended in the area**

Windsor Castle; Eton College; Legoland; Windsor Great Park.

# BUCKINGHAMSHIRE

All Saints church, Marlow.

# Villiers Hotel

★★★★ 73% ⊛⊛ HOTEL

Address:    3 Castle Street,
            BUCKINGHAM MK18 1BS
Tel:        01280 822444
Fax:        01280 822113
Email:      buckingham@villiershotels.com
Website:    www.villiershotels.com
Map ref:    3, SP63
Directions: M1 junct 13 (N) or 15 (S) follow signs to
Buckingham. Castle St by Town Hall

**Rooms:** 46, S £105–£135 D £120–£150 **Facilities:** STV Wi-fi available **Parking:** 40 **Notes:** ⊗ in bedrooms ⊘ in restaurant

Guests can enjoy a town centre location with a high degree of comfort at this 400-year-old former coaching inn. Relaxing public areas feature flagstone floors, oak panelling and real fires whilst bedrooms are modern, spacious and equipped to a high level. Diners can unwind in the atmopsheric bar before taking dinner in the award-winning and newly refurbished restaurant.

**Recommended in the area**

Stowe Landscape Gardens; Silverstone motor racing circuit; Bicester Village designer outlet shopping

# Danesfield House Hotel & Spa

★★★★ 85% HOTEL

Address:    Henley Road, MARLOW SL7 2EY
Tel:        01628 891010
Fax:        01628 890408
Email:      reservations@danesfieldhouse.co.uk
Website:    www.danesfieldhouse.co.uk
Map ref:    3, SU88
Directions: 2m from Marlow on A4155 towards Henley

**Rooms:** 87, S £215 D £260–£355 **Facilities:** ® Sauna Jacuzzi Solarium Gym STV Wi-fi **Parking:** 100 **Notes:** ⊗ in bedrooms ⊘ in restaurant

A magnificent mansion set in 65 acres of elevated landscaped gardens, overlooking the River Thames and, beyond, the Chiltern Hills. Impressive public rooms include the cathedral-like Grand Hall – morning coffee here is an experience – the award-winning Oak Room restaurant and the Orangery, for less formal dining. Both restaurants and the extensive outside terrace are popular with local residents.

**Recommended in the area**

Henley River Cruises; Hambleden Valley; Marlow boutique shopping

Trinity College, Cambridge.

# The Cambridge Belfry

★★★★ 81% ◉ HOTEL

| | |
|---|---|
| Address: | Back Street, CAMBOURNE CB3 6BW |
| Tel: | 01954 714600 |
| Fax: | 01954 714610 |
| Email: | cambridgebelfry@qhotels.co.uk |
| Website: | www.qhotels.co.uk |
| Map ref: | 3, TL35 |

Directions: M11 junct 13 take A428 towards Bedford, follow signs to Cambourne. Exit at Cambourne keeping left. Left at rdbt, hotel on left

Rooms: 120, S £149 D £178 Facilities: ☉ Sauna Jacuzzi Solarium Tennis Gym STV Wi-fi available

Parking: 260 Notes: ⊗ in bedrooms ⊘ in restaurant

Situated in a tranquil lakeside setting on the outskirts of Cambridge, this superior QHotels-owned hotel offers the very highest standards of accommodation. The tastefully decorated bedrooms include Executive rooms, suites, twins and doubles, some interconnecting. There are also six individually-styled penthouse suites occupying the whole of the third floor. Original artwork adorns the lounge areas creating a spacious, contemporary atmosphere that extends throughout. The award winning Bridge Restaurant offers fine dining complemented by an impressive array of wines whilst Brooks Brasserie has a more informal menu with an attractive terrace overlooking the lake for morning coffee, afternoon tea or al fresco dining during the warmer weather. Guests can relax in the hotel's Reflections Spa and Leisure Club or pamper themselves with a luxury Spa treatment from the wide selection of therapies and body treatments available. Outside, for the more energetic, there is an all weather floodlit tennis court. The Cambridge Belfry is perfect for sightseeing and day trips around Cambridge and the surrounding countryside.

Recommended in the area

Kings College Chapel; Milton Country Park, Linton Zoo

# Arundel House Hotel

★★★ 79% HOTEL

| | |
|---|---|
| Address: | Chesterton Road, CAMBRIDGE CB4 3AN |
| Tel: | 01223 367701 |
| Fax: | 01223 367721 |
| Email: | info@arundelhousehotels.co.uk |
| Website: | www.arundelhousehotels.co.uk |
| Map ref: | 3, TL45 |
| Directions: | City centre on A1303 |

Rooms: 103, S £75–£95 D £95–£120 Parking: 70
Notes: ⊗ in bedrooms ⊘ on premises

By definition, a fine location in the city of Cambridge would surely be one that overlooks the River Cam and open parkland. The Arundel House Hotel does just that. This privately owned hotel, once a row of Victorian townhouses, is only a short walk from the historic centre, and its shops, restaurants and pubs. All bedrooms are en suite, with either a bath, shower, or both. They also have tea and coffee making facilities, TV, radio, hair dryer and direct dial phone; irons, ironing boards and room safes are on the way. Relax in a comfortable armchair in the bar, then move into the adjacent restaurant, decorated in refreshing yellow, orange, gold and green, with upholstered chairs, crisp white and yellow linen, and oak dressers. A wide range of imaginative dishes features on its fixed price, carte, vegetarian and children's menus, all freshly prepared in the hotel's scrupulously clean, award-winning kitchens. Another time, try the all-day Conservatory Brasserie, which offers main meals, snacks and cream teas. The charming garden outside its doors is surprisingly tranquil, despite the proximity of the city centre. While retaining its original façade, the Coach House behind the main building has been completely rebuilt to provide three conference rooms and 22 bedrooms

**Recommended in the area**

Kings College Cambridge; Imperial War Museum Duxford; Anglesey Abbey (NT)

# Best Western The Gonville Hotel

★★★ 77% HOTEL

| | |
|---|---|
| Address: | Gonville Place, CAMBRIDGE CB1 1LY |
| Tel: | 01223 366611 |
| Fax: | 01223 315470 |
| Email: | all@gonvillehotel.co.uk |
| Website: | www.bw-gonvillehotel.co.uk |
| Map ref: | 3, TL45 |

Directions: M11 junct 11, on A1309 follow city centre signs. At 2nd mini rdbt right into Lensfield Rd, over junct with lights. Hotel 25yds on right

Rooms: 73, S £89–£150 D £99–£170 Facilities: Wi-fi available Parking: 80 Notes: ⊗ in restaurant

The hotel is centrally located on the eastern side of the city's historic centre, and overlooks a 25-acre open park. All rooms are en suite, and some are air-conditioned. The hotel's Chancellor's Restaurant and the more informal Atrium Restaurant offer local dishes and wide-ranging cuisine. The Abington Suite and the adjoining Gresham House gardens are a popular venue for social occasions.

**Recommended in the area**

Cambridge University; Imperial War Museum, Duxford; National Horseracing Museum, Newmarket

# Hotel Felix

★★★★ 80% ◉◉ HOTEL

| | |
|---|---|
| Address: | Whitehouse Lane, CAMBRIDGE CB3 0LX |
| Tel: | 01223 277977 |
| Fax: | 01223 277973 |
| Email: | help@hotelfelix.co.uk |
| Website: | www.hotelfelix.co.uk |
| Map ref: | 3, TL45 |

Directions: N on A1307, right at The Travellers Rest

Rooms: 52, S £136–£186 D £168–£275 Facilities: STV Wi-fi in bedrooms Parking: 90 Notes: ⊗ in restaurant

Many of the restored original features in this Victorian mansion built of pale cream brick are complemented by today's simple, clean and contemporary decor and furnishing. The addition of two new wings has created a welcoming central courtyard. In the bedrooms, silk-panelled curtains frame the floor-to-ceiling windows, and the finest linen covers the beds, while the bathrooms are lined with natural stone or slate. Public rooms include an open-plan bar and the Graffiti restaurant. Three first-floor reception rooms can be used for meetings or private dining.

**Recommended in the area**

King's College, Cambridge; Newmarket Racecourse; Imperial War Museum, Duxford

# Bell Inn Hotel

★★★ 77% ❀ HOTEL

| | |
|---|---|
| Address: | Great North Road, STILTON PE7 3RA |
| Tel: | 01733 241066 |
| Fax: | 01733 245173 |
| Email: | reception@thebellstilton.co.uk |
| Website: | www.thebellstilton.co.uk |
| Map ref: | 3, TL18 |
| Directions: | A1(M) junct 16, follow Stilton signs |

Rooms: 22, S £72.50–£79.50 D £99.50–£129.50
Facilities: STV Wi-fi available Parking: 30
Notes: ⊗ in bedrooms ⊘ in restaurant

Just off the Great North Road, this lovely 17th-century coaching inn has served the famous and infamous alike – film star Clark Gable, and highwayman Dick Turpin, for example. The magnificent inn sign is an exact replica of the original and, together with its wrought-iron bracket, weighs an astonishing two and three-quarter tons. Curiously, the famous blue cheese has never been made in Stilton; in coaching days it was extensively sold in the local market and the village's name stuck. Recently refurbished en suite bedrooms, including two with four-posters and several with Jacuzzis, are ranged around the old courtyard. For dining, guests have a choice - the beamed Galleried Restaurant, with its AA-Rosette-awarded menu of modern British cuisine; the softly lit Bistro, offering internationally influenced dishes; and the stone-floored Village Bar, offering bar meals and snacks. Browse over the menus in a comfortable leather armchair in the first-floor Dick Turpin's room, so named because legend says he escaped to his horse, Black Bess, from the window. In favourable weather eat, or just have a drink, in the courtyard. Byron's Room (another famous guest) adjoins the Marlborough Suite, which can accommodate up to 100 business delegates theatre style.

### Recommended in the area

Peterborough Cathedral; Imperial War Museum, Duxford; Flag Fen

Wisbech.

# Crown Lodge Hotel

★★★ 77% ⬢ HOTEL

| | |
|---|---|
| Address: | Downham Road, Outwell, |
| | WISBECH PE14 8SE |
| Tel: | 01945 773391 |
| Fax: | 01945 772668 |
| Email: | office@thecrownlodgehotel.co.uk |
| Website: | www.thecrownlodgehotel.co.uk |
| Map ref: | 3, TF40 |
| Directions: | On A1122/A1101 approx 5m from Wisbech |

Rooms: 10, S £66 D £88 Facilities: Free Wi-fi
Parking: 55 Notes: ⊗ in restaurant

A small hotel, off the beaten track, on the banks of the meandering Well Creek, with a warm, contemporary style. Public areas include a lounge bar and large sitting room with plush sofas. The brasserie restaurant menu reflects the hotel's desire for flexibility in every respect, so that a guest fancying either a simple healthy meal or something richer will not be disappointed. The chef sources the best local produce, including fresh fish from the man who supplies the Queen at Sandringham.

**Recommended in the area**

Sandringham; Ely Cathedral; Welney Wildfowl & Wetlands Trust

Cholmondley Castle.

# Alderley Edge Hotel

★★★  83% ⊛⊛  HOTEL

| | |
|---|---|
| **Address:** | Macclesfield Road, |
| | ALDERLEY EDGE SK9 7BJ |
| **Tel:** | 01625 583033 |
| **Fax:** | 01625 586343 |
| **Email:** | sales@alderleyedgehotel.com |
| **Website:** | www.alderleyedgehotel.com |
| **Map ref:** | 6, SJ87 |

**Directions:** Off A34 in Alderley Edge onto B5087 towards Macclesfield. Hotel 200yds on right

**Rooms:** 50 **Facilities:** STV Wi-fi in bedrooms **Parking:** 90 **Notes:** ⊗ in bedrooms ⊘ in restaurant

Built of local sandstone in 1850 by a Manchester cotton king, this well-furnished hotel in charming grounds has grand views over the Cheshire Plain at the front, and the lovely garden at the rear. Room goodies include bowls of fruit, bathrobes, trouser press, hairdryer and tea and coffee making facilities. Some even have sofa beds too – great for families. The bar and adjacent lounge lead into the split-level conservatory restaurant, where a combined carte and fixed price menu offers welcome flexibility.

**Recommended in the area**

Jodrell Bank; Quarry Bank Mill; Tatton Park

# Best Western Manor House Hotel

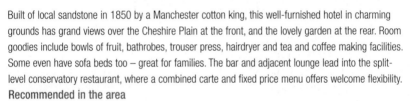

★★★  82% ⊛  HOTEL

| | |
|---|---|
| **Address:** | Audley Road, ALSAGER, |
| | Stoke-on-Trent ST7 2QQ |
| **Tel:** | 01270 884000 |
| **Fax:** | 01270 882483 |
| **Email:** | mhres@compasshotels.co.uk |
| **Website:** | www.compasshotels.co.uk |
| **Map ref:** | 6, SJ86 |

**Directions:** M6 junct 16/A500 toward Stoke. After 0.5m take 1st slip road to Alsager and left at top.

**Rooms:** 57, S £70–£98 D £90–£145 **Facilities:** ⓣ Jacuzzi STV Wi-fi in bedrooms 4 conference rooms available **Parking:** 150 **Notes:** ⊗ in bedrooms ⊘ in restaurant

Developed around a 17th-century farmhouse this hotel has much for the modern traveller. The Ostler Restaurant offers fixed-price and à la carte menus, and uses local produce in season; the wine list is extensive. Informal meals can be enjoyed in the warm atmosphere of the oak-beamed Stables Bar.

**Recommended in the area**

The Potteries; Alton Towers; Rode Hall and gardens.

Beeston Castle.

# The Chester Grosvenor & Spa

★★★★★ ◉◉◉ HOTEL

| | |
|---|---|
| Address: | Eastgate, CHESTER CH1 1LT |
| Tel: | 01244 324024 |
| Fax: | 01244 313246 |
| Email: | hotel@chestergrosvenor.com |
| Website: | www.chestergrosvenor.com |
| Map ref: | 5, SJ46 |

Directions: Off M56 for M53, then A56. Follow signs for city centre hotels.

Rooms: 80, S D £190–£850 Facilities: Sauna Spa and steam room Gym STV Notes: ⊗ ⊘ in hotel

This half-timbered Grade II listed building, dating from 1865 lies in Chester's historic centre. Its suites and bedrooms are furnished with high-quality fabrics and queen- or king-sized beds. The Arkle Restaurant offers gourmet cuisine and has a wine cellar of nearly 600 bins; the more informal La Brasserie offers international dishes. Traditional English afternoon tea can be taken in the Library.

Recommended in the area

Chester Cathedral; Roman walls; Chester Zoo

# Crewe Hall

★★★★  80% ⊛⊛ HOTEL

**Address:** Weston Road,
CREWE CW1 6UZ
**Tel:** 01270 253333
**Fax:** 01270 253322
**Email:** crewehall@qhotels.co.uk
**Website:** www.qhotels.co.uk
**Map ref:** 6, SJ75
**Directions:** M6 junct 16 follow A500 to Crewe. Last exit at rdbt onto A5020. 1st exit next rdbt to Crewe. Crewe Hall 150yds on right
**Rooms:** 65, S £154.50 D £194 **Facilities:** Tennis STV **Parking:** 140 **Notes:** ⊗ in bedrooms ⊗ in restaurant

Set in 35 acres of parkland, Crewe Hall is a majestic Jacobean stately home dating back to 1615. Originally built by the Earl of Crewe to entertain on the most lavish scale, it was previously owned by the Queen in the guise of the Duchy of Lancaster. The accommodation features 26 Superior rooms within the Hall itself. Individually furnished and designed, they include 10 four-poster rooms, 5 suites and the sumptuous Royal Suite where King George V and Queen Mary stayed in 1913. A further 39 classically-modern rooms are situated in the 'West Wing', connected to the original Hall with a glass link. All are air-conditioned and spacious with most having lovely views of the gardens. The Ranulph restaurant features intimate fine dining, where the finest ingredients are coupled with a fresh and innovative style. The contemporary award-winning Brasserie offers a modern menu and is a popular venue for locals and residents to meet and enjoy a drink at the famous revolving bar. Richly designed ceilings, exquisite marble fireplaces, ornate carved wood and stained glass features all add to the air of magnificence at Crewe Hall.

**Recommended in the area**

Tatton Park; Alton Towers; Chester Zoo

# The Park Royal Hotel

★★★★ 77% HOTEL

| | |
|---|---|
| Address: | Stretton Road, STRETTON WA4 4NS |
| Tel: | 01925 730706 |
| Fax: | 01925 730740 |
| Email: | parkroyalreservations@qhotels.co.uk |
| Website: | www.qhotels.co.uk |
| Map ref: | 6, SJ68 |

Directions: M56 junct 10, A49 to Warrington, at lights turn right to Appleton Thorn, hotel 200yds on right
Rooms: 144, S £125–200 D £135–210 Facilities: ⓢ
Sauna Jacuzzi Solarium Tennis Gym STV Parking: 400 Notes: ⊗ in bedrooms ⊘ in restaurant

The Park Royal is a modern hotel in the heart of Cheshire's delightful countryside, with its sleepy villages, meandering rivers and mirror-smooth canals. The en suite bedrooms are spacious and incorporate Wi-fi access. The Topiary in the Park restaurant is open daily for lunch and dinner, serving pastas, fresh fish, game and grilled steaks. Snacks are offered in the Lounge Bar. Attractive public areas include extensive conference and function facilities, and a comprehensive leisure centre.

**Recommended in the area**

Chester Zoo; Gateway Theatre (Chester); Beeston Castle

# Stanneylands Hotel

★★★★ 79% ⑳⑳ HOTEL

| | |
|---|---|
| Address: | Stanneylands Road, WILMSLOW SK9 4EY |
| Tel: | 01625 525225 |
| Fax: | 01625 537282 |
| Email: | reservations@stanneylandshotel.co.uk |
| Website: | www.stanneylandshotel.co.uk |
| Map ref: | 6, SJ88 |

Directions: from M56 for Airport turn off, follow signs to Wilmslow. Left into Station Rd, onto Stanneylands Rd.
Rooms: 56, S £68–£110 D £90–£140 Facilities: STV
Wi-fi available in bedrooms Parking: 108 Notes: ⊗ in bedrooms

Stanneylands is surrounded by woodlands and landscaped gardens extending over four acres. The oak-panelled restaurant offers both traditional English fare and a range of modern world cuisine. Private functions can cater for up to 120 guests in one of the three dining suites. The hotel offers conference facilities and the accommodation includes top-class executive rooms with modern decor. It is a short drive from Manchester city centre, and only 3 miles from Manchester International Airport.

**Recommended in the area**

Old Trafford (Manchester United football stadium); the Peak District; Tatton Park

St Germans Viaduct in the Tamar Valley.

# Hell Bay Hotel

★★★ ◎◎ HOTEL

| | |
|---|---|
| Address: | BRYHER, Isles of Scilly TR23 0PR |
| Tel: | 01720 422947 |
| Fax: | 01720 423004 |
| Email: | contactus@hellbay.co.uk |
| Website: | www.hellbay.co.uk |
| Map ref: | 1, SV63 |
| Directions: | Take helicopter or plane from mainland |

Rooms: 25, S £150–£237.50 D £240–£380
Facilities: ⤫ Sauna Jacuzzi Gym STV

In extensive private, tranquil grounds on the smallest of the inhabited Scillies, Hell Bay Hotel is filled with original works by locally-connected artists, including Barbara Hepworth, and decorated in cool blues and greens to create a sort of New England-meets-Cornwall atmosphere. The bedrooms are equally stylish and many have stunning Atlantic views. Eating here is a delight; seafood features strongly on the menus.

**Recommended in the area**

Tresco Abbey Garden; Gallery Tresco; Old Blockhouse

# The Falcon Hotel

★★★ 77% HOTEL

| | |
|---|---|
| Address: | Breakwater Road, BUDE EX23 8SD |
| Tel: | 01288 352005 |
| Fax: | 01288 356359 |
| Email: | reception@falconhotel.com |
| Website: | www.falconhotel.com |
| Map ref: | 1, SS20 |
| Directions: | Off A39 into Bude, follow road to |

Widemouth Bay. Hotel on right over canal bridge
Rooms: 29, S £55 D £110 Facilities: STV Wi-fi in bedrooms Parking: 40 Notes: ⊗ in bedrooms ⊘ in restaurant

This old coaching-house has been welcoming guests for nearly 200 years. The bedrooms are individually decorated in country-house style, with en suite facilities. The candlelit air-conditioned restaurant provides modern English cuisine with international twists. Local produce in season is offered on both the a la carte and fresh fish menus, and there is a long wine list. The beer garden has fine views over the canal and harbour. Private functions can be held in the Acland Suite.

**Recommended in the area**

Clovelly; Tintagel; Boscastle

# Crantock Bay Hotel

★★★ 75% HOTEL

Address: West Pentire, CRANTOCK TR8 5SE
Tel: 01637 830229
Fax: 01637 831111
Email: stay@crantockbayhotel.co.uk
Website: www.crantockbayhotel.co.uk
Map ref: 1, SW76
Directions: At Newquay A3075 to Redruth. After 500yds right towards Crantock, follow signs to West Pentire
Rooms: 31, S £59–£105 D £118–£210 **Facilities:** ⊗ Sauna Jacuzzi Tennis Gym Wi-fi in bedrooms Beauty Spa
Parking: 40 **Notes:** ⊘ in restaurant

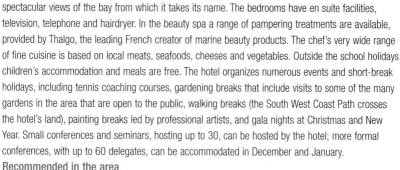

This family-owned hotel stands on a headland, enjoying spectacular views of the bay from which it takes its name. The bedrooms have en suite facilities, television, telephone and hairdryer. In the beauty spa a range of pampering treatments are available, provided by Thalgo, the leading French creator of marine beauty products. The chef's very wide range of fine cuisine is based on local meats, seafoods, cheeses and vegetables. Outside the school holidays children's accommodation and meals are free. The hotel organizes numerous events and short-break holidays, including tennis coaching courses, gardening breaks that include visits to some of the many gardens in the area that are open to the public, walking breaks (the South West Coast Path crosses the hotel's land), painting breaks led by professional artists, and gala nights at Christmas and New Year. Small conferences and seminars, hosting up to 30, can be hosted by the hotel; more formal conferences, with up to 60 delegates, can be accommodated in December and January.

**Recommended in the area**

The Eden Project; The Lost Gardens of Heligan; Jamie Oliver's Fifteen Cornwall restaurant, Watergate Bay; Rick Stein's Seafood Restaurant, Padstow.

# Best Western Falmouth Beach Resort Hotel

★★★ 78% HOTEL

**Address:** Gyllyngvase Beach, Seafront, FALMOUTH TR11 4NA
**Tel:** 01326 310500
**Fax:** 01326 319147
**Email:** info@falmouthbeachhotel.co.uk
**Website:** www.falmouthbeachhotel.co.uk
**Map ref:** 1, SW83
**Directions:** A39 to Falmouth, follow seafront signs
**Rooms:** 120, S £62–£85 D £124–£170
**Facilities:** ⊗ Sauna Jacuzzi Solarium Tennis Gym STV Wi-fi in bedrooms **Parking:** 88
**Notes:** ⊗ in restaurant

Enjoying wonderful views across Falmouth Bay, this popular hotel is situated opposite sandy Gyllyngvase beach. It is within easy walking distance of this attractive little town's sometimes quite quirky shops and pubs. The port, frequently visited these days by cruise ships, is not far away either. The hotel exudes a friendly atmosphere and guests have a good choice of leisure and fitness, entertainment and dining options. Many of the 120 en suite bedrooms not only have balconies and sea views, but also are within earshot of the waves breaking on the shore. All rooms are well equipped and comfortable. Sandpipers restaurant offers both fixed menu and carvery dining, with fish fresh from the sea given pride of place, as well as

specialities from award-winning chefs that range from the familiar to the exotic. The smart Feathers Bar is ideal for an informal snack before a night out or for a bistro-style meal, such as a delicious steak with all the trimmings. Beach Club amenities include a stunning indoor pool with back and neck massage jets, Jacuzzis, sauna, solarium, beauty salon and tennis courts. In its role as a leading conference venue provider it can accommodate up to 300 delegates. The hotel has good facilities for guests with disabilities including a hoist for entrance to the swimming pool and a fully-equipped room can be reserved.

**Recommended in the area**

National Maritime Museum; Eden Project; Pendennis Castle; South West Coast Path; Argal and College Water Park

Falmouth.

# Falmouth Hotel

★★★  75% ⊚  HOTEL

| | |
|---|---|
| **Address:** | Castle Beach, FALMOUTH TR11 4NZ |
| **Tel:** | 01326 312671 |
| **Fax:** | 01326 319533 |
| **Email:** | reservations@falmouthhotel.com |
| **Website:** | www.falmouthhotel.com |
| **Map ref:** | 1, SW83 |
| **Directions:** | Take A30 to Truro then A390 to Falmouth |

Rooms: 69, S £60–£85 D £39–£100pp **Facilities:** ☜

Sauna Jacuzzi Solarium Gym STV **Parking:** 120

Notes: ⊘ in restaurant

Falmouth's first Victorian-era hotel is opposite a sandy beach, with five acres of beautiful leafy gardens. Many of its comfortable bedrooms, some with balconies, look across Falmouth Bay to Pendennis Point. Roomy public areas include the bar/lounge, an outdoor terrace and the grand Trelawney Restaurant. The Falmouth offers a choice of dining experiences, including gourmet dishes, showcasing the full talents of the chef and his team, along with plenty for those who enjoy the simpler things in life.

**Recommended in the area**

Pendennis Castle; National Maritime Museum of Cornwall; Gweek Seal Sanctuary

# Green Lawns Hotel

★★★   75%   HOTEL

Address:    Western Terrace, FALMOUTH TR11 4QJ
Tel:        01326 312734
Fax:        01326 211427
Email:      info@greenlawnshotel.com
Website:    www.greenlawnshotel.com
Map ref:    1, SW83
Directions: On A39
Rooms: 39, S £60–£115 D £110–£180 **Facilities:** ⊗
Sauna Jacuzzi Solarium Tennis Gym **Parking:** 60
Notes: ⊗ in restaurant

The lawns that give this ivy-clad hotel its name are long-matured grounds that take full advantage of the subtropical climate of the region. In summer they blaze with a profusion of flowers and shrubs, and have won prizes for the hotel in garden competitions over many years. Among the hotel's top-of-the-range rooms are some that are equipped with four-poster beds, jacuzzis, and Victorian roll-top baths. All rooms are equipped with colour television, radio, hairdriers, irons and trouser presses, and room service is available 24 hours a day. Residents can enjoy free use of a large heated indoor swimming pool, a sauna, a jacuzzi spa, a solarium and a small gymnasium. There are further facilities for such sports as squash, tennis and snooker at the Falmouth Club, which is adjacent to the hotel. The Garras Restaurant complements its fine cuisine with a wide range of vintage wines. A range of special offers for stays of two nights or more are available throughout the year. The hotel caters for wedding parties, conferences and other functions, and on-site car parking can accommodate 60 cars. A short walk brings the visitor to Gyllynvase Beach on Falmouth Bay.

### Recommended in the area

National Maritime Museum, Cornwall; Tate St Ives; The Eden Project, St Austell;
Pendennis Castle; Gweek Seal Sanctuary

# The Greenbank Hotel

★★★ 77% ◉ HOTEL

| | |
|---|---|
| Address: | Harbourside, FALMOUTH TR11 2SR |
| Tel: | 01326 312440 |
| Fax: | 01326 211362 |
| Email: | sales@greenbank-hotel.com |
| Website: | www.greenbank-hotel.com |
| Map ref: | 1, SW82 |

Directions: 500yds past Marina on Penryn River

Rooms: 58, S £70–£100 D £105–£150 Facilities:
Parking: 44 Notes: ⊗ in bedrooms ⊗ in restaurant and bedrooms

With a private mid-17th century quay, this smart hotel's maritime heritage is indisputable, since it served as a base for captains of the packet ships that once carried mail around the world. The entrance foyer has a flagstone floor and sweeping staircase, while the lounge and many of the luxuriously appointed bedrooms look across the harbour to Flushing and the Roseland Peninsula. Naturally, fresh seafood, with catches landed only hours before arriving daily in the kitchen, features prominently in the Harbourside Restaurant, from which, it is worth emphasising, the view is terrific.

**Recommended in the area**

National Maritime Museum of Cornwall; Pendennis Castle; Eden Project

# Bedruthan Steps Hotel

★★★★ 75% ◉ HOTEL

| | |
|---|---|
| Address: | MAWGAN PORTH TR8 4BU |
| Tel: | 01637 860555 |
| Fax: | 01637 860714 |
| Email: | office@bedruthan.com |
| Website: | www.bedruthan.com |
| Map ref: | 1, SW86 |

Directions: From A39/A30 follow signs to Newquay
Airport. Right at T-junct, past airport, to Mawgan Porth

Rooms: 101, S £80–£124 D £160–£248 Facilities: ⊗
⊀ Sauna Jacuzzi Tennis Gym Parking: 100 Notes: ⊗ on premises ⊗ on premises

While the exterior of the Bedruthan pays homage to the 1970s, the interior is more 21st–century, with public areas large enough in which to lie low with a cappuccino and homemade cake. Rooms offer huge comfortable beds and the usual goodies; from most, watch those Atlantic rollers end their journey. The award-winning Indigo Bay restaurant - soft suede chairs, crisp white linen and candlelight - focuses on fine Cornish seafood and other local produce. Facilities for children are excellent.

**Recommended in the area**

Eden Project; Padstow Harbour; Cornish Gardens

# Meudon Hotel

★ ★ ★   85% ◉  COUNTRY HOUSE HOTEL

| | |
|---|---|
| **Address:** | MAWNAN SMITH TR11 5HT |
| **Tel:** | 01326 250541 |
| **Fax:** | 01326 250543 |
| **Email:** | wecare@meudon.co.uk |
| **Website:** | www.meudon.co.uk |
| **Map ref:** | 1, SW72 |

**Directions:** From Truro A39 towards Falmouth at Hillhead (anchor and cannons) rdbt, follow signs to Maenporth Beach. Hotel on left 1m after beach
**Rooms:** 29, S £70–£120 D £140–£240 **Facilities:** Wi-fi available **Parking:** 50 **Notes:** ⊘ in restaurant

There's good reason for the hotel not sounding Cornish. It takes its name from the nearby farmhouse, which Napoleonic prisoners of war named after Meudon, their French village. The private mansion, incorporating two 17th–century coastguard's cottages, which forms the basis of this family-owned hotel came many years later. It stands in a sub-tropical valley leading to private Bream Cove, from where the coastal path leads round Rosemullion Head to the Helford River. Surrounded by its own 'hanging gardens' and National Trust land, it houses a reception area, comfortable lounges, cocktail bar and restaurant, with antiques, oil paintings, log fires, Wilton carpets and fresh flowers everywhere. All guest rooms are in quiet new wings overlooking the gardens, each one with private bathroom (many with bidet), as well as TV, radio, and tea and coffee facilities. Nowhere, says the hotel, will you hear canned music. The restaurant, which harbours a fruiting vine, offers 'English at its best' cooking, with the accent on fresh fish and seafood, game, vegetables and other produce grown to Meudon's requirements by local producers. The wine list extends to some 200 fine wines from around the world. In summer months many guests spend their time relaxing in the exotic gardens.

**Recommended in the area**

Eden Project; National Maritime Museum, Cornwall; Trebah Gardens

# Headland Hotel

★★★★ 77%  HOTEL

| | |
|---|---|
| Address: | Fistral Beach, NEWQUAY TR7 1EW |
| Tel: | 01637 872211 |
| Fax: | 01637 872212 |
| Email: | office@headlandhotel.co.uk |
| Website: | www.headlandhotel.co.uk |
| Map ref: | 1, SW86 |

Directions: Off A30 onto A392 at Indian Queens, approaching Newquay follow signs for Fistral Beach
Rooms: 104, S £80–£130 D £90–£320 Facilities: ⓩ ⌇ Sauna Tennis STV Parking: 400 Notes: ⊘ in restaurant

This palatial Victorian hotel overlooks the surfers' paradise of Fistral Bay. Impressively floral public areas include quiet sitting rooms. The en suite guest rooms range from Budget to Best, some furnished as family suites. In addition to the genteel dining room, Sand Brasserie offers an extensive menu. Winter storm-watching breaks are popular here.

**Recommended in the area**

Lappa Valley Steam Railway; Lanhydrock (NT); Tate St Ives

---

# Hotel Penzance

★★★ 82%  HOTEL

| | |
|---|---|
| Address: | Britons Hill, PENZANCE TR18 3AE |
| Tel: | 01736 363117 |
| Fax: | 01736 350970 |
| Email: | enquiries@hotelpenzance.com |
| Website: | www.hotelpenzance.com |
| Map ref: | 1, SW40 |

Directions: From A30 pass heliport on right, left at next rdbt for town centre. 3rd right and hotel on right
Rooms: 24, S £55–£74 D £100–£132 Facilities: ⌇ STV Wi-fi available Parking: 14 Notes: ⊘ in restaurant

This Edwardian house is an ideal base from which to explore the west of Cornwall. In its thoughtfully and tastefully decorated bedrooms, find a generous supply of extras, and sea views from many. The contemporary Bay Restaurant & Gallery, around whose walls are paintings by local artists, offers award-winning modern European cuisine based on fresh produce from local fish markets, farms and gardens, and a few Cornish wines from the Camel Valley. The lounge offers a lighter all-day menu.

**Recommended in the area**

Eden Project; Land's End; Minack Open Air Theatre

# Rosevine Hotel

★★★ 80% ◉ COUNTRY HOUSE HOTEL

| | |
|---|---|
| Address: | PORTSCATHO, Truro TR2 5EW |
| Tel: | 01872 580206 |
| Fax: | 01872 580230 |
| Email: | info@rosevine.co.uk |
| Website: | www.rosevine.co.uk |
| Map ref: | 1, SW85 |

Directions: From St Austell take A390 for Truro. Left onto B3287 to Tregony. Then A3078 through Ruan High Lanes. Hotel 3rd left

Rooms: 17, S £86–£171 D £172–£276 Facilities: ⊗ Jacuzzi Wi-fi available Parking: 20
Notes: ⊗ in restaurant

The superb location of this small, family-run hotel affords breathtaking views across the sandy Porthcurnick Beach. The hotel's Classic rooms include en suite bathrooms, televisions and telephones; the Superior-grade rooms, available for a supplement, are larger and have fine sea-facing positions. The hotel has an indoor swimming pool, jacuzzi and paddling pool for all-weather family relaxation. The restaurant uses local produce in all its meals, and is happy to cater for children and diners with special dietary requirements. The hotel's therapist can offer rejuvenating and revitalizing massages and other treatments in guests' own rooms. Special residential packages offered by the hotel include: Rosevine Gourmet Three-Night Breaks and Weekend Breaks, throughout October and December; a Garden Lovers' Four-Day Break, including admission to three of Cornwall's finest gardens; and a four-night Winter Warmer package, including tickets to the Eden Project and the Lost Gardens of Heligan. During the school holidays, children can enjoy the Art and Play workshops. The hotel puts on special entertainment with many of its festive meals over the Christmas period. A ten-minute walk along the beautiful coastal path to the unspoilt fishing village of Portscatho is recommended.

### Recommended in the area

The Lost Gardens of Heligan; the Eden Project; Gull Rock seabird colony

# Penventon Park Hotel

★★★ 77% HOTEL

| | |
|---|---|
| Address: | REDRUTH TR15 1TE |
| Tel: | 01209 203000 |
| Fax: | 01209 203001 |
| Email: | hello@penventon.com |
| Website: | www.penventon.com |
| Map ref: | 1, SW64 |

Directions: Off A30 at Redruth. Follow signs for Redruth West, hotel 1m S

Rooms: 68, S £35–£100 D £64–£138 Facilities: ⓡ Sauna Jacuzzi Solarium Gym Parking: 100 Notes: ⊘ in restaurant

The Penventon Park Hotel is a splendid Georgian mansion, now adapted to the highest standards of modern convenience and luxury. Although large – it sits in fully 10 acres of private grounds – it is a private hotel run by the Pascoe family. Its accommodation includes 20 newly built garden suites, two of which are equipped with four-poster beds. All rooms have en suite facilities, and television, including satellite TV, direct-dial telephone and drinks-making facilities. The hotel has a health and leisure spa, which includes a heated indoor swimming pool, a sauna, a gymnasium and a sunroom. A staff beautician and a masseuse are available. The Dining Galleries Restaurant features Cornish dishes in addition to its English, French and Italian cuisines. The restaurant also offers vegetarian menus and a wide range of fish dishes. Two function rooms are available for private parties, conferences, civil ceremonies and wedding receptions. Special breaks are available at Christmas, New Year and St Valentine's Day, and at other times of year. Being located centrally in the county, it is within an hour of all of Cornwall's attractions. The hotel is conveniently situated close to the A30 road, giving easy access to Truro, St Ives and other locations. Children of all ages are welcome at the hotel.

**Recommended in the area**

St Michael's Mount; National Maritime Museum, Falmouth; Tate Gallery.

# Idle Rocks Hotel

★★★ 86% ◉◉ HOTEL

| | |
|---|---|
| **Address:** | Harbour Side, ST MAWES TR2 5AN |
| **Tel:** | 01326 270771 |
| **Fax:** | 01326 270062 |
| **Email:** | reception@idlerocks.co.uk |
| **Website:** | www.idlerocks.co.uk |
| **Map ref:** | 1, SW83 |
| **Directions:** | Off A390 onto A3078, 14m to St Mawes. |

Hotel on left

**Rooms:** 33, D £158–£318 **Parking:** 6

**Notes:** ⊘ in restaurant

The fishing village of St Mawes is situated on the tip of Cornwall's Roseland Peninsula, in an officially designated Area of Outstanding Natural Beauty. Thanks to the harbourside location of the Idle Rocks Hotel, most of the bedrooms enjoy a view of the water. The rooms are of four grades: Premier, Select, Standard (sea view) and Standard (non-view). All rooms have en suite facilities, direct-dial telephones, television, hairdryers and tea- and coffee-making facilities. The hotel boasts two restaurants – the Water's Edge and the On the Rocks Brasserie – with a team of chefs who have developed a reputation for fine cuisine over many years. Dishes are based on local produce and are constantly changing. The Water's Edge is the more formal of the restaurants, with a dress code of smart casual wear. Its tables are set on three levels to enable diners to enjoy the view of the harbour. The On The Rocks Brasserie offers a less formal eating experience, and offers morning coffee, lunch, afternoon tea, and dinner. Drinks and meals can be taken on the large terrace perched over the water. Falmouth can be reached by the passenger ferry from St Mawes and visitors can make day trips by boat. Many of Cornwall's major attractions are within a 45-minute drive of the hotel and the South West Coach Path is nearby.

**Recommended in the area**

St Mawes Castle; The Eden Project; The Lost Gardens of Heligan; Trelissick Garden (NT)

# The Island Hotel

★★★ ◉◉ HOTEL

| | |
|---|---|
| Address: | TRESCO, Isles of Scilly TR24 0PU |
| Tel: | 01720 422883 |
| Fax: | 01720 423008 |
| Email: | islandhotel@tresco.co.uk |
| Website: | www.tresco.co.uk/holidays/island_hotel.asp |
| Map ref: | 1, SV81 |
| Directions: | Helicopter service Penzance to Tresco |

**Rooms:** 48 S £125–£165 D £260–£440 **Facilities:** ↖
Tennis STV **Notes:** ⊗ in bedrooms ⊘ in restaurant

This delightful colonial-style hotel stands by the waterside, ringed by uninhabited islands and the Golden Ball reef. Spacious, comfortable lounges, the airy restaurant and many of the bedrooms look over Atlantic backwaters. The Flower Rock and Castle Wings make up the majority of the brightly furnished rooms. From the Terrace Bar and Lounge, decking leads down to the extensive lawns. The first-floor, balconied Garden Wing looks towards Crow Sound and the Eastern Isles. Carefully prepared cuisine showcases locally caught fish, island vegetables and Tresco-reared beef.

**Recommended in the area**

Isles of Scilly Heritage Coast, Blockhouse Castle, Ravens Porth Sailing Centre

# Trenython Manor Hotel and Spa

★★★ 80% ◉ COUNTRY HOUSE HOTEL

| | |
|---|---|
| Address: | Castle Dore Road, TYWARDREATH, Fowey PL24 2TS |
| Tel: | 01726 814797 |
| Fax: | 01726 817030 |
| Email: | trenython@clublacosta.com |
| Website: | www.trenython.co.uk |
| Map ref: | 1, SX05 |

**Directions:** A390/B3269 towards Fowey, after 2m right into Castledore. Hotel 100mtrs on left
**Rooms:** 24, S £105–£195 D £125–£225 **Facilities:** ⊛ Sauna Jacuzzi Solarium Tennis Gym
**Parking:** 50 **Notes:** ⊗ in bedrooms ⊘ in restaurant

Trenython, a successful marriage of Italian style and English charm, stands in 25 acres overlooking St Austell Bay. The 17th century hotel retains its original staircases and colonnades and many of the bedrooms have sea views. TM's Restaurant serves a range of meats and fish, including fresh lobster.

**Recommended in the area**

Eden Project; Pine Lodge Gardens; Lanhydrock House

Veryan.

# The Nare Hotel

★★★★ 82% ❀ COUNTRY HOUSE HOTEL

| | |
|---|---|
| Address: | Carne Beach, VERYAN TR2 5PF |
| Tel: | 01872 501111 |
| Fax: | 01872 501856 |
| Email: | office@narehotel.co.uk |
| Website: | www.narehotel.co.uk |
| Map ref: | 1, SW93 |

Directions:From Tregony follow A3078 for approx 1.5m. Left at Veryan sign, through village towards sea & hotel)
Rooms: 39, S £100–£206 D £190–£380 Facilities: ↘ ⓧ Sauna Jacuzzi Tennis Gym STV Hair & Beauty Salon Parking: 80 Notes: ⊘ in restaurant

The Nare Hotel, standing in its own extensive grounds above Carne Beach, is a hotel in the traditional country-house style, its bedrooms decorated with flowers, and providing such traditional services as shoe-cleaning and daily laundry. The hotel's chef of many years creates traditional English fare from local produce, including seafood specialities such as Portloe lobster and crab. Desserts and cakes are home-made. The main dining-room commands views of the sea on three sides.

**Recommended in the area**

The Eden Project; The National Maritime Museum, Falmouth; The Lost Gardens of Heligan

Ullswater, Lake District National Park.

# Rothay Manor

★ ★ ★  82% 🏵 HOTEL

| | |
|---|---|
| **Address:** | Rothay Bridge, AMBLESIDE LA22 0EH |
| **Tel:** | 015394 33605 |
| **Fax:** | 015394 33607 |
| **Email:** | hotel@rothaymanor.co.uk |
| **Website:** | www.rothaymanor.co.uk/aa |
| **Map ref:** | 5, NY30 |

**Directions:** In Ambleside follow signs for Coniston (A593). Hotel 0.25m SW of Ambleside opposite
**Rooms:** 19 S £85–£130 D £135–£210 **Parking:** 45
**Notes:** ⊗ in bedrooms ⊘ in restaurant

For 40 years the same family has run this hotel, a Regency house built in 1825 and set in its own landscaped gardens, a quarter of a mile from Lake Windermere. The bedrooms are individually designed, with en suite facilities, telephone, television, hairdryer and tea-and coffee-making facilities. Several of the highest-quality rooms have balconies and a view of the fells. Flowers and antiques create the atmosphere of a traditional country house. Meals are prepared from local produce and complemented by a wine list selected with unusual care; cakes and desserts are home-made by the hotel's own pastry chef. The hotel is a 10-minute walk from the centre of Ambleside, and is a good starting-point for walking, riding and cycling in the surrounding National Park. Guests have complimentary access to the exercise facilities and beauty treatments of the nearby Low Wood Leisure Club. The hotel offers a number of packages, devoted to such special interests as antiques, bridge, gardening, Lake District literary heritage and painting. Midweek three-night short breaks are available round the year and there are house parties at Christmas and New Year. Small meetings of up to 22 people can be accommodated in the Brathay Room.

### Recommended in the area

Lake Windermere; Dove Cottage (Wordsworth); Hill Top (Beatrix Potter).

# Best Western Appleby Manor Country House Hotel

★★★  85% ◉  HOTEL

| | |
|---|---|
| **Address:** | Roman Road, |
| | APPLEBY-IN-WESTMORLAND CA16 6JB |
| **Tel:** | 017683 51571 |
| **Fax:** | 017683 52888 |
| **Email:** | reception@applebymanor.co.uk |
| **Website:** | www.applebymanor.co.uk |
| **Map ref:** | 6, NY62 |
| **Directions:** | M6 junct 40 and on A66 towards Brough |

**Rooms:** 30, S £87–£97 D £134–£220 **Facilities:** ⊗
Sauna Jacuzzi Solarium STV Wi-fi in bedrooms **Parking:** 50 **Notes:** ⊗ in bedrooms ⊖ in restaurant

From the gardens at Appleby Manor, residents have a fine view over the Eden Valley. Inside, the decor is in pitch-pine or oak. The bedrooms are furnished in rich traditional styles, and some have four-poster beds. The restaurant uses local produce and features an extensive selection of wines.

**Recommended in the area**

Rheged Discovery Centre; Weatheriggs Pottery; Lake District National Park.

# Farlam Hall Hotel

★★★  ◉◉  HOTEL

| | |
|---|---|
| **Address:** | BRAMPTON CA8 2NG |
| **Tel:** | 016977 46234 |
| **Fax:** | 016977 46683 |
| **Email:** | farlam@relaischateaux.com |
| **Website:** | www.farlamhall.co.uk |
| **Map ref:** | 6, NY56 |
| **Directions:** | On A689 (to Alston). Hotel 2m on left |

**Rooms:** 12, S £147–£167 D £275–£315 **Parking:** 35
**Notes:** ⊖ in restaurant & bedrooms

This hotel, occupying a large manor house in 12 acres of grounds, enjoys a tranquil setting. Rooms are tastefully furnished and have en suite bathrooms. The restaurant opens to the general public in the evenings and for prebooked lunches for parties of 10 or more. Light lunches are always available during the day for residents only. The menu changes daily, and makes the most of local produce. Smart dress is requested for the evening meal. There is no bar, but drinks are served in the gardens, the two drawing-rooms, or bedrooms. No children under five years.

**Recommended in the area**

Northern Pennines (Area of Outstanding Natural Beauty); Hadrian's Wall; Eden Valley

Holker Hall.

# Clare House

★ ◉ HOTEL

| | |
|---|---|
| **Address:** | Park Road, |
| | GRANGE-OVER-SANDS LA11 7HQ |
| **Tel:** | 015395 33026 |
| **Fax:** | 015395 34310 |
| **Email:** | info@clarehousehotel.co.uk |
| **Website:** | www.clarehousehotel.co.uk |
| **Map ref:** | 1, SD47 |
| **Directions:** | Off A590 onto B5277, through Lindale into |

Grange, keep left, hotel 0.5m on left past Crown Hill

**Rooms:** 19 (18 en suite), S £68 D £136 **Parking:** 18 **Notes:** ⊗ in bedrooms ⊘ in restaurant

A family-run hotel, with Morecambe Bay to the south and the Lake District to the north; most rooms enjoy a view over the bay. They are all centrally heated, have tea- and coffee-making facilities, TV and direct dial telephones, and some have balconies. A full English breakfast is the ideal start to the day, before setting off along the mile-long promenade at the foot of the garden. Return for a light lunch or skilfully prepared dinner chosen from a menu of English and French traditional and speciality dishes.

**Recommended in the area**

Holker Hall; Windermere Steamboat Centre; Cumberland Pencil Museum

# Best Western Castle Green Hotel in Kendal

★★★ 81% ®® HOTEL

| | |
|---|---|
| **Address:** | KENDAL LA9 6RG |
| **Tel:** | 01539 734000 |
| **Fax:** | 01539 735522 |
| **Email:** | reception@castlegreen.co.uk |
| **Website:** | www.castlegreen.co.uk |
| **Map ref:** | 5, SD59 |

**Directions:** M6 junct 37 follow A684 towards Kendal. Hotel on right after 5m

**Rooms:** 100, S £79–£129 D £88–£158 **Facilities:** ® Solarium Gym STV Wi-fi available

**Parking:** 200 **Notes:** ® in bedrooms ® in restaurant & bedrooms

The Castle Green, with Kendal on its doorstep, is well placed for exploring the southern end of the beautiful Lake District. Standing in 14 acres of woodlands and gardens, this smart modern hotel offers comfort and convenience in all its en suite rooms. They all look bright and fresh, and all have soft duvets, satellite TV and tempting room service menu. Those wanting more space and a little more luxury might opt for an Executive room, while the two rooms with a four-poster will appeal to those after something different. The bustling Greenhouse restaurant offers a choice of things to look at – in one direction, through huge panoramic windows, are the landscaped gardens and Kendal Castle; in the other, the chefs at work in the theatre-style kitchen. The produce is the best the region can provide – try Cumbrian lamb, for example, or Morecambe Bay shrimps. Alexander's, in the grounds, is the hotel's genuine real-ale pub, serving hearty meals and snacks. Work out in the leisure club's fully equipped gym, swim in the indoor pool, or relax in the steam room. A large conference and training centre offers a wide range of rooms to accommodate up to 300 people.

**Recommended in the area**

Abbot Hall Art Gallery; Lake District National Park; Levens Hall & Topiary Gardens

# Dale Head Hall Lakeside Hotel

★★★  78% ◉◉  COUNTRY HOUSE HOTEL

Address:     Lake Thirlmere, KESWICK CA12 4TN
Tel:         017687 72478
Fax:         017687 71070
Email:       onthelakeside@daleheadhall.co.uk
Website:     www.daleheadhall.co.uk
Map ref:     5, NY22
Directions:  Between Keswick & Grasmere. Off A591
and onto private drive
Rooms: 12, S £127.50–£135 D £205–£260 Parking: 30 Notes: ⊗ in bedrooms ⊘ in restaurant

The oldest part of the main house dates from the early 16th century, although it has been much extended over the centuries. It stands alone on the edge of Thirlmere with Helvellyn, England's third highest mountain, rising behind. For much of the 20th century it was the summer residence of the Mayor of Manchester, until in 1990 the city council sold the property and the long process of restoration and transformation into a private hotel began. Comfortable and inviting public areas include a choice of lounges, but no bar, and an atmospheric beamed restaurant. There are three styles of bedroom – the Fellside in the original house, the Lakeside in the Victorian wing, and, in a new extension, the particularly spacious Superior Lakeside, some with hand-crafted four-posters. Whichever style you choose, the gardens can be seen sloping gently towards the shore of the lake which, incidentally, supplies Manchester with 50 million gallons of water a day. The restaurant has two AA Rosettes awarded for excellence of cuisine and service for seven years running, and features a short, daily-changing menu based on fresh local produce, such as Borrowdale trout, and salt marsh lamb. The stable block at the rear has been converted into self-catering accommodation.

## Recommended in the area

Lake District National Park; Ravenglass and Eskdale Railway; Cumberland Pencil Museum

# Swinside Lodge

★★ ◉◉ COUNTRY HOUSE HOTEL

| | |
|---|---|
| Address: | Grange Rd, Newlands, KESWICK CA12 5UE |
| Tel: | 017687 72948 |
| Fax: | 017687 73312 |
| Email: | info@swinsidelodge-hotel.co.uk |
| Website: | www.swinsidelodge-hotel.co.uk |
| Map ref: | 5, NY22 |

Directions: Off A66 left at Portinscale. Follow road to Grange for 2m ignoring Swinside & Newlands Valley signs

Rooms: 8 (7 en suite) S £98 D £156–£196 Facilities: Wi-fi in bedrooms Parking: 12
Notes: ⊗ in bedrooms ⊘ in hotel

Swinside Lodge is a Georgian country house hotel in the Newlands Valley, just west of Derwentwater, known as the Queen of the Northern Lakes. It stands alone, surrounded by hills, valleys and woodlands, at the foot of a mountain called Cat Bells, in one of the most unspoilt areas of the Lake District National Park. A short stroll takes you to the lakeside, from where the Keswick launch provides a regular service. Pastel blues and yellows in the reception rooms give them a fresh, clean look, while the sitting rooms offer books, maps and fresh flowers. Seven attractively decorated bedrooms offer a high degree of comfort and good views. All have a private bath and/or shower, TV, radio, hair dryer, hospitality tray and other extras. In the restaurant, candlelight accentuates the richness of the red walls and ceiling. Very much a Lake District favourite, with fresh, local produce used as much as possible in everything, from the home-baked breads, soups and puddings to the petits fours served with coffee. A four-course dinner is served at 7.30 each evening, preceded by aperitifs and canapés. Those who enjoy sailing, bird watching and fell walking will certainly be in their element at Swinside Lodge.

### Recommended in the area

Ospreys at Whinlatter Forest; Castlerigg Stone Circle; Borrowdale

# Macdonald Leeming House

★★★★ 76% ◉◉ HOTEL

| | |
|---|---|
| Address: | WATERMILLOCK CA11 0JJ |
| Tel: | 0870 400 8131 |
| Fax: | 017684 86443 |
| Email: | leeminghouse@macdonald-hotels.co.uk |
| Website: | www.macdonald-hotels.co.uk |
| Map ref: | 5, NY42 |

Directions: M6 junct 40, take A66 to Keswick. At rdbt take A592 toward Ullswater

Rooms: 41, S £150–£185 D £260–£330 **Facilities:** STV Wi-fi in bedrooms **Parking:** 50 **Notes:** ⊗ in restaurant

The 22-acre, south-facing location is superb, with lush gardens sloping down to Ullswater. Many rooms, more than half with balconies, offer views of the lake and the towering fells. All are furnished to a high standard, with private en suite bathroom. Public rooms include three lounges, cosy bar and library. The Regency restaurant has an excellent reputation for its modern British and classic food, with just about everything homemade. The Conservatory serves an informal lunch and afternoon tea.

**Recommended in the area**

Aira Force Waterfall; Carlisle Cathedral; Dalemain House

# Rampsbeck Country House Hotel

★★★ ◉◉◉ COUNTRY HOUSE HOTEL

| | |
|---|---|
| Address: | WATERMILLOCK, Penrith CA11 0LP |
| Tel: | 017684 86442 |
| Fax: | 017684 86688 |
| Email: | enquiries@rampsbeck.fsnet.co.uk |
| Website: | www.rampsbeck.fsnet.co.uk |
| Map ref: | 5, NY42 |

Directions: M6 junct 40, signs for A592 to Ullswater, at T-junct with lake in front, turn right

Rooms: 19, S £75–£150 D £120–£250 **Facilities:** Wi-fi available **Parking:** 30 **Notes:** ⊗ in restaurant

This fine 18th-century country house, furnished with antiques, lies in 18 acres of parkland on Ullswater's western shore. There are three reception rooms: the Panelled Hall, with comfortable settees and log fire; the Drawing Room, with marble fireplace and ornate ceiling; and an intimate lounge. The elegant restaurant offers attractively presented food. In good weather, have lunch on the bar terrace.

**Recommended in the area**

Lowther Wildlife Park; Rheged Discovery Centre; Lake District National Park

# Gilpin Lodge Country House Hotel & Restaurant

★★★★ ◎◎◎ HOTEL

| | |
|---|---|
| Address: | Crook Road, WINDERMERE LA23 3NE |
| Tel: | 015394 88818 |
| Fax: | 015394 88058 |
| Email: | hotel@gilpinlodge.co.uk |
| Website: | www.gilpinlodge.co.uk |
| Map ref: | 5, SD49 |

Directions: M6 junct 36, take A590/A591 to rdbt north of Kendal, take B5284, hotel 5m on right

Rooms: 20, S £175 D £250–£350 Parking: 30 Notes: ✖ in hotel ⊘ on premises

An elegant, friendly hotel in 20 tranquil acres of gardens, moors and woodland, owned and run by two generations of the Cunliffe family. The en suite bedrooms all have bath and shower, Molton Brown toiletries and bath robes. Individually and stylishly decorated to a high standard, they are quiet, with delightful views. Each room has a sitting area, TV, direct-dial phone, radio, hair dryer, and beverage tray with home-made biscuits; some rooms also have a trouser press. The Garden Suites have enormous beds, walk-in dressing areas, large sofas, modern fireplaces, flatscreen TVs and sensual bathrooms. Glass-fronted lounge areas lead to individual gardens with cedarwood hot tubs. Food is important at Gilpin Lodge. The nine chefs are passionate about using the finest local, organic ingredients as extensively as possible. It's hard to put a label on the food - classically based, yes, yet thoroughly modern and imaginative, without being too experimental. Tables have fresh flowers, candles at night, crisp white linen, fine china and glass, and gleaming silver. The wine list, featuring over 300 wines from 13 countries, reflects real interest rather than a desire to sell high priced vintages. Residents have free use of a local leisure club, although on-call spa therapists will visit guest rooms.

### Recommended in the area

Lake Windermere; Beatrix Potter Gallery; Dove Cottage and Wordsworth Museum

# Holbeck Ghyll Country House Hotel

★★★★ ◉◉◉  COUNTRY HOUSE HOTEL

Address:     Holbeck Lane, WINDERMERE LA23 1LU
Tel:         015394 32375
Fax:         015394 34743
Email:       stay@holbeckghyll.com
Website:     www.holbeckghyll.com
Map ref:     5, SD49
Directions:  3m N of Windermere on A591, right into Holbeck Lane (signed Troutbeck), hotel 0.5m on left
Rooms: 23, S £135–£175 D £220–£270 **Facilities:** Sauna Spa Steam room Tennis Gym STV Wi-fi available **Parking:** 28 **Notes:** ⊗ in restaurant

If stunning Lakeland scenery is what you want – and why visit this part of England otherwise – the Holbeck Ghyll has it all. Lord Lonsdale, who coincidentally was the AA's first president, certainly thought so when he bought it in 1888 as his hunting lodge. The peaceful setting is truly seductive, with extensive grounds and views across the lawns to Lake Windermere and the Langdale Fells. In the welcoming oak-panelled entrance hall a log fire burns in an inglenook fireplace most of the year. There's more oak panelling in the two elegant restaurants, both of which look out over the lake and mountains. Here a typical menu might offer John Dory with cauliflower beignets, or roast squab pigeon with confit cabbage and Madeira sauce. In the individually designed en suite bedrooms you'll find every amenity, including exquisite furnishings, Egyptian cotton sheets and, in many, a balcony or patio from which to gaze out over the lake and countryside. Additional rooms are in an adjacent, more private lodge. Sports and spa facilities include a gym, sauna, treatment rooms, tennis court, croquet lawn and putting green.

### Recommended in the area

Dove Cottage; Rydal Mount; Lake Windermere Cruises

# Lindeth Howe Country House Hotel & Restaurant

★★★ 85% ◉ HOTEL

Address: Lindeth Drive, Longtail Hill,
WINDERMERE LA23 3JF
Tel: 015394 45759
Fax: 015394 46368
Email: hotel@lindeth-howe.co.uk
Website: www.lindeth-howe.co.uk
Map ref: 5, SD49
Directions: Off A592, onto B5284 1m S of Bowness
Rooms: 36 (including 2 for disabled guests), S £59–£84 D £118–£0 **Facilities:** ⊕ Sauna Solarium
Gym STV **Parking:** 50 **Notes:** ⊗ in bedrooms ⊘ in restaurant

Once owned by Beatrix Potter, Lindeth Howe enjoys views across Lake Windermere. Public areas
include a sun terrace, the Hilltop Lounge and the library. Canapés and drinks in the lounge may be
followed by a five-course dinner in the Dining Room. The bedrooms are furnished to a high standard.
**Recommended in the area**
World of Beatrix Potter; Windermere Lake Cruises; Mountain Goat mini-coach tours

# Linthwaite House Hotel & Restaurant

★★★ ◎◎◎ COUNTRY HOUSE HOTEL
Address: Crook Road, WINDERMERE LA23 3JA
Tel: 015394 88600
Fax: 015394 88601
Email: stay@linthwaite.com
Website: www.linthwaite.com
Map ref: 5, SD49
Directions: A591 to The Lakes, at rdbt, take B5284
Rooms: 27, S £130–£160 D £170–£320 **Facilities:** STV Wi-fi in bedrooms **Parking:** 40
**Notes:** ⊗ in bedrooms ⊘ in restaurant

A beautiful country house hotel in a sublime hilltop setting overlooking Lake Windermere and the fells.
Inviting public rooms include an attractive conservatory, adjoining lounge and smokers' bar. Individually
decorated en suite bedrooms combine contemporary furnishings with classical styles. The restaurant
serves modern British food, using top quality local produce. Voted the 'most romantic' hotel by the AA.
**Recommended in the area**
Lake District National Park; Dove Cottage; Scafell Pike

# The Samling

★★★ ◉◉◉ HOTEL

| | |
|---|---|
| Address: | Ambleside Road, WINDERMERE LA23 1LR |
| Tel: | 015394 31922 |
| Fax: | 015394 30400 |
| Email: | info@thesamling.com |
| Website: | www.thesamling.com |
| Map ref: | 5, SD30 |
| Directions: | Turn right off A591, 300mtrs after Low Wood Hotel |

**Rooms:** 11, S £195–£395 D £195–£395 **Facilities:** Jacuzzi STV Parking: 15 **Notes:** ⊗ in bedrooms ⊘ in restaurant

This three-gabled gem is situated in 67 acres of grounds, several hundred feet above Lake Windermere. Built in the early 1780s, it is, the owners emphasise, a hotel in the country, not a country-house hotel. By the 1800s, The Samling was owned by the landlord of poet William Wordsworth, who lived nearby. The spacious, beautifully furnished bedrooms and suites are split between the main house and some converted cottages. All are startlingly different and all but two overlook the lake. Room names, such as Methera, Tethera and Hovera, are traditional words once used by Lake District shepherds to count sheep. Public rooms include a sumptuous drawing room, a small library and an elegant, award-winning dining room where the food, made from only the best local ingredients, is light and full of good ideas. The wine selection can hold its own under the scrutiny of some pretty expert noses. The breakfast, by common consent, is best taken in bed. Outdoor activities include water-skiing, paragliding, canoeing and croquet. The Conference Centre in the old stables seats 14; there are also several syndicate rooms, while the Dutch Barn Theatre can comfortably seat up to 60. Contemporary works of art can be found located in different parts of the grounds.

**Recommended in the area**

Sailing on Lake Windermere; Dove Cottage; Jenkins Crag

Whitehaven Harbour.

# Washington Central Hotel

★★★ 85% ❀ HOTEL

| | |
|---|---|
| Address: | Washington Street, WORKINGTON CA14 3AY |
| Tel: | 01900 65772 |
| Fax: | 01900 68770 |
| Email: | kawildwchotel@aol.com |
| Website: | www.washingtoncentralhotelworkington.com |
| Map ref: | 5, NY02 |
| Directions: | M6 junct 40, follow A66 to Workington |

Rooms: 46, S £85 D/T £125 Facilities: ⓧ Pool Sauna Jacuzzi Solarium Gym STV Parking: 10 Notes: ⊗ in bedrooms ⊘ in restaurant

The distinctive red-brick Washington includes super rooms, fine restaurant, conference facilities and leisure club. The en suite bedrooms are all provided with those extras that guests look for. The Carlton Restaurant, painted in soft pastels, recently won its first AA Rosette, while bar meals are available in the lounge, snug and conservatory. For a private dinner, the Clock Tower is unique, since it is actually inside the clock face, with long-distance views of the Isle of Man, Scotland and the Lake District.

**Recommended in the area**

St Bees Head Heritage Coast; Ravenglass and Eskdale Railway; Sellafield Visitors Centre

The valleys of Dovedale, Peak District National Park.

# Callow Hall

★★★  80% ●● COUNTRY HOUSE HOTEL

Address:  Mappleton Road, ASHBOURNE DE6 2AA
Tel:  01335 300900
Fax:  01335 300512
Email:  reservations@callowhall.demon.co.uk
Website:  www.callowhall.co.uk
Map ref:  7, SK14
Directions:  A515 through Ashbourne towards Buxton, left at Bowling Green pub, then 1st right
Rooms: 16, S £95–£120 D £140–£190 Parking: 20
Notes: ⊗ in bedrooms ⊘ in restaurant

A charming, much loved country house hotel in a tranquil valley, 'just over the hill' from the attractive market town of Ashbourne. Enveloped by 44 acres of gardens, fields and woodland overlooking the Bentley Brook and valley of the River Dove, this restored Victorian hall meets 21st-century expectations in old world surroundings. Owners, the Spencer family are still much in evidence with the younger generation, Anthony and Emma, now enthusiasticallly running day-to-day operations. The hotel's en suite bedrooms are all as tastefully decorated as the public rooms, and some have uninterrupted views across the countryside. After an aperitif in the cosy bar, or maybe in the elegant drawing room, transfer to the restaurant to dine on freshly prepared, award-winning food prepared by accomplished head chef, Anthony Spencer, and his team. Their innovative menus change daily, accompanied, of course, by an extensive wine list. Expect to find dishes making full use of the baking, smoking and curing skills passed down through the Spencer family, master bakers in Ashbourne, since 1724. As somewhere to leave the city behind for, celebrate a family occasion, or maybe brief the sales reps on the new ad campaign, Callow Hall could be quite hard to beat.

**Recommended in the area**

Peak District National Park; Chatsworth House; Alton Towers

Chatsworth House and the Derwent River.

# Cavendish Hotel

★★★  86% ⍟⍟  HOTEL

| | |
|---|---|
| Address: | BASLOW DE45 1SP |
| Tel: | 01246 582311 |
| Fax: | 01246 582312 |
| Email: | info@cavendish-hotel.net |
| Website: | www.cavendish-hotel.net |
| Map ref: | 7, SK27 |

Directions: M1 junct 29/A617 W to Chesterfield & A619 to Baslow. Hotel in village centre, off main road
Rooms: 24, S £119–£153 D £152–£230
Facilities: STV Parking: 50 Notes: ⊗ in bedrooms ⊘ in restaurant

The hotel's location on the Duke of Devonshire's Chatsworth Estate, in the heart of the Peak District, makes it an ideal centre for walking. Over 300 paintings, from all periods and schools, together with antiques and tasteful furnishings, lend elegance to the hotel's interior. All bedrooms have magnificent views over the Chatsworth Estate. The Gallery Restaurant bases its dishes on local ingredients and offers about 70 wines. The Boardroom is available for business meetings of 16-20 participants.
Recommended in the area
Chatsworth House; Haddon Hall; Peak District National Park.

# Fischer's Baslow Hall

★★★ ◎◎◎◎ HOTEL

| | |
|---|---|
| Address: | Calver Road, BASLOW DE45 1RR |
| Tel: | 01246 583259 |
| Fax: | 01246 583818 |
| Email: | reservations@fischers-baslowhall.co.uk |
| Website: | www.fischers-baslowhall.co.uk |
| Map ref: | 7, SK27 |

Directions: On A623 between Baslow & Calver
Rooms: 11, S £100–£130 D £140–£180
Facilities: Wi-fi in bedrooms Parking: 40
Notes: ⊗ in bedrooms ⊘ in restaurant & bedrooms

Standing at the end of a winding, chestnut-lined driveway, on the edge of the Chatsworth Estate, Baslow Hall enjoys an enviable location. Even someone with architectural knowledge may be forgiven for dating its gabled wings, mullioned and transomed windows and splendid shell porch to the 17th century. In fact, it was built in 1907, but the locally quarried gritstone has weathered as nicely in 100 years as it would have in three hundred. Max and Sue Fischer bought the hall in 1988 as a fitting setting for an already successful restaurant business, but with the added benefit of guest accommodation. Rooms in the main house feature ornate plasterwork ceilings, lavish fabrics, quality Egyptian cotton bedding and well-appointed, traditionally-styled bathrooms. In the Garden House they are more contemporary, more minimalist in style, with 'dramatic' bathrooms and every convenience. Max and his head chef, Rupert Rowley, have collected a clutch of accolades for their imaginative seasonal cuisine that makes use of the very best local produce, typically Derbyshire spring lamb, Chatsworth venison, and wild hare, alongside imported desirables such as foie gras and truffles. Public rooms can all be used for weddings, meetings and conferences. The Fischers also own Rowleys Restaurant and Bar in the village.

### Recommended in the area

Chatsworth House; Peak District National Park; Blue John Cavern; Haddon Hall

# Best Western Midland Hotel

★★★★  84% HOTEL

Address:   Midland Road, DERBY DE1 2SQ
Tel:       01332 345894
Fax:       01332 293522
Email:     sales@midland-derby.co.uk
Website:   www.midland-derby.co.uk
Map ref:   7, SK33
Directions: Opposite Derby railway station
Rooms: 100, S £68–£130 D £68–£140
Facilities: Wi-fi in bedrooms **Parking:** 90
Notes: ⊗ in bedrooms ⊖ in restaurant

This early Victorian, Grade II-listed hotel is situated in a conservation area opposite Derby mainline station. It is now the world's oldest operating railway hotel, venerable enough for Queen Victoria to have visited it several times during the 1840s. One of the menus served is mounted on the wall in the Wyvern Bar. Derby has a long association with Rolls-Royce and from 1921 to 1945 most of the company's AGMs were held here. All 50 en suite standard bedrooms have colour TV, radio, Wi-Fi, hospitality tray, hair dryer and a choice of bedspreads or duvets, while an equal number of executive rooms have, additionally, a separate desk and working area, walk-in shower cubicle and decent-sized bath. Public areas include a comfortable lounge and a walled, tree-lined garden. Service throughout the hotel is skilled, attentive and friendly. The Wyvern Restaurant is noted locally for what it calls 'back to basics' English and Continental cuisine, using the freshest and best ingredients available, complemented by an excellent wine cellar. For more intimate dining guests can try the air-conditioned Mirror Room. A resident pianist plays in the Lounge Bar most evenings. Eight air-conditioned conference suites, three of which overlook the garden, can cater for up to 150 delegates.

#### Recommended in the area

Chatsworth House; Royal Crown Derby; Peak District National Park

# Riber Hall

★★★  81% ◉◉  Country House Hotel

Address:     MATLOCK DE4 5JU
Tel:          01629 582795
Fax:          01629 580475
Email:        info@riber-hall.co.uk
Website:      www.riber-hall.co.uk
Map ref:      7, SK30
Directions:   1m off A615 at Tansley
Rooms: 14, S £98–£116 D £145–£188
Facilities: Tennis STV Parking: 50
Notes: ⊘ in restaurant

The Riber Hall Hotel is a manor house whose origins go back to the 15th century, with its own walled garden, fountain and orchard. It enjoys spectacular views of the Derbyshire countryside and is a good centre for walking in the Peak District National Park. The bedrooms have en suite facilities and are furnished with antiques. The beds too are antique, and most are four-posters. Period furniture is found throughout the hotel, and log fires blaze indoors in the winter. The hotel has received AA awards for both its wine list and cuisine and the Head Chef changes the menus monthly to make optimum use of the seasonal and local produce, some of which is sourced from an organic vegetable supplier in Riber village. A full menu is available for vegetarian guests. Conference facilities for between 6–30 delegates, supported with slide projection, photocopying, fax and other services, can be held in any of a selection of period rooms. The hotel and its grounds provide a beautiful backdrop for wedding receptions and other private functions. In addition, the hotel is licensed as a place where wedding ceremonies can be conducted. Riber Hall is close to Matlock, an attractive old town that is a centre for caving and hill-walking. It is also 20 minutes' drive from the M1 motorway and has easy access to Chesterfield, Derby, Mansfield, Nottingham and Sheffield.

**Recommended in the area**

Chatsworth House; Haddon Hall; Peak District National Park.

# DEVON

Torquay harbour.

# Northcote Manor

★★★ ◉◉ COUNTRY HOUSE HOTEL

| | |
|---|---|
| Address: | BURRINGTON, Umberleigh EX37 9LZ |
| Tel: | 01769 560501 |
| Fax: | 01769 560770 |
| Email: | rest@northcotemanor.co.uk |
| Website: | www.northcotemanor.co.uk |
| Map ref: | 2, SS61 |

Directions: Off A377 opposite Portsmouth Arms, into hotel drive. NB. Do not enter Burrington village

Rooms: 11, S £100–£170 D £150–£250

Facilities: Tennis STV Parking: 30 Notes: ⊗ in restaurant

This beautiful, early 18th-century hotel stands surrounded by 20 acres of woodlands and lawns, including a newly reinstated Victorian water garden, much to the delight of local dragonflies. Suites and bedrooms are all very appealing, and while no two are identical in size, decor or furnishings. The restaurant's seasonal gourmet menu offers well-prepared, locally sourced dishes such as Exmoor lamb or rod-caught Cornish turbot, with exceptional wines to accompany each course.

**Recommended in the area**

Exmoor Bird Gardens; RHS Garden Rosemoor; Marshall Falcons

# Mill End Hotel

★★ ◉◉ HOTEL

| | |
|---|---|
| Address: | Dartmoor National Park, |
| | CHAGFORD TQ13 8JN |
| Tel: | 01647 432282 |
| Fax: | 01647 433106 |
| Email: | info@millendhotel.com |
| Website: | www.millendhotel.com |
| Map ref: | 2, SX79 |

Directions: From A30 at Whiddon Down follow A382. After 3.5m, Hotel on right by river.

Rooms: 15, S £80–£115 D £110–£160 Parking: 25 Notes: ⊘ in restaurant

Situated on a river bank and lulled by the sound of a working waterwheel, this former flour mill provides classic comfort for its residents. The upstairs rooms enjoy fine views, while the downstairs rooms have private patios. The restaurant offers award-winning food, with continually changing menus making the most of local and seasonal ingredients. There are three meeting rooms for up to 40 people. Guests can play croquet on the lawns, and anglers can use the hotel's private fishing licence.

**Recommended in the area**

Castle Drogo; Chagford; Dartmoor National Park

# Langstone Cliff Hotel

★ ★ ★   77% HOTEL

| | |
|---|---|
| **Address:** | Dawlish Warren, DAWLISH EX7 0NA |
| **Tel:** | 01626 868000 |
| **Fax:** | 01626 868006 |
| **Email:** | reception@langstone-hotel.co.uk |
| **Website:** | www.langstone-hotel.co.uk |
| **Map ref:** | 2, SX97 |
| **Directions:** | 1.5m NE off A379 Exeter road |

**Rooms:** 66 S £64–£79 D £108–£150 **Facilities:** ⊗ ⚲
Tennis Gym STV Wi-fi in bedrooms **Parking:** 200
**Notes:** ⊘ in restaurant

It was the Rogers family who welcomed the first guests here in 1947. They're still here, although it's generations two and three now, and still welcoming some of those pioneering visitors. Such loyalty is understandable: the views of the sea from the lawn, verandah and lounges are breathtaking, and a two-mile stretch of beach is five-minutes' walk away. The service is attentive, the public rooms spacious, the lounges are comfortable and the bars friendly. Bedrooms undergo frequent updating to reflect changing expectations of comfort and convenience. Many are designed as family rooms, some have balconies, and all are en suite, with TV, radio, baby-listening, phone and other amenities. The extensive breakfast menu in the Lincoln Restaurant gets guests off to a good start. Coffee shop-style service offers anything from a sandwich, baguette or Danish pastry to a selection of hot and cold meals, with dinner chosen from a fixed price menu or the carvery. Many of the sensibly priced wines are available by the glass. There are indoor and outdoor heated pools, a hard tennis court, compact leisure centre and full-size snooker table. An 18-hole golf course is nearby, but you can practise your swing beforehand in the hotel grounds.

**Recommended in the area**

Paignton Zoo; Powderham Castle; Miniature Pony Centre

# The Horn of Plenty

★ ★ ★  85% ◉◉◉  HOTEL

**Address:**    GULWORTHY PL19 8JD
**Tel:**    01822 832528
**Fax:**    01822 834390
**Email:**    enquiries@thehornofplenty.co.uk
**Website:**    www.thehornofplenty.co.uk
**Map ref:**    1, SX47
**Directions:** From Tavistock take A390 W for 3m. Right at Gulworthy Cross. After 400yds turn left and hotel on right
**Rooms:** 10, S £150–£240 D £160–£250 **Parking:** 25

Turn into the driveway to be greeted by fantastic views over the Tamar Valley. This creeper-clad hotel, set in five acres of gardens and orchards, has an intimate feel, attributable in part to the scent from a wealth of fresh flowers mingling with the tang of wood smoke from winter log fires. The bedrooms are well equipped with TV, DVD and mini-bar, as well as fluffy towels, soft robes and homemade chocolates. The Coach House rooms have balconies overlooking the walled gardens. Head Chef, Peter Gorton, is passionate about creating superb food and certainly maintains exceedingly high standards.

**Recommended in the area**

Eden Project; Lost Gardens of Heligan; Buckland Abbey

# Combe House Hotel & Restaurant

★ ★ ★  ◉◉  HOTEL

**Address:**    Gittisham, HONITON EX14 3AD
**Tel:**    01404 540400
**Fax:**    01404 46004
**Email:**    stay@thishotel.com
**Website:**    www.thishotel.com
**Map ref:**    2, ST10
**Directions:**    Off A30 1m S of Honiton
**Rooms:** 15, S £125–£158 D £168–£180 **Facilities:** Wi-fi in bedrooms **Parking:** 38

This Elizabethan manor stands on high ground, enjoying views over 3,500 acres of estate land. The interior is richly adorned with carved oak panelling and family portraits of those who have owned the house. Some of the local produce that features in the award-winning restaurant's meals comes from the hotel's own gardens. The extensive and interesting wine list includes a fine range of Chablis. Wedding vows can be made at Combe Hall, and, if wished, the House can also be booked for use.

**Recommended in the area**

World Heritage Coast; Exmouth to Lyme Regis; Dartmoor National Park; Honiton; Exeter

Ilsington House, near Puddletown.

# Best Western Ilsington Country House Hotel

★★★  85% ⑳⑳  HOTEL

| | |
|---|---|
| Address: | ILSINGTON, Newton Abbot TQ13 9RR |
| Tel: | 01364 661452 |
| Fax: | 01364 661307 |
| Email: | hotel@ilsington.co.uk |
| Website: | www.ilsington.co.uk |
| Map ref: | 2, SX77 |

Directions: Exit A38 at Bovey Tracey. 3rd exit from rdbt to 'Ilsington', then 1st right. Hotel 5m by Post Office

Rooms: 25, S £92–£98 D £136–£144 Facilities: ⓧ Sauna Jacuzzi Tennis Gym Flatscreen TV and Wi-fi in bedrooms Parking: 100 Notes: ⊗ in restaurant

A friendly, family-owned hotel in 10 acres of Dartmoor's southern slopes, offering tranquillity and far-reaching views. The air-conditioned restaurant serves local fare and classic dishes featuring fresh market produce. Scrumptious Devonshire cream teas are served in the conservatory or garden.

**Recommended in the area**

Castle Drogo; Buckfast Abbey; Dartmoor National Park

# Soar Mill Cove Hotel

★ ★ ★ ★  78% ◉◉  HOTEL

| | |
|---|---|
| Address: | Soar Mill Cove, Marlborough, SALCOMBE TQ7 3DS |
| Tel: | 01548 561566 |
| Fax: | 01548 561223 |
| Email: | info@soarmillcove.co.uk |
| Website: | www.soarmillcove.co.uk |
| Map ref: | 2, SX73 |

Directions: 3m W of town off A381 at Malborough. Follow 'Soar' signs

Rooms: 22, S £94–£150 D £150–£200

Facilities: ⊗ ⟲ Sauna Tennis Wi-fi available

Parking: 30 Notes: ⊘ in restaurant

This family-run establishment, lying near the harbour town of Salcombe, commands breathtaking views in an Area of Outstanding Natural Beauty. This is possibly the most dramatic seaside setting in Devon: directly below the hotel, sandy Soar Mill Cove Beach is surrounded by cliffs and is replete with rock pools. Guests can explore the area on the hotel's free tandem bike. All rooms in this single-storey establishment, built of local slate and stone, open directly onto private terraces and the 10 acres of gardens. The restaurant specializes in local produce, including lobster, crab, beef, chicken and goat's cheese. In the afternoons, cream teas are served. Guests can also enjoy the finest champagne in the only Bollinger Bar in the UK outside London. The hotel welcomes children of all ages, and has changing facilities and a playroom. The hotel arranges a number of different holiday breaks, centred on themes including cookery, painting, walking and bird-watching. There is a cookery master class every Sunday afternoon, and festive events at Christmas and New Year. The Ocean Spa centre is available for pampering health and beauty treatments.

### Recommended in the area

Salcombe; Dartmouth Castle; Dartmoor National Park

Rickham Sands, Salcombe.

# Tides Reach Hotel

★★★ 81% ◉ HOTEL

| | |
|---|---|
| **Address:** | South Sands, SALCOMBE TQ8 8LJ |
| **Tel:** | 01548 843466 |
| **Fax:** | 01548 843954 |
| **Email:** | enquire@tidesreach.com |
| **Website:** | www.tidesreach.com |
| **Map ref:** | 2, SX73 |

**Directions:** Off A38 at Buckfastleigh to Totnes. Then take A381 to Salcombe, follow signs to South Sands

**Rooms:** 35, S £110–£137 D £190–£300 **Facilities:** ⊕ Sauna Jacuzzi Solarium Gym Wi-fi available **Parking:** 100 **Notes:** ⊘ in restaurant

This privately owned and run luxury sea side hotel has superb views of the Salcombe estuary. The bedrooms, many with balconies, are spacious and comfortable. Priorities are placed on friendly, caring and courteous service, fine food and wine in elegant and comfortable surroundings. All of these aspects combine with the extensively equipped Leisure Complex which includes a hair and beauty salon. The resident owners set out to promote an environment for a totally relaxing break.

**Recommended in the area**

South Sands Sailing; South West Coastal Path; Overbecks Garden and Museum (NT)

# Riviera Hotel

★★★★ 80% ◉◉ HOTEL

| | |
|---|---|
| Address: | The Esplanade, |
| | SIDMOUTH EX10 8AY |
| Tel: | 01395 515201 |
| Fax: | 01395 577775 |
| Email: | enquiries@hotelriviera.co.uk |
| Website: | www.hotelriviera.co.uk |
| Map ref: | 2, SY18 |
| Directions: | M5 junct 30 & follow A3052 |

Rooms: 26, S £104–£156 D £208–£290
Facilities: STV Parking: 14 Notes: ⊗ in restaurant

This superb Regency building on Sidmouth's Esplanade dates from the age when the town grew to prominence as a fashionable resort. The hotel overlooks Lyme Bay, yet is close to the town centre. Many of the bedrooms enjoy fine views over the sea, and all have en suite facilities and colour television, radio, direct-dial telephones and hairdryers. The dining room too has fine views over the sea, and emphasizes local seafood in its wide-ranging menus, which are both à la carte and fixed-price. Cream teas can be enjoyed in the lounge or, in summer, on the patio. Light refreshments are always available at any time of the year. A resident pianist enhances the ambiance of the Regency Bar on many evenings. Private functions including wedding parties and business conferences can be accommodated. The hotel can arrange sporting activities in the area: golfing at concessionary fees at the nearby Sidmouth Golf Club and Woodbury Park Golf and County Club; riding; and pheasant- and duck-shooting on local estates. The Heritage Coast Trail passes nearby. The hotel offers packages of weekend and three-day breaks. All the sights of Devon can be reached within a short journey time, and the M5 motorway lies only 13 miles from the hotel. Children of all ages are welcomed.

### Recommended in the area

Bicton Gardens; Killerton House and Gardens; Exeter Cathedral.

# Westcliff Hotel

★★★ 85% HOTEL

| | |
|---|---|
| **Address:** | Manor Road, SIDMOUTH EX10 8RU |
| **Tel:** | 01395 513252 |
| **Fax:** | 01395 578203 |
| **Email:** | stay@westcliffhotel.co.uk |
| **Website:** | www.westcliffhotel.co.uk |
| **Map ref:** | 2, SY18 |

**Directions:** Turn off A3052 to Sidmouth then to seafront and esplanade, turn right, hotel directly ahead
**Rooms:** 40, S £66–£132 D £132–£236
**Facilities:** STV **Parking:** 40 **Notes:** ⊘ in restaurant

The privately owned Westcliff Hotel is set in two beautiful acres of lawns and gardens, right in the middle of the Jurassic Coast, a World Heritage Site since 2001. In fact, the Westcliff's position gives it a natural advantage sheltering it from every wind but the south. Regency Sidmouth is known as the 'Jewel of the West Country' and its town centre, promenade and beaches are a just a short walk away. Locally renowned for excellent food and courteous and efficient service, Westcliff carries the highest AA quality score for a three-star hotel in South Devon, and is one of the few to have won the coveted AA Courtesy and Care Award. Elegant lounges and a cocktail bar open on to a terrace leading to the pool and croquet lawn. The different types of bedroom are well proportioned, tastefully furnished and equipped with all the usual amenities. Most have sea views, some from their balconies. In fact, it is only a few of the single and standard rooms that do not face the sea. The restaurant offers a tempting choice of both carte and fixed price menus, and views of the red cliffs for which this part of Devon is famous.

### Recommended in the area

Bicton Gardens; Crealy Adventure Park; Otterton Mill; Jurassic Coast (World Heritage Site); Sidmouth; red cliffs of Devon

# Corbyn Head Hotel & Orchid Restaurant

★★★ 77% ●●● HOTEL

| | |
|---|---|
| **Address:** | Torbay Road, Sea Front, TORQUAY TQ2 6RH |
| **Tel:** | 01803 213611 |
| **Fax:** | 01803 296152 |
| **Email:** | info@corbynhead.com |
| **Website:** | www.corbynhead.com |
| **Map ref:** | 2, SX96 |

**Directions:** Follow signs to Torquay seafront, turn right on seafront. Hotel on right with green canopies
**Rooms:** 44, S £54–£160 D £108–£198 **Facilities:** ↘ Sauna Solarium Gym  Wi-fi available **Parking:** 50 **Notes:** ⊛ in restaurant

This establishment is sited in a magnificent setting on Torbay's waterfront just a minute's leisurely walk to Livermead Beach. The rooms are all en suite; most have sea views, and many have private balconies. Guests staying seven nights on the standard tariff receive a free extra night's accommodation, and there are accommodation packages at Christmas, New Year and throughout the year. The three AA Rosette air-conditioned Orchid Restaurant offers fine dining on the top floor of the hotel, with magnificent views over Torbay. Smart casual wear is requested here. The traditional English cuisine of the Harbour View Restaurant, made with only the finest local produce, is constantly changing. The Regency Lounge and the Continental Coffee Bar open onto the Poolside Terrace and offer wonderful views to guests enjoying morning coffee and afternoon tea. The Corbyn Head Hotel also offers free onsite parking.

**Recommended in the area**

Paignton Zoo; Kent's Cavern, Torquay; Babbacombe Model Village

The harbour bridge, Torquay

# Orestone Manor Hotel & Restaurant

★★★ ◉◉ HOTEL

| | |
|---|---|
| Address: | Rockhouse Lane, Maidencombe, |
| | TORQUAY TQ1 4SX |
| Tel: | 01803 328098 |
| Fax: | 01803 328336 |
| Email: | info@orestonemanor.com |
| Website: | www.orestonemanor.com |
| Map ref: | 2, SX96 |

Directions: Follow A38 off motorway to A380 then B3192 coast road Teignmouth to Torquay
Rooms: 12, S £89–£149 D £125–£225 Facilities: ⚒ Parking: 40 Notes: ⊗ in restaurant

All rooms at the Orestone are beautifully decorated and have en suite bathrooms. Skilfully prepared contemporary English cuisine makes full use of the superb local seafood. Diners can enjoy pre-dinner drinks and coffee afterwards in one of the large armchairs in the drawing room, conservatory or on the terrace, gazing out at the fine views over the English Channel.
Recommended in the area
Kent's Cavern; Babbacombe Model Village; Dart Valley Railway

# Woodbury Park Hotel Golf & Country Club

★★★★ 75% ◉ HOTEL

| | |
|---|---|
| **Address:** | Woodbury Castle, |
| | WOODBURY, |
| | Exeter EX5 1JJ |
| **Tel:** | 01395 233382 |
| **Fax:** | 01395 234701 |
| **Email:** | reservations@woodburypark.co.uk |
| **Website:** | www.woodburypark.co.uk |
| **Map ref:** | 2, SY08 |

**Directions:** M5 junct 30, A376 then A3052 towards Sidmouth, onto B3180, hotel signed
**Rooms:** 56, S £75–£135 D £85–£185 **Facilities:** ⊗ Sauna Jacuzzi Tennis Gym STV Wi-fi in bedrooms **Parking:** 400 **Notes:** ⊗ in bedrooms ⊘ in restaurant

Woodbury Park stands in 500 acres of Devon's most beautiful countryside, and provides the ultimate in sport and leisure facilities, as well as spacious, luxuriously appointed en suite bedrooms, suites and individual Swiss-style lodges. Many have balconies, with sweeping views across the surrounding greens of the two parkland golf courses and rolling countryside of the Exe Valley. The glass-roofed Atrium Restaurant is flooded with natural light by day and, on clear nights, a canopy of stars encourages a romantic mood. The carte offers a mouth-watering array of freshly cooked seasonal fish, meat and game dishes, and the wine list is impressive. Private dining facilities are available, while light snacks, tea and coffee are served in the Conservatory in the Clubhouse. You can also re-live the thrills of Formula One in the unique 'The Nigel Mansell World of Racing', then stand alongside the actual Formula One racing cars he drove to victory. Enjoy a game of football on the Premier-standard pitch, or a swim in the leisure centre.

**Recommended in the area**

Woodbury Castle; Exeter Cathedral; World of Country Life

Woolacombe.

# Watersmeet Hotel

★★★ 88% ❀ HOTEL

| | |
|---|---|
| **Address:** | Mortehoe, WOOLACOMBE EX34 7EB |
| **Tel:** | 01271 870333 |
| **Fax:** | 01271 870890 |
| **Email:** | info@watersmeethotel.co.uk |
| **Website:** | www.watersmeethotel.co.uk |
| **Map ref:** | 1, SS44 |

**Directions:** Follow B3343 into Woolacombe, turn right onto esplanade, hotel 0.75m on left

**Rooms:** 25 S £72–£198 D £144–£236 **Facilities:** ⓢ ⌇ Jacuzzi Spa STV **Parking:** 36 **Notes:** ⊗ in bedrooms ⊘ in restaurant

Built in 1907 as a gentleman's residence, Watersmeet has been transformed since those far-off Edwardian days into an elegant hotel. Steps lead directly to the beach, so it is no surprise that the attractive, en suite bedrooms enjoy magnificent bay views past Hartland Point to Lundy Island. The atmosphere in the candlelit Pavilion Restaurant is intimate and relaxed, especially when there's a beautiful sunset to watch. The menu takes advantage of excellent seasonal local ingredients.

**Recommended in the area**

Exmoor National Park; Saunton Sands; Tarka Railway Line

# Woolacombe Bay Hotel

★★★ 78% HOTEL

| | |
|---|---|
| **Address:** | South Street, WOOLACOMBE EX34 7BN |
| **Tel:** | 01271 870388 |
| **Fax:** | 01271 870613 |
| **Email:** | woolacombe.bayhotel@btinternet.com |
| **Website:** | www.woolacombe-bay-hotel.co.uk |
| **Map ref:** | SS44 |
| **Directions:** | B3343 to Woolacombe town centre |

**Rooms:** 63 S £55–£147 D £110–£294 **Facilities:** ⊕
⊀ Sauna Steam room Spa bath Solarium Tennis Gym
STV **Parking:** 150 **Notes:** ⊗ in bedrooms ⊘ in
restaurant

This family hotel, built in the late 1880s, is set in 6-acre
grounds leading to Woolacombe's three-mile stretch
of Blue Flag golden sands. The village is in an Area of Outstanding Natural Beauty, surrounded by
National Trust headlands where many little coves abound. Barricane Beach is world renowned for its
variety of exotic sea shells and is a true delight for the serious shell-seeker. The hotel has been
sensitively brought into the 21st century with superb leisure facilities and amenities of which guests
have free unlimited use. In addition to those listed above, these include 9-hole approach golf and a
health suite. Golf and Health spa breaks are available. There is also a fully-equipped gymnasium,
aerobics studio, billiard room, table tennis and squash court as well as a drying room for wetsuits and
weather gear. For children there is an adventure playground, paddling pools, crèche and baby
monitoring. Doyle's restaurant has unbroken views to Lundy Island and, as befits its Edwardian origins,
features chandeliers and high ceilings. It is renowned for its fine dining and ambiance as well as for
the quality of its English and French cusine. The Bay Brasserie is a popular venue for morning coffee,
lunches, Devon cream teas and dinner using local Devon produce.

**Recommended in the area**

Morthoe Heritage Centre; Marwood Hill Gardens; Arlington Court (NT)

Durdle Door.

# Best Western Chine Hotel

★★★  80% ◉  HOTEL

| | |
|---|---|
| Address: | Boscombe Spa Rd, BOURNEMOUTH BH5 1AX |
| Tel: | 01202 396234 |
| | (Central reservations: 0845 337 1550) |
| Fax: | 01202 391737 |
| Email: | reservations@chinehotel.co.uk |
| Website: | www.fjbhotels.co.uk |
| Map ref: | 3, SZ19 |

Directions: Follow A35 to St Pauls rdbt. Take exit onto St Pauls Rd to Christchurch Rd. Rd 3rd on right.
Rooms: 87, S £70–£95 D £140–£180 Facilities: ⊗ ≺ Sauna Jacuzzi Solarium Gym STV Wi-fi in bedrooms Parking: 50 Notes: ⊘ in restaurant

Attention to detail is a hallmark in the well-appointed en suite bedrooms, many with a sea-facing balcony. The charming SeaView Restaurant's mouth-watering menu presents freshly caught fish, carefully selected meats, vegetarian options and a very good wine list. The hotel also caters for conferences, meetings and functions. The beach is just a short walk through the three acre-gardens.
**Recommended in the area**
Bournemouth Shopping Centre; Poole Quay; New Forest National Park

# Mortons House Hotel

★★★  85% ◉◉  HOTEL

| | |
|---|---|
| Address: | 49 East Street, CORFE CASTLE BH20 5EE |
| Tel: | 01929 480988 |
| Fax: | 01929 480820 |
| Email: | stay@mortonshouse.co.uk |
| Website: | www.mortonshouse.co.uk |
| Map ref: | SY98 |
| Directions: | On A351between Wareham & Swanage |

Rooms: 21, S £85–£140 D £144–£255
Facilities: Jacuzzi Wi-fi available Parking: 40
Notes: ⊗ on premises ⊘ in restaurant or bedrooms

Built in the shape of an E to commemorate Elizabeth I, this Tudor house has been skilfully remodelled as a hotel. Relax by its roaring log fire in the oak-panelled drawing room, or on the sun terrace enjoying the carp pond. The spacious Elizabethan Room has a four-poster, spa bath, lounge area and dressing room. The owners are proud of commendations for their well-appointed restaurant's traditional English cuisine. Bar lunches are available, and private parties can dine in the charming Castle Room.
**Recommended in the area**
Lulworth Cove; Swanage Steam Railway; Dorset and East Devon World Heritage Coast

Gold Hill, Shaftesbury.

# Stock Hill Country House Hotel & Restaurant

★★★ ◎◎◎ COUNTRY HOUSE HOTEL

| | |
|---|---|
| Address: | Stock Hill, GILLINGHAM SP8 5NR |
| Tel: | 01747 823626 |
| Fax: | 01747 825628 |
| Email: | reception@stockhillhouse.co.uk |
| Website: | www.stockhillhouse.co.uk |
| Map ref: | 4, ST72 |
| Directions: | 3m E on B3081, off A303 |

Rooms: 9, S £145–£165 D £250–£300 **Facilities:**
Sauna Tennis **Parking:** 20 **Notes:** ⊗ in bedrooms ⊘ in restaurant

This Victorian house is approached along a beech-lined driveway through 11 acres of landscaped gardens. The bedrooms and public rooms are filled with antiques and sumptuous furnishings. The menu uses local ingredients and changes daily. Peter Hausner's cooking is influenced both by classic French cuisine and by that of his Austrian birthplace. Children over seven years are welcome.

**Recommended in the area**

Stourhead House and Garden; Stonehenge; Kingston Lacy Country House; Longleat Safari Park.

# Best Western Mansion House Hotel

★ ★ ★ ◉◉ HOTEL

| | |
|---|---|
| Address: | Thames Street, POOLE BH15 1JN |
| Tel: | 01202 685666 |
| Fax: | 01202 665709 |
| Email: | enquiries@themansionhouse.co.uk |
| Website: | www.themansionhouse.co.uk |
| Map ref: | 3, SZ09 |

Directions: A31 to Poole, follow channel ferry signs.
Left at Poole bridge onto Poole Quay, 1st left into Thames St. Hotel opposite St James Church
Rooms: 32, S £75–£90 D £135–£150 Facilities: STV Wi-fi available throughout hotel Parking: 46
Notes: ⊗ in bedrooms ⊘ in restaurant

This grand Regency townhouse was the Mayoral House when it was built in 1779 and It is located just off the vibrant quayside in Poole's Old Town. The individually-named bedrooms are luxuriously furnished with sumptuous fabrics and furnishings, but also have full modern amenities, including television, direct-dial telephone, hairdryer and en suite bathroom. The cherrywood-panelled restaurant offers fine dining, using local produce wherever possible, and is very popular with diners from Poole and its surroundings. The Bistro offers a more informal setting and menu. Private suites and dining-rooms are available for functions, wedding receptions (the hotel is licensed for civil wedding ceremonies) and business meetings with up to 40 delegates. The hotel offers special rates for its Autumn Breaks, Golfing Breaks, using the facilities of the Dorset Golf and Country Club, and Christmas and New Year Breaks. 'Boomerang Breaks' offer family activities during autumn, winter and spring. Near the hotel is the harbour and the new Dolphin Yacht Haven, fine beaches, fishing, and walking in Dorset's Thomas Hardy country. The hotel is only a mile from Poole's bus and railway stations.

Recommended in the area

Sandbanks Peninsula beach; The New Forest; Compton Acres gardens; Bournemouth

# Harbour Heights Hotel

★★★★  81% ◉◉  HOTEL

| | |
|---|---|
| Address: | 73 Haven Rd, Sandbanks, POOLE BH13 7LW |
| Tel: | 01202 707272 |
| | (Central reservations: 0845 337 1550) |
| Fax: | 01202 708594 |
| Email: | enquiries@harbourheights.net |
| Website: | www.fjbhotels.co.uk |
| Map ref: | 3, SZ09 |

Directions: Follow signs for Sandbanks, hotel on left after Canford Cliffs

Rooms: 38 Facilities: STV Wi-fi available Parking: 50 Notes: ⊗ in bedrooms ⊛ in restaurant

Comfort is clearly the priority in the luxuriously designed bedrooms of this contemporary boutique hotel, many directly overlooking Poole Harbour. The harbar Brasserie offers an impressive menu, relaxing music, funky furniture and myriad cocktails. Hytes is available for private and corporate hire. The bar and restaurant extend onto tiered, landscaped terraces with panoramic views towards the Purbeck Hills.

**Recommended in the area**

Tank Museum; Swanage Railway; Purbeck Heritage Coast

# Haven Hotel

★★★★  73% ◉◉  HOTEL

| | |
|---|---|
| Address: | Banks Road, Sandbanks, POOLE BH13 7QL |
| Tel: | 01202 707333 |
| | (Central reservations: 0845 337 1550) |
| Fax: | 01202 708796 |
| Email: | reservations@havenhotel.co.uk |
| Website: | www.fjbhotels.co.uk |
| Map ref: | 3, SZ09 |

Directions: B3965 towards Poole Bay, left onto the Peninsula. Hotel 1.5m on left next to Swanage Ferry point

Rooms: 78, S £80–£180 D £160–£360 Facilities:⊗ ⊀ Sauna Jacuzzi Solarium Tennis Gym STV Wi-fi in bedrooms Parking: 160 Notes: ⊗ in bedrooms ⊛ in restaurant

For more than 100 years, the Haven has graced the southernmost point of Sandbanks peninsula. Its five lounges are all different, so there's always one to meet the needs of the moment. Guest rooms are exceedingly comfortable, most having balconies overlooking the sea or harbour. The water's edge La Roche restaurant offers a seasonal menu. The informal Seaview Restaurant is no less impressive.

**Recommended in the area**

Brownsea Island; Compton Acres; Corfe Castle

The old lifeboat station, now a museum, Poole Quay.

# Sandbanks Hotel

★★★★  77% ◉ HOTEL

| | |
|---|---|
| **Address:** | 15 Banks Rd, Sandbanks, POOLE BH13 7PS |
| **Tel:** | 01202 707377 |
| | (Central reservations: 0845 337 1550) |
| **Fax:** | 01202 708885 |
| **Email:** | reservations@sandbankshotel.co.uk |
| **Website:** | www.fjbhotels.co.uk |
| **Map ref:** | 3, SZ09 |

**Directions:** A338 from Bournemouth onto Wessex Way, to Liverpool Victoria rdbt. Take 2nd exit onto B3965.

**Rooms:** 110, S £65–£121 D £130–£242 **Facilities:** ⊗ Sauna Jacuzzi Solarium Gym STV Wi-fi available **Parking:** 120 **Notes:** ⊗ in bedrooms ⊗ in restaurant

The Sandbanks is situated on a Blue Flag beach, looking across Poole Bay to the famous Old Harry Rocks. The view can be enjoyed from the terrace, the Peninsula and Sandbanks Suites, the Seaview Restaurant and many of the bedrooms. Depending on the time of year several watersports are offered. Experienced staff are available to assist with all aspects of business or social events.

**Recommended in the area**

Poole Quay; Alice in Wonderland Park; Jurassic Coastal Path

Auckland Castle, Bishop Auckland.

# Ramside Hall Hotel

★★★ 80% HOTEL

| | |
|---|---|
| Address: | Carrville, DURHAM DH1 1TD |
| Tel: | 0191 386 5282 |
| Fax: | 0191 386 0399 |
| Email: | mail@ramsidehallhotel.co.uk |
| Website: | www.ramsidehallhotel.co.uk |
| Map ref: | 7, NZ34 |

Directions: From A1(M) junct 62 take A690 to Sunderland. Straight on at lights. 200mtrs after railway bridge turn right

Rooms: 80, S £125–£195 D £145–£245 Facilities: Sauna STV Wi-fi available Parking: 500
Notes: ⊗ in restaurant

All the bedrooms in this imposing hotel have luxurious furniture and fabrics, and are equipped with satellite television, free in-house films, radio, direct-dial telephones, hairdryers, trouser presses and facilities for making hot drinks. All also have en suite bathrooms. The restaurant offers a menu that changes seasonally, taking as much advantage as possible of local and seasonal produce. The Hotel's Palm Court Trio entertains diners at Sunday lunch. Pemberton's Rotisserie and Carvery offers lighter meals at lunchtime and in the evening, and snacks throughout the afternoon. Private dining is available in boardrooms, the magnificent Green Room, the Fountain Room or the banqueting suites, which cater for up to 360 diners. The hotel has a Civil Marriage Licence, and both wedding ceremonies and receptions can take advantage of the extensive grounds and gardens. Large marquees are also available. The Ramside Hall Golf Club has 27 holes in three loops, a driving range, computerized indoor training areas, and a fine clubhouse. In the heart of the golf course is the Ramside Farmhouse, its five bedrooms providing sole occupancy for up to 10 people. The hotel is conveniently situated just two miles from Durham city centre.

### Recommended in the area

Beamish Open-air Museum; Durham Cathedral; MetroCentre, Gateshead

# Seaham Hall Hotel

★★★★★ ◉◉◉ HOTEL

Address: Lord Byron's Walk,
SEAHAM SR7 7AG
Tel: 0191 516 1400
Fax: 0191 516 1410
Email: reservations@seaham-hall.com
Website: www.seaham-hall.com
Map ref: 8, NZ44
Directions: From A19 take B1404 to Seaham. At lights straight over level crossing. Hotel approx 0.25m on right
Rooms: 19, S £195–£575 D £195–£575 Facilities: ⊗ Sauna Jacuzzi Solarium Gym STV
Parking: 120 Notes: ⊗ in bedrooms ⊛ in restaurant

This imposing house was where, in 1815, Britain's great romantic poet, Lord Byron, married Annabella Milbanke, the younger daughter of Seaham Hall's first owner. Generally regarded as 'mad, bad and dangerous to know' he would have loved the hotel today, now fully restored to its opulent glory, but with the addition of 21st-century amenities. The hotel offers five types of suites including the stunning Penthouse, all offering cutting edge technology, contemporary artwork and an undeniable sense of style. Bathrooms are particularly lavish, with two-person baths a feature that some will find deliciously decadent. The contemporary White Room restaurant offers fine dining with superb fresh produce and daily changing lunch and dinner menus, as well as a full breakfast service. Seaham's original vaulted cellars have stored fine wines for over two centuries; today, under the guidance of sommeliers, they house an eclectic collection of fine and unusual European and New World wines. The award-winning Serenity Spa, reached by a magical underground walkway, has received top accolades from national publications for its more than 55 different treatments. Businesses can stage events in light, air conditioned rooms with ISDN, 50" plasma screen and all the technology they are likely to need.

### Recommended in the area

City of Newcastle & Gateshead; Durham Cathedral; Beamish Open Air Museum

# ESSEX

The Pier, Clacton-on-Sea.

# Maison Talbooth

★★★ ◎◎ COUNTRY HOUSE HOTEL

| | |
|---|---|
| Address: | Stratford Road, DEDHAM C07 6HN |
| Tel: | 01206 322367 |
| Fax: | 01206 322752 |
| Email: | maison@milsomhotels.co.uk |
| Website: | www.milsomhotels.com |
| Map ref: | 4, TM03 |

Directions: A12 towards Ipswich, 1st turning signed
Dedham, follow road until left bend, take right turn
Rooms: 10, S £120–£250 D £170–£350
Facilities: Jacuzzi STV Parking: 20 Notes: ⊗ in bedrooms ⊘ in restaurant

Tranquility is the essence of this Victorian country house hotel in pretty, landscaped grounds. Public areas include a large, comfortable drawing room where tea and snacks are available. The spacious bedrooms are truly luxurious, each one decorated with an expert eye for colour. All have king- or queen-sized bed and en suite facilities. Breakfasts and light meals are available on the premises, while lunch and dinner are a stroll, or short courtesy car ride, away at the riverside Le Talbooth Restaurant.
**Recommended in the area**
Flatford Mill; Colchester Castle; Beth Chatto Gardens

# The Pier at Harwich

★★★ 83% ◎◎ HOTEL

| | |
|---|---|
| Address: | The Quay, HARWICH C012 3HH |
| Tel: | 01255 241212 |
| Fax: | 01255 551922 |
| Email: | pier@milsomhotels.com |
| Website: | www.milsomhotels.co.uk |
| Map ref: | 4, TM23 |

Directions: From A12, take A120 to Quay. Hotel
opposite lifeboat station
Rooms: 14 Facilities: STV Parking: 10 Notes: ⊗ in
bedrooms ⊘ in restaurant

On the quay in the heart of old Harwich, The Pier is owned by the Milsom family, who also own Maison Talbooth (see above). Newly refurbished public rooms include a smart lounge bar, claimed to make the best coffee in town, and plush residents' lounge. The contemporary-style bedrooms are tastefully decorated and thoughtfully equipped, while many overlook the ever-changing activities of this busy port. The first-floor Harbourside restaurant has a well-deserved reputation for seafood.
**Recommended in the area**
Flatford Mill; Suffolk Heritage Coast; Mistley Towers

# GLOUCESTERSHIRE

The River Eye, Upper Slaughter.

The Devil's Chimney, Cheltenham.

# Charlton Kings Hotel

★★★ 77% SMALL HOTEL

| | |
|---|---|
| **Address:** | London Road, Charlton Kings, |
| | CHELTENHAM GL52 6UU |
| **Tel:** | 01242 231061 |
| **Fax:** | 01242 241900 |
| **Email:** | enquiries@charltonkingshotel.co.uk |
| **Website:** | www.charltonkingshotel.co.uk |
| **Map ref:** | 2, SO92 |

**Directions:** From Oxford on A40, 1st on left
**Rooms:** 13 S £65–£85 D £98–£125 **Facilities:** STV
Wi-fi in bedrooms **Parking:** 26 **Notes:** ⊗ in hotel

Quality, comfort and friendliness are the hallmarks of this lovely hotel, standing in an acre of garden with sweeping lawns. All bedrooms have en suite facilities and most have views of the surrounding Cotswold hills. Talented chefs present a varied, weekly changing menu using the finest fresh produce. The Atrium Restaurant offers privacy for an intimate dinner, as well as sufficient space for a family reunion. The bar and conservatory are open all day for snacks and lunches.

**Recommended in the area**

Sudeley Castle; Cheltenham Racecourse; Cotswold villages

# Macdonald Queen's Hotel

★★★★ 76% ◉ HOTEL

Address: The Promenade, CHELTENHAM GL50 1NN
Tel: 0870 400 8107
Fax: 01242 224145
Email: general.queens@macdonald-hotels.co.uk
Website: www.thequeens-cheltenham.co.uk
Map ref: 2, SO92
Directions: Follow town centre signs. Left at Montpellier
Walk rdbt. Entrance 500mtrs right
Rooms: 79, S £80–£140 D £105–£160
Facilities: STV Parking: 80 Notes: ⊗ in restaurant

The hotel occupies a recently refurbished listed building, commanding a fine position at the top of the tree-lined Promenade in the heart of Cheltenham. The bedrooms are furnished to high standards, with comfort cooling in all of them. Two of the bedrooms have four-poster beds, and many command views of the hotel's gardens. All have en suite facilities, television, radio, direct-dial telephones, hairdryers, trouser presses, and facilities for making hot drinks. Most have wireless Internet access, as do the public areas of the hotel. The Napier Restaurant and Conservatory offers fine dining, making use of seasonal produce, and an extensive wine list. Diners in the Conservatory can be seated indoors or on the terrace when the weather is warm. The Queen's Lounge is the place to have traditional afternoon tea, while morning coffee and light snacks can be taken in the lounge and in the Gold Cup Bar. Conference and banqueting facilities for 10 to 100 guests are available in a number of suites, all licensed for civil marriage ceremonies. Wedding receptions include complimentary accommodation for the bride and groom in a feature bedroom for one night. The hotel also hosts a variety of residential packages: the Golf Package, for example, offers a special rate for an overnight stay and 18 holes at the Spa Course at the nearby Brickhampton Court Golf Complex.

### Recommended in the area

Cheltenham Racecourse; the Cotswolds; Sudeley Castle

# Tudor Farmhouse Hotel & Restaurant

★★★ 79% ◉◉ HOTEL

| | |
|---|---|
| **Address:** | High Street, CLEARWELL |
| | Nr Coleford GL16 8JS |
| **Tel:** | 01594 833046 |
| **Fax:** | 01594 837093 |
| **Email:** | info@tudorfarmhousehotel.co.uk |
| **Website:** | www.tudorfarmhousehotel.co.uk |
| **Map ref:** | 2, SO50 |

**Directions:** Off A4136 onto B4228, through Coleford, turn right into Clearwell, hotel on right just before War Memorial Cross

**Rooms:** 22, S £60 D £85–£160 **Facilities:** STV **Parking:** 30 **Notes:** ⊘

The Tudor Farmhouse is located within a picturesque village in the heart of the Forest of Dean. Its 14 acres of grounds have been designated an area of Special Scientific Interest, due to the rare and varied flora found on the banks and rocky outcrops. Although called Tudor Farmhouse, its origins go back to the 13th century although, whatever their age, the oak beams, exposed stonework, inglenook fireplaces and wooden spiral staircase are a delight to see. Well-appointed double, twin and family rooms are located either within the main house or in converted buildings in the grounds. All are en suite, and some have four-poster beds and Jacuzzi corner baths. The award-winning candlelit restaurant offers an excellent selection of dishes, using ingredients sourced from local suppliers, such as venison from Lydney Park, and home-grown vegetables. There is a special menu for children. In good weather, guests can eat outside in the garden. Private parties can also be catered for and business guests can hold meetings for up to 20 delegates in one of the function rooms. The area is renowned for its iron mining heritage such as the Clearwell Caves, within walking distance of the hotel.

**Recommended in the area**

Tintern Abbey; Symond's Yat; Chepstow Castle and Races

# Washbourne Court Hotel

★★★  80% ⚘⚘  HOTEL

Address:    LOWER SLAUGHTER GL54 2HS
Tel:        01451 822143
Fax:        01451 821045
Email:      info@washbournecourt.co.uk
Website:    www.vonessenhotels.co.uk
Map ref:    3, SP12
Directions: Off A429 at signpost 'The Slaughters',
between Stow-on-the-Wold and Bourton-on-the-Water.
Hotel in centre of village
Rooms: 30, S £90–£125 D £120–£190
Parking: 40 Notes: ⊘ in restaurant

Washbourne Court is a trendy, luxury country house hotel in the heart of the Cotswolds. In four acres of immaculate grounds beside the River Eye, it dates from the 17th century, as its beamed ceilings, stone-mullioned windows, flagstone floors and truly majestic fireplace in the bar testify. Ancient features such as these harmonise well with the stylish restaurant, 'designer' bedrooms and cool café bar, where guests can linger over a latte, or something stronger. All bedrooms have private bathrooms, some with double showers or Jacuzzi, and are individually furnished to a high standard. Rooms named Daisy, Iris, Lily and Poppy were once boys' dormitories when Washbourne was a crammer school for Eton. In the grounds, the delightful Cottage Suites have private lounges attached. The exceptionally stylish Riverside Restaurant is a magnet for local foodies who love the high quality modern English style cuisine, based on the best produce the Cotswolds can muster, complemented, of course, by a selection of fine wines. During the summer, guests may have lunch or drinks out on the Riverside Terrace, with the pretty river drifting by just yards away. All meeting rooms have natural daylight and are located on the ground floor.

## Recommended in the area

Batsford Arboretum; Bourton-on-the-Water; Cotswold Falconry Centre

# Manor House Hotel

★★★ 82% ◉◉ HOTEL

Address: High Street,
MORETON-IN-MARSH GL56 0LJ
Tel: 01608 650501
Fax: 01608 651481
Email: info@manorhousehotel.info
Website: www.costswold-inns-hotels.co.uk
Map ref: 3, SP23
Directions: Off A429 at south end of town. Take East
St off High St, hotel car park 3rd on right
Rooms: 38, S £180 D £220 **Parking:** 24 **Notes:** ⊗ in bedrooms ⊘ in restaurant

The Manor House Hotel is a 16th-century retreat with a tranquil garden shaded by a 300-year-old mulberry tree. The bedrooms have modern amenities and are furnished in traditional country-house style and some rooms have four-poster beds, open fireplaces and window seats. The Mulberry Restaurant has a vibrant modern styling serving meals made with fresh local produce. It offers both fine dining and a bistro-style menu. Business facilities can accommodate up to 120 people.

**Recommended in the area**

Royal Shakespeare Company; Stratford-upon-Avon; Batsford Arboretum; Hidcote Manor Gardens

# Calcot Manor

★★★★ ◉◉ HOTEL

Address: Calcot, TETBURY GL8 8YJ
Tel: 01666 890391
Fax: 01666 890394
Email: reception@calcotmanor.co.uk
Website: www.calcotmanor.co.uk
Map ref: 2, ST89
Directions: 3m West of Tetbury at junct A4135/A46
Rooms: 35 D £195–£220 **Facilities:** ⊗ ⇃ Sauna
Jacuzzi Solarium Gym Calcot Spa **Parking:** 120
Notes: ⊗ in bedrooms ⊘ in restaurant

Fourteenth-century Cistercian monks built the ancient barns and stables amid which stands this lovely English farmhouse. While no two rooms or suites are identical, each is beautifully decorated and equipped with contemporary comforts. Sumptuous sitting rooms, with crackling log fires in winter, look out over immaculate gardens. There are two dining options: the coolly elegant Conservatory Restaurant and the gastropubby Gumstool Inn. The luxurious Calcot Spa has outstanding facilities and features a 16-metre pool. For children, a supervised crèche and 'playzone' are available.

**Recommended in the area**

Slimbridge Wildfowl Trust; Westonbirt Arboretum; Tetbury

Rape seed field near Winchcombe.

# Lords of the Manor

★★★ ◉◉◉ HOTEL
**Address:** UPPER SLAUGHTER GL54 2JD
**Tel:** 01451 820243
**Fax:** 01451 820696
**Email:** enquiries@lordsofthemanor.com
**Website:** www.bespokehotels.com
**Map ref:** 3, SP12
**Directions:** 2m W of A429. Turn off A40 onto A429, take 'The Slaughters' turn
**Rooms:** 27, S £110–£140 D £170
**Facilities:** STV **Parking:** 40 **Notes:** ⊘ in restaurant

A 17th-century, honey-coloured rectory in eight acres of gardens and parkland, the Lords is the next best thing to a private retreat. Reception rooms have been preserved with style and character, their log fires blazing throughout the winter, and french windows thrown open to the terrace in summer. Some of the bedrooms overlook the gardens and lake, others the Victorian courtyard. Room extras include DVD player, and luxury soaps and oils. The restaurant serves some of the county's finest food.

**Recommended in the area**

Bourton Model Village; Cotswold Farm Park; Broadway

Sunset over Wigan Pier.

# Hotel Rossetti

★★★★ 68% ◉ TOWN HOUSE HOTEL

**Address:** 107 Piccadilly, MANCHESTER M1 2DB
**Tel:** 0161 247 7744
**Fax:** 0161 247 7747
**Email:** reservationsmanchester@abodehotels.co.uk
**Website:** www.hotelrossetti.co.uk
**Map ref:** 6, SJ89
**Directions:** M62/M602 follow signs for city centre
**Rooms:** 61 S £110–£119 D £110–£119 **Facilities:** STV
Wi-fi available **Notes:** ⊗ in restaurant

ABode's newly acquired hotel is an exciting addition to the city. Situated only minutes from Piccadilly station, this handsome, terracotta-coloured building was once the headquarters of Manchester's textile industry. Rooms feature ABode's trademark hand-built beds, personal DVD player, LCD TV and bathrooms featuring monsoon showers. ABode is also home to Michael Caines restaurants and bars serving Michael's innovative and award-winning modern British cuisine. Below ground are rooms for meetings and private dining.

**Recommended in the area**

Lowry Art Gallery; Trafford Centre; Urbis Exhibition Centre

# Macdonald Kilhey Court

★★★★ 69% HOTEL

**Address:** Chorley Road, Standish, WIGAN WN1 2XN
**Tel:** 0870 1942122
**Fax:** 01257 422401
**Email:** general.kilheycourt@macdonald-hotels.co.uk
**Website:** www.macdonald-hotels.co.uk/kilheycourt
**Map ref:** 6, SD50
**Directions:** M6 junct 27, through Standish. Take B5239
onto A5106. Hotel on right
**Rooms:** 62, S £65–£155 D £80–£170 **Facilities:** ⊗
Sauna Jacuzzi Solarium Gym STV **Parking:** 200 **Notes:** ⊗ in bedrooms ⊗ in restaurant

A grand Victorian house set in 10 acres of award-winning landscaped gardens overlooking Worthington Lakes, Kilhey Court was orginally built in 1884 by a Wigan brewer as a wedding present for his wife. It opened as a hotel in 1984. The bedrooms demonstrate all the qualities of a first-class hotel, with luxury en suite bathrooms. The expertly prepared cuisine of the attractive Laureate Restaurant is combined with an exceptional wine list.

**Recommended in the area**

Camelot Theme Park; Blackpool Pleasure Beach; Samlesbury Hall

# HAMPSHIRE

HMS Victory, Portsmouth.

# The Hampshire Court

★★★★ 78% ❀ HOTEL

**Address:** Centre Drive, Chineham,
BASINGSTOKE RG24 8FY
**Tel:** 01256 319700
**Fax:** 01256 319730
**Email:** hampshirecourt@qhotels.co.uk
**Website:** www.qhotels.co.uk
**Map ref:** SU65
**Directions:** Off A33 (Reading road) behind Chineham
Shopping Centre via Great Binfields Rd
**Rooms:** 90, S £144 D £171
**Facilities:** ⓧ Sauna Jacuzzi Solarium Tennis Gym STV
Wi-fi in bedrooms **Parking:** 200
**Notes:** ⊗ in bedrooms ⊘ in restaurant

The Hampshire Court couples luxury accommodation with leisure facilities that are second to none. With five indoor and four outdoor French soft clay courts, rain will not stop play. Complementing the tennis is an impressive range of facilities including two indoor pools (an adult only swimming pool plus a "fun" pool for all ages), sauna, steam and spa bath plus a state of the art gymnasium. Comfort and style run throughout the hotel from the bedrooms to the lounge areas. Many of the bedrooms have private balconies and all rooms are fully equipped with wireless internet access, tea- and coffee-making facilities, trouser press, hairdryer, direct dial telephone and satellite television as well as a range of toiletries. The modern, attractive Restaurant offers a traditional menu using the finest English sourced meats with a good selection of wines whilst the hotel's stylish Terrace Brasserie also serves a good selection of refreshments and food throughout the day. The hotel offers an ideal base to explore the area's attractions. The Hampshire Centrecourt is ust 45 minutes from London with easy access from the M3.

**Recommended in the area**

Winchester Cathedral; Legoland; Milestones Open Air Museum

Queens Bower near Brockenhurst in the New Forest.

# Careys Manor Hotel

★★★★ 75% ®® HOTEL

| | |
|---|---|
| Address: | BROCKENHURST SO42 7RH |
| Tel: | 01590 623551 |
| Fax: | 01590 622799 |
| Email: | stay@careysmanor.com |
| Website: | www.careysmanor.com |
| Map ref: | 3, SU30 |

Directions: M27 junct 3, then M271, then A35 to Lyndhurst. Then A337 towards Brockenhurst. Hotel on left
Rooms: 80 Facilities: ⓧ Sauna Jacuzzi Gym STV
Wi-fi available Parking: 180 Notes: ⓧ in bedrooms ⊘ in restaurant

Careys Manor is a luxury hotel in the heart of the New Forest. Rooms in the original part are traditionally styled, while those in the garden wing are more modern with lovely views of the grounds and either a balcony or patio. There are three places to eat – the two-Rosette Manor restaurant, Blaireau's French bistro, and the Zen Garden Thai Restaurant. Plus, experience the Orient with the unique Thai spa, SenSpa, offering world-class hydrotherapy facilities and indulgent spa treatments.

**Recommended in the area**

Beaulieu Palace & Motor Museum; Hurst Castle; Exley Gardens

# Le Poussin at Whitley Ridge Hotel

★★★　85% ◉◉◉　HOTEL

| | |
|---|---|
| Address: | Beaulieu Road, |
| | BROCKENHURST SO42 7QL |
| Tel: | 01590 622354 |
| Fax: | 01590 622856 |
| Email: | info@whitleyridge.co.uk |
| Website: | www.whitleyridge.com |
| Map ref: | 3, SU30 |

Directions: At Brockenhurst onto B3055 Beaulieu Road. 1m on left up private road

Rooms: 20, S £75–£95 D £95–£195 Facilities: Tennis Parking: 35 Notes: ⊘ in restaurant

This 18th-century Georgian house, extended in Victorian times, lies in the New Forest. The hotel has been given its present name to highlight its restaurant, Le Poussin, which is at the core of its attraction. Alex Aitken, who owns and runs the hotel with his wife Caroline, is a master chef who utilises local ingredients whenever possible. His offerings include a special gastronomic menu with such speciality dishes as turbot with wild fungi, terrine of roast poussin with foie gras and prunes, and pork brined in beer and pot-roasted in honey and cloves. Tea is served in one of the hotel's sitting-rooms or on the terrace. The hotel's bedrooms are individually styled and furnished, and most offer views across gardens and open forest. Among the top-grade rooms there is one with a four-poster bed and a steam cabin, and there are a number of suites. The hotel offers many residential packages – breaks of two, three or four nights, which include dinners on several nights at Le Poussin. They range from the 'Quiet Sunday for Food-Lovers' to a romantic midweek two-night break, or the 'Ultimate New Forest Stay' weekend. Golf, horse-riding and beauty therapy at nearby locations and visits to local attractions can be arranged by staff.

### Recommended in the area

National Motor Museum, Beaulieu; Exbury Gardens; Lymington

# Esseborne Manor

★★★ 78% ®® HOTEL

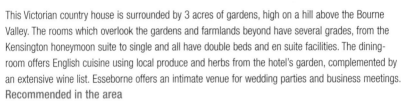

| | |
|---|---|
| Address: | HURSTBOURNE TARRANT, |
| | Andover SP11 0ER |
| Tel: | 01264 736444 |
| Fax: | 01264 736725 |
| Email: | info@esseborne-manor.co.uk |
| Website: | www.esseborne-manor.co.uk |
| Map ref: | 3, SU34 |
| Directions: | Between Andover & Newbury on A343 |

Rooms: 20, S £98–£130 D £125–£180

Facilities: Tennis STV Internet in rooms **Parking:** 50 **Notes:** ⊘ in restaurant

This Victorian country house is surrounded by 3 acres of gardens, high on a hill above the Bourne Valley. The rooms which overlook the gardens and farmlands beyond have several grades, from the Kensington honeymoon suite to single and all have double beds and en suite facilities. The dining-room offers English cuisine using local produce and herbs from the hotel's garden, complemented by an extensive wine list. Esseborne offers an intimate venue for wedding parties and business meetings.

**Recommended in the area**

Stonehenge; Highclere Castle; Salisbury; Newbury Racecourse; North Wessex Downs

# Stanwell House Hotel

★★★ 77% ® HOTEL

| | |
|---|---|
| Address: | 14-15 High Street, LYMINGTON SO41 9AA |
| Tel: | 01590 677123 |
| Fax: | 01590 677756 |
| Email: | sales@stanwellhousehotel.co.uk |
| Website: | www.stanwellhousehotel.co.uk |
| Map ref: | 3, SZ39 |
| Directions: | A337 to town centre, on right of High St, |
| | before descent to quay |

Rooms: 29, S £85 D £110 **Notes:** ⊘ in restaurant

This privately owned boutique hotel enjoys a central position in this picturesque Regency town. Every surface is covered with fruity colours; velvets and silks adorn windows and cover plump cushions to create an appealingly Bohemian impression. Bedrooms are quirky, comfortable and very well equipped; in the older part of the building some have four-posters. Lunch may be taken on the terrace, afternoon tea in the Conservatory, a pre-dinner drink in the bar, and dinner in the Bistro. Neighbouring Stanwells is the hotel's designer clothing and accessory store.

**Recommended in the area**

New Forest National Park; Beaulieu Palace & Motor Museum; The Solent

Bournemouth beach.

# Westover Hall Hotel

Address: Park Lane, MILFORD ON SEA SO41 0PT
Tel: 01590 643044
Fax: 01590 644490
Email: info@westoverhallhotel.com
Website: www.westoverhallhotel.com
Map ref: 3, SZ29
Directions: M3 & M27 W onto A337 to Lymington.
Follow signs to Milford-on-Sea onto B3058.
Rooms: 12, S £95–£180 D £120–£260 Parking: 50
Notes: ⊗ in restaurant

A beautiful, Grade II-listed Victorian country house hotel, 150 metres from the beach, beyond which the Isle of Wight and The Needles take centre stage. Inside, admire the magnificent stained-glass windows, extensive oak panelling, decorated ceilings, and the art gallery-like main hall. Stylish bedrooms have private bathroom, tasteful furnishings, luxury Italian bed linen, phone, radio and TV. Six of them look clear across Christchurch Bay. The restaurant is open daily for lunch and dinner, with the kitchen making full use of fresh and abundant New Forest produce.

**Recommended in the area**

Hurst Castle; Hengistbury Head; Beaulieu Palace & Motor Museum

# Chewton Glen Hotel

★★★★★ ◉◉◉ HOTEL

**Address:** Christchurch Road, NEW MILTON BH25 5QS
**Tel:** 01425 275341
**Fax:** 01425 272310
**Email:** reservations@chewtonglen.com
**Website:** www.chewtonglen.com
**Map ref:** 3, SZ29
**Directions:** A35 from Lyndhurst for 10m, left at staggered junct. Follow tourist sign for hotel through Walkford, take 2nd left
**Rooms:** 58, S £290–£435 D £290–£775 **Facilities:** ☒ ⚲ Sauna Tennis Gym Croquet Golf STV
**Parking:** 100 **Notes:** ⊗ in bedrooms ⊘ in restaurant No facilities for pets

The sea is just 10 minutes' walk from this superb country-house hotel, which originated as a mansion in the 18th century. Bedrooms are individually styled with luxurious fabrics and furnishings. All bedrooms enjoy the benefits of air-conditioning, satellite television, radio, DVD and CD players, and direct-dial telephone. There are also a number of suites, some duplex, and all with secluded private gardens. Guests can enjoy the health and beauty treatments, both traditional and modern, of the elegant high-tech spa, where everything from a massage to a facial or a body polish is offered. The restaurant offers a wide variety of cuisines, using as much fresh local produce as possible. The nearby New Forest offers wild mushrooms, vegetables and game; seafood may come from Christchurch and Lymington nearby. The wine list is drawn from a cellar of over 600 bins. Vegetarian and low-calorie dishes can be provided. Short residential packages include: Gourmet Dining Breaks; Spa Breaks; Golf Breaks, in which there is unlimited use of the hotel's nine-hole par-3 course and a round at either of the fine local clubs at Barton-on-Sea or Ferndown; and Tennis Breaks with coaching from the hotel's resident tennis professional. Children over five are welcome at the hotel.

### Recommended in the area
New Forest National Park; National Motor Museum, Beaulieu; Buckler's Hard historic village

Basing House ruins.

# Tylney Hall Hotel

★★★★ ◉ HOTEL

| | |
|---|---|
| Address: | ROTHERWICK, Hook RG27 9AZ |
| Tel: | 01256 764881 |
| Fax: | 01256 768141 |
| Email: | sales@tylneyhall.com |
| Website: | www.tylneyhall.com |
| Map ref: | 3, SU75 |

Directions: M3 junct 5, A287 to Basingstoke, over junct with A30 and right at Newnham Green

Rooms: 112, S £150–£455 D £195–£500 Facilities: ⊗
↝ Sauna Solarium Tennis Gym STV Wi-fi Parking: 120 Notes: ⊗ in bedrooms ⊗ in restaurant

A Grade II-listed, grand Victorian house in 66 acres of beautiful parkland this hotel offers a high level of comfort, as a quick peek into the Library Bar, Wedgwood Drawing Room, Italian Lounge or panelled Oak Room Restaurant will confirm. The hotel prides itself on a modern cooking style, yet one retaining classical hallmarks.Open to non-residents, it offers a full carte menu, with roasts from a carving trolley. The bedrooms are traditionally furnished with telephone, trouser press, hair dryer and toiletries.

**Recommended in the area**

Stratfield Saye; Legoland; Jane Austen's House

The garden at Hatfield House.

# St Michael's Manor

★★★★ 74% ◉◉ HOTEL

**Address:** Fishpool Street, ST ALBANS AL3 4RY
**Tel:** 01727 864444
**Fax:** 01727 848909
**Email:** reservations@stmichaelsmanor.com
**Website:** www.stmichaelsmanor.com
**Map ref:** 3, TL10
**Directions:** From St Albans Abbey follow Fishpool Street toward St Michael's village. Hotel 0.5m on left
**Rooms:** 30, S £145–£240 D £180–£320 **Facilities:** STV Wi-fi in bedrooms **Parking:** 70 **Notes:** ⊗ in bedrooms ⊘ in restaurant

This magnificent country house hotel stands in five acres of country gardens overlooking a lake, yet is still within walking distance of modern St Albans and its Roman predecessor. The house, which is over 500 years old, only became a hotel in the early 1960s, when the Newling Ward family bought it, and they're still the owner/managers today. Many of the individually designed rooms overlook the lake and garden and, as well as providing the generally accepted extras, thoughtfully include board games, biscuits, sweets, books and magazines too, not to mention 24-hour room service. From the restaurant there are excellent views across the gardens and lake which, together with the award-winning modern British cuisine, is responsible for drawing in food lovers from a wide area. Two examples from the carte illustrate the style: Lapsang tea-smoked salmon, and rump of lamb with sweetbreads. Dining can also be enjoyed on the garden terrace, by the lake, in the bar, or in one of the private dining rooms. St Michael's is a romantic house and thus in great demand for weddings, but businesses, with possibly a different sort of merger in mind, could make good use of its conference and meeting rooms.

**Recommended in the area**

Roman Verulamium; St Albans Cathedral & Abbey; Hatfield House

# Marriott Hanbury Manor Hotel & Country Club

★★★★★ 82% ◉◉ HOTEL

Address: WARE SG12 0SD
Tel: 01920 487722
Fax: 01920 487692
Email: mhrs.stngs.guestrelations@marriotthotels.com
Website: www.marriotthanburymanor.co.uk
Map ref: 3, TL31
Directions: M25 junct 25, take A10 north for 12m, take A1170 exit, turn right at rndbt, hotel is on the left
Rooms: 161, D £140–£529 **Facilities:** ⊗ Sauna Jacuzzi Solarium Golf Tennis Gym STV Wi-fi available **Parking:** 200

A stately Jacobean-style country house, with fragrant walled gardens, standing in 200 acres of beautiful Hertfordshire countryside. The estate dates back to the 14th century, although the current property was built in 1890. It later spent 60 years as a convent and boarding school, before opening in 1990 as the stunning hotel and country club it is today. Its appeal extends from the sculptured chimneystacks, richly panelled library, historic tapestries and stained glass to the 161 individually designed guest rooms. These offer Marriott's new Revive bedding package of down comforters, designer duvets and fluffier pillows, plus business-savvy touches such as high-speed internet. Eat contemporary Mediterranean cuisine in Oakes Grill, or more wide-ranging international dishes in the elegant Zodiac Restaurant. Drinks are served in the Oak Hall. Take on the par-defying PGA championship golf course designed by Jack Nicklaus II. For business and social events there are 14 versatile conference suites. Guests may use the health club, romanesque pool, sauna, steam room and cardio and resistance gym, jog around the fitness trail or play tennis.

**Recommended in the area**

Hatfield House; Knebworth House; Woburn Safari Park

# ISLE OF WIGHT

The Needles.

Botanic Gardens at Ventnor.

# The Royal Hotel

★★★★  76%  ◉◉  HOTEL

| | |
|---|---|
| **Address:** | Belgrave Road, VENTNOR, |
| | Isle of Wight PO38 1JJ |
| **Tel:** | 01983 852186 |
| **Fax:** | 01983 855395 |
| **Email:** | enquiries@royalhoteliow.co.uk |
| **Website:** | www.royalhoteliow.co.uk |
| **Map ref:** | 3, SZ57 |

**Directions:** A3055 into Ventnor follow one-way system
**Rooms:** 55, S £85–£150 D £140–£200
**Facilities:** ⌁ Conferences for up to 80 **Parking:** 56 **Notes:** ⊗ in bedrooms

The largest of the Isle of Wight's premier-class hotels is set in large and colourful gardens, with views of the island's south coast. All rooms are en suite and individually furnished, with tea and coffee-making facilities, television and direct-dial telephone. Guests can take their morning coffee in the conservatory. The bar is cosy, and the lounges are sumptuously furnished. Packages of three to seven nights are available throughout the year, together with Christmas and New Year packages.

**Recommended in the area**

Ventnor Botanic Garden; Appuldurcombe House; Osborne House.

# KENT

Leeds Castle.

# Eastwell Manor

★★★★ ◎◎ HOTEL

| | |
|---|---|
| Address: | Eastwell Park, Boughton Lees, ASHFORD TN25 4HR |
| Tel: | 01233 213000 |
| Fax: | 01233 635530 |
| Email: | enquiries@eastwellmanor.co.uk |
| Website: | www.eastwellmanor.co.uk |
| Map ref: | 4, TR04 |
| Directions: | On A251, 200yds on left when entering Boughton Aluph |

**Rooms:** 62, S £110–£415 D £140–£445 **Facilities:** ⑤ ↝ Sauna Jacuzzi Solarium Tennis Gym STV complimentary Wi-fi throughout complex **Parking:** 200 **Notes:** ⊘ in restaurant

Eastwell Manor, with a history going back to the Norman Conquest, lies in 62 acres of grounds, including a formal Italian garden, attractive lawns and parkland, all part of a three thousand acre estate. In the 16th century Richard Plantagenet, illegitimate son of Richard III, lived here, and centuries later Queen Victoria and King Edward VII were frequent visitors. Its age is apparent in the lounges, restaurant and bar, with their original baronial fireplaces, carved panelling and abundance of fine antiques. Twenty-three individually designed bedrooms, all with private bathrooms, bear witness to the Manor's long history, with rooms named after previous owners and other worthies. Eastwell Mews cottages in the grounds have been converted from Victorian stables, all with bathroom, kitchen, sitting room and dining facilities. The informal, all-day Brasserie in The Pavilion looks out across the Kent countryside, while the more formal dining destination is the Manor Restaurant, where the choice is from an extensive menu of French and modern English cuisine. The Pavilion Spa houses a 20-metre pool in a Roman baths-like setting, hydrotherapy pool, sauna, Jacuzzi, steam room and technogym. The beauty and therapy area, Dreams, pampers both men and women. There is also a 20-metre outdoor swimming pool and an all weather tennis court.

**Recommended in the area**

Canterbury Cathedral; Sissinghurst Castle; Leeds Castle

# Bridgewood Manor

★★★★ 74% ◉◉ HOTEL

| | |
|---|---|
| Address: | Bridgewood Roundabout, |
| | Walderslade Woods, |
| | CHATHAM ME5 9AX |
| Tel: | 01634 201333 |
| Fax: | 01634 201330 |
| Email: | bridgewoodmanor@qhotels.co.uk |
| Website: | www.qhotels.co.uk |
| Map ref: | 4, TQ76 |

Directions: Adjacent to Bridgewood rdbt on A229.
Take 3rd exit signed Walderslade and Lordswood. Hotel 50mtrs on left
Rooms: 100, S £132.50 D £171
Facilities: ⊗ Sauna Jacuzzi Solarium Tennis Gym STV
Wi-fi available Parking: 170 Notes: ⊗ in bedrooms ⊘ in restaurant

Situated on the edge of the historic city of Rochester, close to the ancient Pilgrims Way and near to many places of interest, Bridgewood Manor has 100 delightful bedrooms including twins, doubles, suites and inter-connecting rooms that are ideal for families. Guests at this hotel can enjoy an al fresco drink during the Summer months in the attractive central courtyard or relax in the comfortable lounge areas. The excellent Reflections Spa and Leisure Club boasts a heated indoor pool, spa bath, steam/sauna and gymnasium as well as a full-size snooker table. There is a luxurious range of Spa body/beauty/ holistic treatments available by fully trained therapists for those wishing to indulge in a pampering session. Renowned for its fine food, guests can enjoy the elegant atmosphere of the award winning Squires restaurant or choose to take lighter meals throughout the day in the attractive Terrace Bistro. Bridgewood Manor is conveniently situated and close to many places of interest including the Bluewater Shopping Centre.

**Recommended in the area**

Chatham Dockyards; Leeds Castle

# Rowhill Grange Hotel & Utopia Spa

★★★★ 80% ◉◉ HOTEL

**Address:** DARTFORD DA2 7QH
**Tel:** 01322 615136
**Fax:** 01322 615137
**Email:** admin@rowhillgrange.co.uk
**Website:** www.rowhillgrange.co.uk
**Map ref:** 4, TQ57
**Directions:** M25 junct 3 take B2173 to Swanley, then B258 to Hextable
**Rooms:** 38, S £165–£245 D £190–£350 **Facilities:** ⓢ Sauna Jacuzzi Gym Aerobics studio 19 treatments rooms STV Wi-fi in bedrooms **Parking:** 150 **Notes:** ⊗ in bedrooms ⊘ in restaurant

A partly thatched hotel in nine acres of grounds encompassing a lake with Australian black swans, Victorian walled garden, private woodlands and sweeping lawns. From one exceptional setting to another - the hotel itself, built in 1868 as a 'summer house' for a seemingly very fortunate 18-year-old girl. Original period features, solid-wood furniture, top-end designer fabrics and attractive artwork all contribute to Rowhill's stylish character. The bedrooms and suites feel homely, in no small measure due to their comfortable beds, upholstered armchairs, elegant side tables and cushioned window seats. Many of the en suite bathrooms are lined with Italian marble. Diners in Truffles Restaurant, the informal Brasserie, or out on the terrace, may choose from an extensive international menu. In the Utopia spa, one of the world's top 50 according to a national newspaper, qualified therapists offer beauty treatments, massage and aromatherapy. The indoor swimming pool is surrounded by a convincing Tuscan trompe l'oeil. The hotel is fully geared up for business seminars and corporate events, either in the oak-panelled boardroom, or in the thatched Clockhouse Suite, whose impressive former town-hall clock weighs over a ton.

**Recommended in the area**

Leeds Castle; Brands Hatch; Bluewater Shopping Centre

# The Hythe Imperial

★★★★ 80% ⚜ HOTEL

**Address:** Princes Parade,
HYTHE CT21 6AE
**Tel:** 01303 267441
**Fax:** 01303 264610
**Email:** hytheimperial@qhotels.co.uk
**Website:** www.qhotels.co.uk
**Map ref:** 4, TR13
**Directions:** M20, junct 11 onto A261. In Hythe follow
Folkestone signs. Right into Twiss Rd to hotel

**Rooms:** 100 S £112 D £171 **Facilities:** ⓧ Sauna Jacuzzi Solarium Tennis Gym STV **Parking:** 200
**Notes:** ⊗ in bedrooms ⊘ in restaurant

Occupying an unspoilt seafront location in the historic Cinque Port of Hythe, virtually all of the 100 comfortable, well-appointed bedrooms (including suites and family rooms) enjoy wonderful views over either the English Channel, golf course or mature and manicured gardens offered by The Hythe Imperial. There is excellent food served in the award winning restaurant and guests can also try the lighter innovative menus of the more informal Terrace Bar/Bistro. All of these features will ensure a warm welcome at one of Kent's friendliest hotels. The extensive leisure facilities of the Reflections Spa and Leisure Club include the heated indoor pool and all weather tennis courts plus a range of luxurious Spa body/beauty treatments in which to indulge. The par 68, 18 tee, 13 green links golf course is bounded by the Royal Military Canal on one side and the sea on the other and is a challenge for all keen golfers. Located just a short drive from the Channel Tunnel The Hythe Imperial is also ideally suited as a base from which to enjoy a day in France. Children are especially welcome, staying free of charge when sharing a room with their parents. A playroom is also available and special entertainment and activities are organised at certain times of the the year.

**Recommended in the area**

Port Lympne and Howlett Wild Animal parks; Romney; Hythe; Dymchurch Railway; Canterbury

# LANCASHIRE

Blackpool Pleasure Beach.

# Garstang Country Hotel & Golf Club

★★★ 75% HOTEL

| | |
|---|---|
| Address: | Garstang Road, Bowgreave, GARSTANG PR3 1YE |
| Tel: | 01995 600100 |
| Fax: | 01995 600950 |
| Email: | reception@ghgc.co.uk |
| Website: | www.garstanghotelandgolf.co.uk |
| Map ref: | 6, SD44 |

Directions: M6 junct 32 take 1st right after Rogers Esso garage on A6 onto B6430

Rooms: 32, S £60–£95 D £85£100 Facilities: STV Parking: 172 Notes: ⊗ in bedrooms

This modern, family-owned hotel has the golfer very much in mind. It possesses its own 18-hole, par 68 course, designed by former PGA Cup captain, Richard Bradbeer, and a floodlit driving range. Guests can watch the play from the en suite bedrooms and then dine on Goosnargh duck breast in the Kingfisher Restaurant. Seven meeting rooms can accommodate up to 180 delegates.

**Recommended in the area**

National Football Museum; Blackpool Pleasure Beach; Hoghton Tower

# Chadwick Hotel

★★★ 77% HOTEL

| | |
|---|---|
| Address: | South Promenade, LYTHAM ST ANNES FY8 1NP |
| Tel: | 01253 720061 |
| Fax: | 01253 714455 |
| Email: | sales@thechadwickhotel.com |
| Website: | www.thechadwickhotel.com |
| Map ref: | 5, SD32 |

Directions: M6 junct 32 take M55 to Blackpool then A5230 to South Shore. Follow signs for St Annes

Rooms: 75, S £50–£52 D £69–£78 Facilities: ⊗ Sauna Jacuzzi Solarium Gym STV Wi-fi in bedrooms Parking: 40 Notes: ⊗ in bedrooms ⊗ in restaurant

From the bright, comfortable lounges and front-facing bedrooms of the Chadwick Hotel the uninterrupted views extend over the Ribble Estuary south to Wales. Some of the thoughtfully equipped en suite bedrooms have spa baths. The Four Seasons restaurant offers a wide choice of traditional English and popular international dishes, including local seafood specialities.

**Recommended in the area**

Blackpool Pleasure Beach; Blackpool Zoo; Royal Lytham St Annes Golf Club

# The Grand Hotel

★★★★ 76% HOTEL

| | |
|---|---|
| **Address:** | South Promenade, LYTHAM ST ANNES FY8 1NB |
| **Tel:** | 01253 721288 |
| **Fax:** | 01253 714459 |
| **Email:** | book@the-grand.co.uk |
| **Website:** | www.the-grand.co.uk |
| **Map ref:** | 5, SD32 |

**Directions:** M6 junct 32 take M55 to Blackpool then A5230 to South Shore. Follow signs for St Annes

**Rooms:** 55, S £75–£125 D £80–£160 **Facilities:** ⓩ Sauna Steam Room Jacuzzi Solarium Gym STV **Parking:** 75 **Notes:** ⊗ in bedrooms ⊘ throughout the hotel

Situated in its own grounds on the South Promenade of a traditional seaside resort, The Grand Hotel is a Victorian building that commands fine and uninterrupted views of the Ribble Estuary and the Irish Sea. Its rooms are of a variety of grades, ranging up to three suites with balconies, four turret rooms and a penthouse suite. All rooms have en suite bathrooms, and are fully equipped with television, direct-dial telephone, and facilities for making hot drinks. There is a 24-hour room service and night porter service. The restaurant, lounge and bar have recently been completely refurbished. The Café Grand restaurant offers all-day dining with traditional English cuisine, while private dining is available in the hotel's salon. The luxurious spa boasts a 17-metre (56-foot) swimming-pool, together with health and beauty treatment rooms. Three function rooms are available to host events including business meetings and wedding receptions with up to 200 participants. Residential packages of two to four nights are available throughout the year if booked online. Golf enthusiasts can take one of the hotel's golf breaks, taking advantage of the three superb golf courses close by: Royal Lytham & St Annes, St Annes Old Links and Fairhaven.

## Recommended in the area

Fylde coastline; Golden Mile, Blackpool; RSPB Discovery Centre, Fairhaven Lake

# LEICESTERSHIRE

Town Hall Square, Leicester.

# Stapleford Park

★★★★ @@ HOTEL

**Address:** Stapleford, MELTON MOWBRAY LE14 2EF
**Tel:** 01572 787000
**Fax:** 01572 787651
**Email:** reservations@stapleford.co.uk
**Website:** www.staplefordpark.com
**Map ref:** 3, SK81
**Directions:** 1m SW of B676, 4m E of Melton Mowbray and 9m W of Colsterworth
**Rooms:** 55, S £195 D £250–£560 **Facilities:** ⊛ Sauna Jacuzzi Tennis Gym STV **Parking:** 120 **Notes:** ⊘ in restaurant

A magnificent 17th-century house in 500 acres of parkland, lake and woods, originally created by the celebrated Lancelot 'Capability' Brown. As one of England's finest stately homes, Stapleford Park offers a stunning blend of architecture, history and landscape. Although no longer in regular use, the Church of St Mary Magdalene graces the gardens. But there is far more to it than its magical environment. The splendid reception rooms, for example, mirror the traditional character of the house, while the 55 individually designed and furnished bedrooms reflect the styles of their creators, among them Crabtree & Evelyn, David Hicks, Pirelli, Sanderson and Zoffany, to ensure that every guest has a unique experience. Just choose your favourite. The Grinling Gibbons dining room offers inspired traditional English and European dishes, while the more relaxed and informal Pavilion Brasserie is housed within the new award-winning golf club. The challenging golf course itself was designed by Donald Steel, but if golf doesn't appeal, try the falconry school, clay pigeon shooting, fishing, archery, giant chess or tennis. The Spa's numerous facilities include a 22-metre mosaic swimming pool, steam room, Jacuzzi, gymnasium, and individually designed beauty therapy rooms. There are facilities for business meetings, conferences and private dining celebrations.

**Recommended in the area**

Rutland Water; Burghley House; Rockingham Castle

Market Harborough.

# Kilworth House Hotel

★★★★ 81% ®® HOTEL

| | |
|---|---|
| Address: | Lutterworth Road, |
| | NORTH KILWORTH LE17 6JE |
| Tel: | 01858 880058 |
| Fax: | 01858 880349 |
| Email: | info@kilworthhouse.co.uk |
| Website: | www.kilworthhouse.co.uk |
| Map ref: | 3, SP68 |

Directions: A4304 towards Market Harborough, after Walcote, hotel 1.5m on right

Rooms: 44, S £135–£180 D £135–£180 Facilities: Gym STV Wi-fi in bedrooms Parking: 140
Notes: ⊗ in bedrooms ⊗ in hotel

Built in the 19th century, Kilworth House is set in 38-acre and exudes grace at every turn. For example, climb the impressive staircase to 11 palatial en suite bedrooms, or cross the courtyard to the equally stately Garden Rooms. For formal dining choose the Wordsworth Restaurant, with its amazing ceiling and stained glass windows, or head for the Orangery and a more casual meal.

**Recommended in the area**

Foxton Locks; Rockingham Castle; Stanford Hall

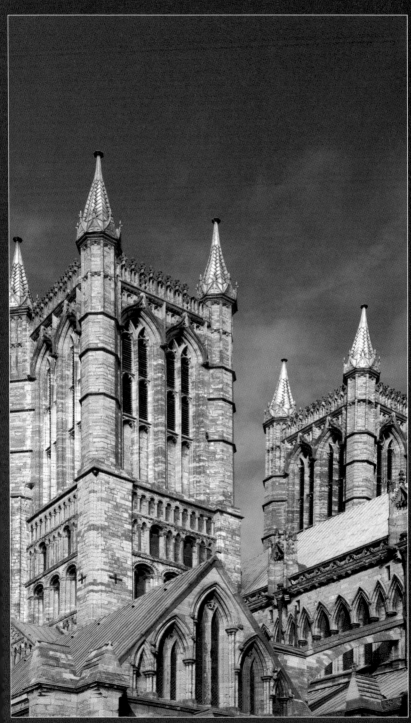

Lincoln Cathedral.

# Grantham Marriott Hotel

★★★★ 76% HOTEL

**Address:** Swingbridge Road, GRANTHAM NG31 7XT
**Tel:** 01476 593000
**Fax:** 01476 592592
**Email:** mhrs.emamc.sales.mgr@marriotthotels.com
**Website:** www.granthammarriott.co.uk
**Map ref:** 8, SK83
**Directions:** Exit A1at Grantham/Melton Mowbray junct onto A607. From N: 1st exit at mini rdbt, hotel on right. From S: at rdbt 2nd exit. Next left at T-junct. At mini rdbt 2nd exit. Hotel on right
**Rooms:** 90, S £65–£85 D £65–£85 **Facilities:** ⊗ Sauna Solarium Gym STV Wi-fi in bedrooms
**Parking:** 150 **Notes:** ⊗ in bedrooms ⊘ in all public areas

Friendly staff at the reception desk in the open lobby welcome you into this smart, modern hotel on the edge of town. Public rooms, which extend into a pretty terraced courtyard, include a serviced lounge, function rooms and a small leisure club. Bedrooms feature Marriott's new range of luxury beds, with down comforters, designer duvets and especially fluffy pillows. The rooms are also provided with en suite bathroom, mini-bar, wireless internet and work area. Superior rooms additionally offer a king-size bed, robe and slippers, premium toiletries, bottled spring water and chocolates. The hotel is happy to recommend local places to eat, including a Thai and a Chinese, but why go out when delicious traditional English and classical international food is served in the Restaurant? And fine wines too. Lunch and dinner are also served in the more informal Lounge. Swim a length or two in the Leisure Club's indoor pool, shed a pound in the sauna, tone up in the fitness centre, or ask staff to fix an outdoor activity from biking to water-skiing. Ten meeting rooms, the largest of which can seat 200, can be used for business meetings, weddings and social events.

**Recommended in the area**

Grimsthorpe Castle; Belvoir Castle; Belton House

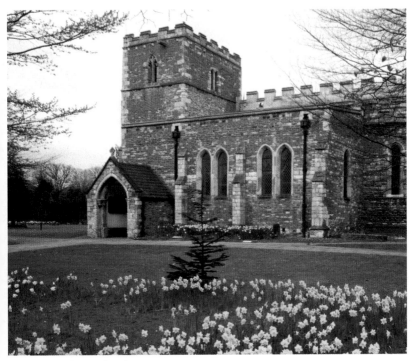

St Lawrence's Church, Scunthorpe.

# Winteringham Fields

★ ★ ★ HOTEL

**Address:** WINTERINGHAM DN15 9PF
**Tel:** 01724 733096
**Fax:** 01724 733898
**Email:** wintfields@aol.com
**Website:** www.winteringhamfields.com
**Map ref:** 8, SE92
**Directions:** In the centre of the village at the crossroads
**Rooms:** 10 **Parking:** 14 **Notes:** ⊘ in restaurant

A 16th-century manor house transformed into a highly regarded restaurant with rooms, not far from the mighty Humber Bridge. Individually designed luxury en suite rooms, some in renovated barns and cottages, are named after former owners and local dignitaries. The Lord Fitz-Hugh, for example, features a huge four-poster and an unexpected beamed bathroom. But it is Robert Thompson's inspired cooking that probably receives most acclaim. He knows the local provenance of everything he uses in each skilfully crafted dish which include fresh fish daily from Grimsby, game from nearby shoots, vegetables and herbs from the gardens. Friendly staff anticipate each guest's request.

**Recommended in the area**

Thornton Abbey; Spurn Head Heritage Coast; Gainsthorpe Deserted Medieval Village

The London Eye and Big Ben.

St Katherine's Dock, London Docklands.

# The Landmark London

★★★★★ ⊛⊛ HOTEL

**Address:** 222 Marylebone Road, LONDON NW1 6JQ
**Tel:** 020 7631 8000
**Fax:** 020 7631 8080
**Email:** reservations@thelandmark.co.uk
**Website:** www.landmarklondon.co.uk
**Map ref:** 3, TQ27
**Directions:** Adjacent to Marylebone Station
**Rooms:** 299, S £260–£370 D £285–£395
**Facilities:** ⊗ Health Club and Spa Sauna Jacuzzi Gym
STV Wi-fi available **Notes:** ⊗ in bedrooms

The Landmark was built in 1899 opposite Marylebone Station. Classic Victorian opulence combine with contemporary Thai influences (it has a sister hotel in Bangkok), most evidently in the eight-storey atrium, where the Winter Garden Restaurant is an impressive place to dine underneath towering palm trees. The bedrooms feature a king-sized bed (except Superior and Twin), executive desk, private bar, and on-command video, radio, three phone lines, bathrobe, hair dryer and quality bath products.

**Recommended in the area**

Madame Tussauds Waxwork Museum; Regent's Park; Lords Cricket Ground

# The Goring

★★★★★ ◉◉ HOTEL

| | |
|---|---|
| Address: | Beeston Place, Grosvenor Gardens, LONDON SW1W 0JW |
| Tel: | 020 7396 9000 |
| Fax: | 020 7834 4393 |
| Email: | reception@goringhotel.co.uk |
| Website: | www.goringhotel.co.uk |
| Map ref: | 3, TQ27 |
| Directions: | Off Lower Grosvenor Place |

Rooms: 71, S £212–£323 D £258–£382 **Facilities:** STV Wi-fi available **Parking:** 12 **Notes:** ⊗ in bedrooms

The Goring opened in 1910, in a distinguished building harmonizing with its Belgravia neighbours. It offers a range of individually decorated rooms of luxurious quality, from queen-bedded single rooms to the garden-view deluxe and balcony rooms, and the family-room suites. Some overlook the hotel's quiet, leafy garden. The sumptuous dining-room was recently refurbished, preserving and enhancing the Edwardian appointments of the original – including its arched windows, elaborate ceiling mouldings and marble fireplace. The fine menu is predominantly British, with occasional Continental touches. It includes such little-known delicacies as eggs Drumkilbo, smoked Somerset eel with beetroot and horseradish, and cauliflower rarebit tart with roasted cherry tomatoes and new potatoes. The range of cheeses available is notable. The wine list is outstanding - The Goring even lays down wines for the benefit of the guests of the future. Light meals can be enjoyed throughout the day in the Garden Bar, which comprises the bar proper, a lounge, the Terrace and the Veranda, an open space seating 24. Functions can be arranged, ranging from private dinner parties for six people to marquee wedding receptions in the hotel's gardens.

**Recommended in the area**

Royal Parks; Central London shopping areas; Houses of Parliament; Buckingham Palace.

# Jumeirah Carlton Tower

★★★★★ ◉◉ HOTEL

| | |
|---|---|
| **Address:** | Cadogan Place, |
| | LONDON SW1X 9PY |
| **Tel:** | 020 7235 1234 |
| **Fax:** | 020 7235 9129 |
| **Email:** | JCTinfo@jumeirah.com |
| **Website:** | www.jumeirah.com |
| **Map ref:** | 3, TQ27 |

**Directions:** A4 towards Knightsbridge, turn right onto Sloane St. Hotel on left before Cadogan Place
**Rooms:** 220, D from £299 **Facilities:** ⊗ Sauna Steam room Sound therapy Massage Tennis Gym STV
**Notes:** ⊗ in bedrooms

Jumeirah Carlton Tower, the essence of Knightsbridge, is only moments from Harvey Nichols, Harrods and Sloane Street's exclusive boutiques. This luxurious hotel offers 59 suites including the spacious Presidential Suite on the 18th floor, featuring stunning panoramic views over London. For the ultimate in sophistication and glamour, have a drink in the opulent GILT Champagne Lounge, or the glamorous Rib Bar. Three restaurants offer a wide range of mouth-watering cuisine, including the Rib Room, renowned since 1961 for serving 'the best English breakfast' London has to offer and succulent Aberdeen Angus beef at lunch and dinner. For a lighter meal, try the elegant Chinoiserie at the heart of the hotel, or the relaxing Club Room on the ninth floor. Private dining can be arranged in the private Boardroom or the contemporary Maple Room; and the Ballroom, glittering in tradition and the stylish Garden Rooms are perfect for special events. The indulgent Peak Health Club & Spa includes a tropical-style, heated indoor pool under a vast glass canopy and a state-of-the-art fitness facility and aerobics studio.

**Recommended in the area**

Hyde Park; Royal Albert Hall; Victoria & Albert Museum

# Jumeirah Lowndes Hotel

| | |
|---|---|
| Address: | 21 Lowndes Street, Knightsbridge |
| | LONDON SW1X 9ES |
| Tel: | 020 7823 1234 |
| Fax: | 020 7235 1154 |
| Email: | contact@lowndeshotel.com |
| Website: | www.jumeirah.com |
| Map ref: | 3, TQ27 |

Directions: M4 onto A4 into London. Left from
Brompton Rd into Sloane St. Left into Pont St and
Lowndes St next left. Hotel on right
Rooms: 87, D from £250 Facilities: STV Wi-fi available Notes: ⊗ in bedrooms

Jumeirah Lowndes Hotel, an oasis in Belgravia, is set in fashionable Knightsbridge close to the
prestigious department stores, Harrods and Harvey Nichols. This chic, contemporary boutique hotel,
overlooking leafy Lowndes Square, offers de luxe service and a high standard of facilities. The hotel,
which launched in November 2006, bears all the hallmarks of Jumeirah properties worldwide.
Calming seasonal colours and an impressive use of space and light create a sense of well-being
and tranquillity. The 87 sumptuous bedrooms, including spacious suites on the dedicated all-suite
6th floor, feature marble bathrooms with luxurious Temple Spa toiletries and other amenities including
plasma-screen TVs, internet access and i-Pod docks. Distinguished by its originality and style, the
Mimosa Bar & Restaurant offers delectable Mediterranean-style cuisine all day, and offers al fresco
dining on the terrace during the summer months. The vibrant, welcoming bar area offers light
refreshments as well as cocktails and afternoon tea. For private entertaining or small business
meetings, the exclusive and flexible event room is available. Guests have complimetary access to
all facilities at nearby sister hotel, the Jumeirah Carlton Tower, including the renowned Peak Health
Club & Spa.

### Recommended in the area

Hyde Park; Kensington Gardens; Victoria & Albert Museum

# The Capital

★★★★★ ◉◉◉◉ TOWN HOUSE HOTEL

| | |
|---|---|
| **Address:** | Basil Street, Knightsbridge, LONDON SW3 1AT |
| **Tel:** | 020 7589 5171 |
| **Fax:** | 020 7225 0011 |
| **Email:** | reservations@capitalhotel.co.uk |
| **Website:** | www.capitalhotel.co.uk |
| **Map ref:** | 3, TQ27 |
| **Directions:** | 20yds from Harrods and Knightsbridge tube station |

**Rooms:** 49, S £245 D £335 **Facilities:** STV Wi-fi in bedrooms
**Parking:** 3 **Notes:** ⊗ in bedrooms ⊘ in restaurant

This small family-owned hotel is in Knightsbridge, in the heart of fashionable London. The rooms available include eight suites, seven de luxe double rooms and a two-bedroom suite with its own dining area, kitchen, and private entrance with security entryphone. Rooms are individually furnished with original artworks and antique furniture, the matresses are handmade and the sheets are made of the finest Egyptian cotton. The marble bathrooms all contain well-proportioned baths and powerful showers. Facilities in the rooms include radio, satellite television, hairdryer, mini-bar and safe and there is wireless Internet access throughout the hotel. Special rates for short stays are available throughout the year and can be viewed on the hotel website. The restaurant offers the finest in gourmet cuisine, with options including a three-course lunch menu, a three-course dinner menu and a five-course 'Dégustation menu'. Eric Chavot and his committed brigade continue to cook to a consistently high standard. The restaurant's fine wine list includes vintages from the hotel's own vineyard, the Levin

Winery in the Loire. Cocktails are a speciality and can be enjoyed in the stylish bar, and afternoon tea can be taken in the sitting room. The hotel will even provide a personal shopper for Harvey Nichols and Harrods, two of the many upmarket stores nearby. Guests have access to The Peak, an exclusive health and fitness spa within walking distance of the hotel. Mountain bikes are available to residents. Business functions can be accommodated in any of the three meeting rooms, with up to 24 participants in a theatre- or boardroom-style event, or up to 40 in reception style.

**Recommended in the area**

Harrods; Harvey Nichols; Hyde Park; Kensington Gardens Serpentine Gallery; Natural History Museum; Victoria and Albert Museum; Science Museum; Royal Albert Hall; Buckingham Palace

# The Draycott Hotel

★★★★★ 82% TOWN HOUSE HOTEL

| | |
|---|---|
| Address: | 26 Cadogan Gardens, |
| | LONDON SW3 2RP |
| Tel: | 020 7730 6466 |
| Fax: | 020 7730 0236 |
| Email: | reservations@draycotthotel.com |
| Website: | www.draycotthotel.com |
| Map ref: | 3, TQ27 |

Directions: From Sloane Sq station towards Peter Jones, keep to left. At Kings Rd. take first right Cadogan Gdns, 2nd right, hotel on left

Rooms: 35, S £125–£135 D £180–£290 Facilities: STV Wi-fi in bedrooms

Notes: ⊘ in restaurant

Combining Edwardian grandeur with the feel of a private residence, albeit a luxurious one, the hotel is a skilful conversion of three elegant town houses. It is part of the Cadogan estate, built by the eponymous peer around Sloane Square, the hub of this ever-fashionable district. The bedrooms all have high ceilings, fireplaces and carefully selected antiques. Each is named after a theatrical personality and decorated around a print, poster or other memento associated with that character. More practical considerations include a well-proportioned en suite bathroom, air conditioning, satellite TV and CD music system, and Sea Island sheets covering the specially made large beds, some rooms look out over the peaceful garden below. Start the day in the Breakfast Room, adorned with masks of famous artistes, such as Dame Kiri Te Kanawa, and framed programmes of plays performed at the nearby Royal Court Theatre. Although The Draycott does not have a formal restaurant, a 24-hour room

service menu offers a selection of seasonal meals and snacks. There is also a private dining room that combines the decadence of The Draycott Hotel with the cosiness of a private home. In addition, the local eating scene is varied and vibrant – see the hotel's recommendations list. The fully-airconditioned Donald Wolfit Suite is a conference room with a beautiful oak-panelled room interior that, via patio doors, opens up into a private garden square. Equipped with the latest audio-visual equipment it can take up to 12 people boardroom style. Further rooms are available if required.

### Recommended in the area

Harrods; Hyde Park; Kensington Gardens Serpentine Gallery; Natural History Museum; Victoria and Albert Museum; Science Museum; Royal Albert Hall; Buckingham Palace

# Brown's Hotel

★★★★★ 88% ◉◉ HOTEL

| | |
|---|---|
| **Address:** | Albemarle Street, Mayfair, LONDON W1S 4BP |
| **Tel:** | 020 7493 6020 |
| **Fax:** | 020 7493 9381 |
| **Email:** | reservations.browns@roccofortehotels.com |
| **Website:** | www.roccofortehotels.com |
| **Map ref:** | 3, TQ27 |
| **Directions:** | A short walk from Bond St & Piccadilly |

**Rooms:** 117, S or D £310–£2700
**Facilities:** Gym STV Wi-fi in bedrooms Functions for up to 120 **Notes:** ⊗ in bedrooms

This ancient and famous hotel has recently been completely refurbished. Original paintings and a selection of books personalize the rooms, which are individually decorated and furnished, with digital flat-screen television. The wood-panelled Grill restaurant serves both traditional British and modern Continental dishes. It includes some banquette booths for secluded dining. The Donovan Bar has a wide selection of cocktails, and the English Tea Room claims to serve London's best afternoon tea.

**Recommended in the area**

New Bond Street shopping; West End theatres; Buckingham Palace

# Millennium Hotel London Mayfair

★★★★ 79% ◉ HOTEL

| | |
|---|---|
| **Address:** | Grosvenor Square, LONDON W1K 2HP |
| **Tel:** | 020 7629 9400 |
| **Fax:** | 020 7629 7736 |
| **Email:** | sales.mayfair@mill-cop.com |
| **Website:** | www.millenniumhotels.com |
| **Map ref:** | 3, TQ28 |
| **Directions:** | On S side of Grosvenor Square - near Park Lane and Oxford St |

**Rooms:** 348, S £160–£250 D £206–£323 **Facilities:** Gym STV Internet **Notes:** ⊗ in bedrooms

Many rooms in this de luxe hotel have fine views over Grosvenor Square, in the heart of Mayfair. The spacious en suite bedrooms have many facilities including radio, direct-dial telephone and mini-bar. The Brian Turner Mayfair restaurant offers British cuisine and the Shogun Restaurant has a wide menu of traditional Japanese dishes. Ten function rooms provide facilities for events with up to 700 guests.

**Recommended in the area**

West End shopping; West End theatres; Hyde Park

Hampton Court.

# Royal Lancaster Hotel

★★★★ 81% ❀ HOTEL

| | |
|---|---|
| **Address:** | Lancaster Terrace, LONDON W2 2TY |
| **Tel:** | 020 7262 6737 |
| **Fax:** | 020 7724 3191 |
| **Email:** | book@royallancaster.com |
| **Website:** | www.royallancaster.com |
| **Map ref:** | 3, TQ27 |

**Directions:** Adjacent to Lancaster Gate Underground
**Rooms:** 416, S £85–£259 D £85–£259 **Facilities:** STV
Function rooms **Parking:** 100 **Notes:** ⊗ in bedrooms

The Standard rooms at this centrally placed hotel have en suite bathrooms and also include satellite television, air-conditioning, a safe, drinks-making facilities, Internet access, direct-dial telephones and en suite marble bathrooms with power showers. Superior rooms have stunning views of Hyde Park and the London skyline from the 13th floor and above. The hotel houses two outstanding restaurants: Nipa serves Thai cuisine, while the Island Restaurant and Bar, overlooking Hyde Park, serves British food. Traditional afternoon tea and light snacks are served in the lounge.

**Recommended in the area**

Royal Albert Hall; Portobello Road market; Hyde Park; Kensington Palace.

# Royal Garden Hotel

★★★★★ ❀❀❀ HOTEL

| | |
|---|---|
| Address: | 2-24 Kensington High Street, LONDON W8 4PT |
| Tel: | 020 7937 8000 |
| Fax: | 020 7361 1991 |
| Email: | sales@royalgardenhotel.co.uk |
| Website: | www.royalgardenhotel.co.uk |
| Map ref: | 3, TQ27 |

**Directions:** Next to Kensington Gardens and close to High Street Kensington Underground

**Rooms:** 396, S £270–£317 D £330–£388

**Facilities:** Sauna Gym STV **Notes:** ⊗ in bedrooms

The views from the upper floors of the Royal Garden Hotel extend over Hyde Park and Kensington Gardens to the financial district of the City and London's riverside landmarks. The bedrooms in the hotel are of modern design, all with high-speed wireless Internet connection, interactive television and radio, DVD and CD player, mini-bar, air-conditioning and safe. Room grades range from Standard through Superior to Deluxe. Deluxe rooms are for double occupancy and all enjoy views over the gardens and the park. They are light and spacious, with work and lounge areas. There are numerous suites, the four highest-grade being on the hotel's highest floors, with unequalled views. The hotel's major restaurant is The Tenth, serving modern European cuisine. Throughout the day guests can also get meals at the Park Terrace Restaurant, with its famous British Speciality Menu. Residents wanting a drink have a choice: perhaps champagne and romantic views of London in the Tenth Bar on the top floor, or an English beer in Bertie's. The hotel offers various promotions, including, on selected

dates, Manhattan Nights, evoking a 1950s New York nightclub. Festive occasions at the hotel include not only Christmas and New Year but also Thanksgiving. The fully equipped business facility has a centre open round the clock and offers 12 meeting rooms, able to accommodate events with up to 550 delegates. The Soma Centre is the hotel's health club and spa, offering a wide range of beauty and fitness treatments, a steam room, a sauna, and coaching in yoga, martial arts, aerobics, Pilates and much else.

### Recommended in the area

Harrods; Hyde Park; Kensington Gardens Serpentine Gallery; Natural History Museum; Victoria and Albert Museum; Science Museum; Royal Albert Hall; Buckingham Palace

The Houses of Parliament.

# Jurys Great Russell Street

★★★★ 79% ◉ HOTEL

**Address:** 16-22 Great Russell St, LONDON WC1B 3NN
**Tel:** 020 7347 1000
**Fax:** 020 7347 1001
**Email:** restaurant_grs@jurysdoyle.com
**Website:** www.jurysdoyle.com
**Map ref:** 3, TQ28
**Directions:** From Gower St turn onto right Bedford Sq, then first left to end of road
**Rooms:** 170, S £95–£240 D £95–£240 **Facilities:** STV Wi-fi in bedrooms 12 conference rooms **Notes:** ⊗ in bedrooms ⊘ in restaurant

Designed by Sir Edwin Lutyens for the YWCA, Jurys Doyle Group bought and converted the building in 1998. Original features have been retained throughout the major interior spaces, particularly in the grand reception lobby and lounge. A choice of accommodation includes classic and executive rooms and junior suites. Lutyens Restaurant is recommended for impressive European cuisine. Pre-theatre menu available.

**Recommended in the area**

British Museum; Oxford Street; Covent Garden; Theatreland; Dominion Theatre

# Renaissance Chancery Court London

★★★★★ 86% ◉◉ HOTEL

| | |
|---|---|
| **Address:** | 252 High Holborn, LONDON WC1V 7EN |
| **Tel:** | 020 7829 9888 |
| **Fax:** | 020 7829 9889 |
| **Email:** | sales.chancerycourt@renaissancehotels.com |
| **Website:** | www.renaissancechancerycourt.co.uk |
| **Map ref:** | 3, TQ27 |

**Directions:** A4 along Piccadilly onto Shaftesbury Av. Into High Holborn, hotel on right
**Rooms:** 356 **Facilities:** Sauna Spa Gym STV Wi-fi available **Notes:** ⊗ in bedrooms ⊘ in restaurant

Sublime old-world class links arms here with contemporary standards of five-star luxury. Enter the beautiful classical courtyard and this grand building makes an immediate impression with its stunning public areas, decorated in rich mahogany, rare marble and fine crystal. The exceptionally spacious, luxurious bedrooms are among the largest in London. More rare marble is to be found in the bathrooms, many with double basins and separate showers. Walking into the Pearl restaurant means being momentarily mesmerised by breathtaking chandeliers and shimmering cascades of real pearls. This sophisticated room is the domain of world-renowned head chef, Jun Tanaka, who brings to the tables a menu of international cuisine. The CC Bar, embellished with restored period features, feels like an exclusive members' club, while the marble-columned Lounge must be one of the finest open spaces to be found in a hotel. Indulge in a relaxation and therapy programme in the Spa at Chancery Court. A superbly appointed business centre is accessible day and night and there are facilities for corporate use.

**Recommended in the area**

London Eye; Somerset House; British Museum

# Richmond Gate Hotel

★★★★ 76% ◎◎ HOTEL

| | |
|---|---|
| **Address:** | 152-158 Richmond Hill, |
| | RICHMOND UPON THAMES TW10 6RP |
| **Tel:** | 020 8940 0061 |
| **Fax:** | 020 8332 0354 |
| **Email:** | richmondgate@foliohotels.com |
| **Website:** | www.foliohotels.com/richmondgate |
| **Map ref:** | 3, TQ17 |
| **Directions:** | Top of Richmond Hill opposite Star & Garter |

**Rooms:** 68, S £180 D £190 **Facilities:** ⓧ Sauna Jacuzzi
Solarium Gym STV Wi-fi in bedrooms **Parking:** 150 **Notes:** ⊗ in bedrooms ⊘ in restaurant

This former Georgian country house stands on top of Richmond Hill, close to the Royal Park. The
bedrooms, many with air-conditioning, combine every comfort of the present with the elegance of the
past including several four-poster rooms and suites. Exceptional and imaginative cuisine, featuring an
extensive wine list is served in the sophisticated surroundings of the Gates on the Park Restaurant.
Guests may relax in the beautiful Victorian walled garden and use the Cedars Health and Leisure Club.

**Recommended in the area**

Kew Gardens; Ham House; Hampton Court Palace; Twickenham Rugby Stadium

# Richmond Hill Hotel

★★★★ 71% ◎ HOTEL

| | |
|---|---|
| **Address:** | 144–150 Richmond Hill, |
| | RICHMOND UPON THAMES TW10 6RW |
| **Tel:** | 020 8940 2247 |
| **Fax:** | 020 8940 5424 |
| **Email:** | richmondhill@foliohotels.com |
| **Website:** | www.foliohotels.com/richmondhill |
| **Map ref:** | 3, TQ17 |
| **Directions:** | Top of Richmond Hill |

**Rooms:** 138, S £90–£165 D £120–£175 **Facilities:** ⓧ
Sauna Jacuzzi Solarium Gym STV Wi-fi in bedrooms **Parking:** 150 **Notes:** ⊘ in bedrooms & restaurant

This attractive Georgian manor is only seven miles from the centre of London, yet standing majestically
on the Richmond hill's crest. The en suite bedrooms are equipped with refreshment facilities, hair
dryer and wireless broadband; most are now air conditioned, and some have balconies. In the newly
refurbished, Grade II-listed Pembrokes restaurant an all-day modern European menu is offered. The
extensive facilities of the Cedars Health and Leisure Club can be used by guests.

**Recommended in the area**

Kew Gardens; Ham House; Hampton Court Palace; Twickenham Rugby Stadium

The Catholic Cathedral of Christ The King, Liverpool.

HMS Plymouth and the submarine HMS Onyx, Birkenhead.

# The RiverHill Hotel

★★★ 79% HOTEL

| | |
|---|---|
| **Address:** | Talbot Road, Prenton, |
| | BIRKENHEAD CH43 2HJ |
| **Tel:** | 0151 653 3773 |
| **Fax:** | 0151 653 7162 |
| **Email:** | reception@theriverhill.co.uk |
| **Website:** | www.theriverhill.co.uk |
| **Map ref:** | 5, SJ38 |

**Directions:** 1m from M53 junct 3, along A552. Turn left onto B5151 at lights hotel 0.5m on right

**Rooms:** 15, S £69.75 D £79.75 **Facilities:** STV **Parking:** 32 **Notes:** ⊗ in bedrooms

The RiverHill stands in its own beautiful grounds in Oxton, a quiet residential neighbourhood near Birkenhead. It is run by Nick and Michelle Burn, who also run the Grove House Hotel in nearby Wallasey. The attractively furnished en suite bedrooms, all have TV, phone, hot drinks facilities, trouser press and hair dryer. The RiverHill has two bridal suites, each with four-poster bed. An excellent choice of carte and fixed price menus and good quality wines can be found in the Bay Tree Restaurant.

**Recommended in the area**

Speke Hall (NT); Bidston Observatory; Ness Botanic Gardens

# Radisson SAS Hotel Liverpool

★★★★ 81% ◉ HOTEL

| | |
|---|---|
| Address: | 107 Old Hall Street, LIVERPOOL L3 9BD |
| Tel: | 0151 966 1500 |
| Fax: | 0151 966 1501 |
| Email: | info.liverpool@radissonsas.com |
| Website: | www.radissonsas.com |
| Map ref: | 5, SJ39 |
| Directions: | Left from Leeds Street dual carriageway |

Rooms: 194, D £160 Business class £180 Junior £290 River £800 Facilities: ⓧ Sauna Jacuzzi Solarium Beauty lounge Gym STV Free Wi-fi Parking: 25 Notes: ⊗ in bedrooms ⊘ in restaurant

A nine-storey atrium features in this ultra modern building on Liverpool's waterfront. Bedrooms range from standard rooms to the River Suite, Liverpool's largest. Residents can dine in the Filini Restaurant, which serves Italian cuisine and drink in the fashionably styled White Bar. They can use the Ark health and fitness club. A floor with fully equipped meeting rooms is available for business functions.

**Recommended in the area**

Tate Liverpool; Merseyside Maritime Museum; The Beatles Story

# The Grove House Hotel

★★★ 78% HOTEL

| | |
|---|---|
| Address: | Grove Road, WALLASEY CH45 3HF |
| Tel: | 0151 639 3947 |
| Fax: | 0151 639 0028 |
| Email: | reception@thegrovehouse.co.uk |
| Website: | www.thegrovehouse.co.uk |
| Map ref: | 5, SJ29 |
| Directions: | M53 junct 1, A554, right after church onto Harrison Drive, left after Windsors Garage onto Grove Rd |

Rooms: 14, S £65 D £80–£90 Facilities: STV Parking: 28 Notes: ⊗ in bedrooms

Pretty lawns and gardens are the setting for this friendly hotel, situated in a quiet residential area of Wallasey. Nick and Michelle Burn have owned it since 1998; they also own the nearby RiverHill Hotel. The attractively furnished ground floor, family and four-poster en suite bedrooms have TV, phone, hot drinks facilities, trouser press and hair dryer. Relax with an aperitif in the cocktail bar before dinner; a liqueur in the cocktail lounge afterwards. The Oak Tree Restaurant offers a wide choice of dishes.

**Recommended in the area**

Speke Hall (NT); Bidston Observatory; Ness Botanic Gardens

# NORFOLK

Blickling Hall.

# Hoste Arms Hotel

★ ★ ★  80% ◉◉  HOTEL

**Address:**   The Green, BURNHAM MARKET,
King's Lynn PE31 8HD
**Tel:**   01328 738777
**Fax:**   01328 730103
**Email:**   reception@hostearms.co.uk
**Website:**   www.hostearms.co.uk
**Map ref:**   4, TF84
**Directions:**   On B1155, 5m W of Wells-next-the-Sea
**Rooms:** 35, S £88–£260 D £117–£260 **Facilities:** STV
Wi-fi available **Parking:** 45

In a few years the Hoste Arms has gone from a pub with
no bedrooms and a dining area for 35, to a 35-bedroom
hotel with a brasserie serving up to 150 diners a night. It
was built in 1550 as a manor house, although by 1651 it had become an inn, later visited weekly
by Horatio Nelson to receive his dispatches. In late Victorian times it was a brothel, and a busy one
too apparently. The bedrooms, among them some with four-posters, junior suites and a penthouse,
were all designed by co-owner Jeanne Whittome. The Zulu Wing, named for her homeland of Zululand,
contains a magnificent boardroom, two luxurious suites and six double bedrooms, each decorated
with Zulu artefacts. The en suite bedrooms in the old Burnham railway station, a five-minute walk
away, are quite small, but well decorated. Inspired by first-hand experience of some of the world's
great restaurants, the Hoste's chefs create imaginative menus based on fine local produce. A list of
over 300 wines features the world's finest. In his book, 'A Hoste of Ideas', Paul Whittome describes
an extraordinary tour of the world in search of the best ideas from over 300 hotels and restaurants.
Managing Director Emma Tagg will be pleased to welcome you to The Hoste Arms.

**Recommended in the area**

Holkham Hall; Sandringham; Wells & Walsingham Light Railway

# Elderton Lodge Hotel & Langtry Restaurant

★★★ 86% ● HOTEL

**Address:** Gunton Park, CROMER NR11 8TZ
**Tel:** 01263 833547
**Fax:** 01263 834673
**Email:** enquiries@eldertonlodge.co.uk
**Website:** www.eldertonlodge.co.uk
**Map ref:** 4, TG24
**Directions:** At North Walsham take A149 towards Cromer, hotel 3m on left, just before Thorpe Market
**Rooms:** 11, S £65 D £100–£120 **Parking:** 50 **Notes:** ⊘ in hotel

Positioned in beautiful wooded grounds, and overlooking 800 acres of deer park, this 200-year-old former shooting lodge to Gunton Hall is lovingly run as a country house hotel. Rachel and Pat, both natives of Norfolk, have worked hard refurbishing the property and training staff. Enjoy pre-dinner drinks or after-dinner coffee in the comfortable lounge. En suite bedrooms are individually decorated and furnished, with careful attention to detail. Every room has TV, DVD player (free DVDs from Reception), phone, alarm clock, tea-making facilities and hair dryer. The candlelit Langtry Restaurant, named after Lillie, the celebrated Victorian beauty and mistress of the Prince of Wales, is open daily to residents and non-residents, with seasonal and regularly changing fixed price menus. The emphasis is on fresh, locally sourced produce, particularly fish and seafood from the nearby coast, and seasonal game from neighbouring estates, including Gunton itself. Adjoining the Langtry is the Conservatory, used also for breakfast and lunch. The hotel building and grounds provide a wonderful backdrop for wedding photographs (it is licensed for civil ceremonies). For large functions there is a top-of-the-range marquee with wooden dance floor and chandeliers.

**Recommended in the area**

Norfolk Broads; Norwich City Centre and Cathedral; Blickling Hall

# The Kings Head Hotel

★★★ 85% ⊕ HOTEL

**Address:** GREAT BIRCHAM, King's Lynn PE31 6RJ
**Tel:** 01485 578265
**Fax:** 01485 578635
**Email:** welcome@the-kings-head-bircham.co.uk
**Website:** www.the-kings-head-bircham.co.uk
**Map ref:** 4, TF73
**Directions:** From King's Lynn take A149 towards Fakenham. After Hillington, turn left onto B1153 and continue to Great Bircham.
**Rooms:** 12, S £69.50–£99.50 D £125–£225 **Parking:** 25 **Notes:** ⊘ in restaurant

The Kings Head Hotel is a converted inn with a modern extension in a peaceful village close to the north Norfolk coast, and bordering the Royal Sandringham estate. Contemporary, spacious bedrooms have king-sized beds, co-ordinated furnishings and welcoming touches such as fresh flowers. The stylish restaurant overlooking the sheltered courtyard offers unfussy brasserie and a la carte menus based on local produce. There's a relaxing lounge and a friendly bar serving local ales, light meals and snacks.

**Recommended in the area**

Houghton Hall; RSPB Titchwell; Norfolk Lavender

# Congham Hall Country House Hotel

★★★ ⊕⊕ HOTEL

**Address:** Lynn Road, GRIMSTON,
King's Lynn PE32 1AH
**Tel:** 01485 600250
**Fax:** 01485 601191
**Email:** info@conghamhallhotel.co.uk
**Website:** www.vonessenhotels.co.uk
**Map ref:** 4, TF72
**Directions:** Take A148 NE of King's Lynn for 100yds. Right to Grimston, hotel 2.5m on left
**Rooms:** 14, S £105–£295 D £185 **Parking:** 50 **Notes:** ⊗ in bedrooms ⊘ in restaurant

This Georgian manor house, set in parklands and gardens, has a homely feel, with log fires and antique furniture. The bedrooms, individually decorated in traditional English style, all overlook the gardens or parkland. In the intimate Orangery restaurant, with its french windows giving on to the terrace, the cuisine features seasonal local produce including specialities such as Cromer crab.

**Recommended in the area**

Sandringham House and Estate; Holkham Hall; Norfolk Lavender and wildflowers

# Beechwood Hotel

★★★ ⍟⍟ HOTEL

Address:     Cromer Road, NORTH WALSHAM NR28 0HD
Tel:     01692 403231
Fax:     01692 407284
Email:     enquiries@beechwood-hotel.co.uk
Website:     www.beechwood-hotel.co.uk
Map ref:     4, TG23
Directions: B1150 from Norwich. At North Walsham left
at 1st lights, then right at next
Rooms: 17, S £70 D £90–£160 Parking: 20
Notes: ⊗ in hotel

The bedrooms in this creeper-clad redbrick 18th-century town house close to the town centre are individually decorated with period furniture and antiques. They range in grade from small double to four-poster. All have en suite bathrooms, CD players and direct-dial telephones. Superior rooms have Victorian-style bathrooms with freestanding slipper baths and separate walk-in showers. The restaurant bases its dinners as far as possible on local produce including Cromer fish.

**Recommended in the area**

Sandringham House; Norwich; Norfolk Broads; East Ruston Old Vicarage gardens

# The Old Rectory

★★ ⍟⍟ HOTEL

Address:     103 Yarmouth Road, Thorpe St Andrew,
                NORWICH NR7 0HF
Tel/Fax:     01603 700772/01603 300772
Email:     enquiries@oldrectorynorwich.com
Website:     www.oldrectorynorwich.com
Map ref:     4, TG20
Directions: From A47 southern bypass onto A1042
towards Norwich N & E. Left at mini rdbt onto A1242.
After 0.3m through lights. Hotel 100mtrs on right
Rooms: 8, S £82–£105 D £110–£135 Facilities: ↘ Wi-fi in bedrooms Parking: 15 Notes: ⊗ in bedrooms ⍟ in restaurant, Drawing Room and bedrooms

Home of the Entwistle family, this handsome Georgian property stands in mature gardens overlooking the Yare Valley. Guest rooms have the finest bed linen, widescreen digital TV, wireless broadband, warm bathrobes, luxury toiletries and other thoughtful finishing touches. Chef James Perry offers a daily changing, seasonal fixed price dinner menu served in the candlelit Dining Room.

**Recommended in the area**

Norfolk Broads; Norwich Cathedral; Blickling Hall

Tresham Lodge, Rushton.

# Hellidon Lakes

★★★★ 78% ☻ HOTEL

| | |
|---|---|
| **Address:** | HELLIDON |
| | NN11 6GG |
| **Tel:** | 01327 262550 |
| **Fax:** | 01327 262559 |
| **Email:** | hellidonlakes@qhotels.co.uk |
| **Website:** | www.qhotels.co.uk |
| **Map ref:** | 3, SP55 |
| **Directions:** | Off A361 between Daventry and Banbury, |

(the hotel is signed)

**Rooms:** 110, S £132.50 D £171 **Facilities:** ☻ Solarium
Tennis Gym STV Wi-fi available
**Parking:** 150 **Notes:** ☻ in bedrooms ☻ in restaurant

Set amidst 220 acres of rolling countryside on the borders of Warwickshire and Northamptonshire, Hellidon Lakes is situated in one of England's most central locations. Guests are offered the choice of 110 comfortable, well-equipped bedrooms and suites, many of which have wonderful vistas over the surrounding countryside as far as the eye can see. A delectable menu bursting with choice and accompanied by a wonderful selection of wines is available in the award-winning restaurant. Alternatively, you can choose to eat in the more informal bar bistro, overlooking the golf course and lakes, which has an excellent range of light meals, snacks and drinks served throughout the day. For relaxation, guests can enjoy the amenities at the Reflections Spa and Leisure Club which has a swimming pool and a 40 station gymnasium or indulge in one of the luxurious Spa body and beauty treatments which are available. For fun, there is a 10-pin bowling alley with computerised scoring and an indoor golf simulator with 22 top golf courses to play. The hotel also boasts a spectacular 27-hole golf course with rolling valleys, picturesque lakes and challenging fairways.

**Recommended in the area**

Warwick Castle; Althorp; Heritage Motor Centre

Cragside House and gardens.

# Langley Castle Hotel

★★★★ 80% HOTEL

| | |
|---|---|
| Address: | Langley on Tyne, HEXHAM NE47 5LU |
| Tel: | 01434 688888 |
| Fax: | 01434 684019 |
| Email: | manager@langleycastle.com |
| Website: | www.langleycastle.com |
| Map ref: | 7, NY86 |

Directions: From A69 S on A686 for 2m. Castle on right

Rooms: 19, S £99.50–£189.50 D £129–£249

Facilities: STV Parking: 70 Notes: ⊗ in bedrooms ⊘ in restaurant and Drawing Room

This really is a castle. It was built in 1350 and is now a rare example of an English medieval fortified castle hotel. A local historian, Cadwallader Bates, bought it as a near ruin in 1882 and spent the rest of his life restoring it; after he died his widow, Josephine, continued the task, rebuilding the original chapel on the castle roof in memory of her husband. She died in 1933 and is buried alongside him in the 10-acre woodland estate. The building preserves what are probably Europe's finest examples of 14th-century garderobes, the name our ancestors gave to their toilets. All the bedrooms have private facilities, four-poster beds and window seats set into the 7-foot thick walls, while additional luxury features may include a sauna or spa bath. Castle View and the Lodge, restored listed buildings situated in the grounds, contain a further 10 rooms and suites decorated and furnished to the same high standard as rooms in the Castle. In the candlelit Josephine Restaurant a fixed-rate menu of continental, regional and local dishes specialises in fresh fish and local game and the wine list extends to vintage Château Lafite. Afterwards guests can retire to the magnificent Drawing Room for a coffee or liqueur in front of a crackling log fire. Not surprisingly, the hotel makes a fine setting for a wedding reception.

### Recommended in the area

Hadrian's Wall; Bamburgh Castle; Hexham Abbey

Matfen.

# Matfen Hall

★★★★  81% ❀❀  HOTEL

| | |
|---|---|
| **Address:** | MATFEN, Newcastle-upon-Tyne NE20 0RH |
| **Tel:** | 01661 886500 |
| **Fax:** | 01661 886055 |
| **Email:** | info@matfenhall.com |
| **Website:** | www.matfenhall.com |
| **Map ref:** | 7, NZ07 |
| **Directions:** | Off A69 to B6318. Hotel just before village |

**Rooms:** 53, S £105–£160 D £160–£255 **Facilities:** ℞
Sauna Jacuzzi Solarium Gym STV Wi-fi in bedrooms
**Parking:** 150 **Notes:** ⊘ in restaurant

Matfen Hall is a magnificent country house set in the Northumberland countryside. Bedrooms are furnished in a combination of traditional and modern styles, some have four-poster beds. The Library and Print Room Restaurant offers fine dining, and light snacks are served in the Conservatory Bar. A range of health and beauty treatments are available in the new spa. The hotel has a fine 6,569-yard golf course with 18 holes, and a 9-hole par-3 course for less experienced players.

**Recommended in the area**

Newcastle; Hadrian's Wall; Northumberland Moors

Wollaton Hall (Nottingham's Natural History Museum).

# Langar Hall

★★★ 79% ◉◉ HOTEL

Address:    LANGAR NG13 9HG
Tel:        01949 860559
Fax:        01949 861045
Email:      info@langarhall.co.uk
Website:    www.langarhall.com
Map ref:    8, SK73
Directions: Via Bingham from A52 or Cropwell Bishop
from A46, both signed. Hotel behind church
Rooms: 12, S £80–£115 D £95–£210 Facilities: Wi-fi
in bedrooms Parking: 20 Notes: ⊘ in restaurant

Langar Hall was built in 1837 on the site of a great historic house, the home of Admiral Lord Howe.
It stands in quiet seclusion in the Vale of Belvoir, overlooking lovely gardens beyond which sheep
graze among ancient trees. Below the croquet lawn lies a network of medieval fishponds stocked with
carp. Langar is the family home of Imogen Skirving, who has built a reputation for good hotel keeping
combined with the hospitality of an informal country house. Most of the bedrooms have super
countryside views, every one is quiet, comfortable and well-equipped and one has a four-poster bed.
The chalet, on the croquet lawn just a short walk from the house, has its own veranda and is a small,
warm and private option. Downstairs is the study, a quiet room for reading and meetings; the white
sitting room, perfect for afternoon tea and pre-dinner drinks; and the Indian Room, ideal for private
parties and conferences. The restaurant, an elegant pillared hall, is well regarded in the neighbourhood
for fresh seasonal food with an emphasis on game in winter and fish in summer. The Garden Room
and Potting Shed Bar is open on weekdays for meals, wines and juices, and in summer meals may
be eaten in the sheltered garden just outside. An interesting wine list offers sympathetically priced
wines from around the world. Langar is a popular venue for civil marriages.

### Recommended in the area

Belvoir Castle; Trent Bridge Cricket Ground; Newark International Antiques and Collectors Fair

# The Grange Hotel

★ ★ ★  80%  HOTEL

| | |
|---|---|
| Address: | 73 London Road, NEWARK-ON-TRENT NG24 1RZ |
| Tel: | 01636 703399 |
| Fax: | 01636 702328 |
| Email: | info@grangenewark.co.uk |
| Website: | www.grangenewark.co.uk |
| Map ref: | 8, SK75 |

Directions: From A1 follow signs to town centre. At castle rdbt follow signs to Balderton. Over 2 sets of lights. Hotel 0.25m on left

Rooms: 19, S £72–£100 D £96–£150 Parking: 17 Notes: ⊗ in bedrooms ⊘ in restaurant

A family-run, Victorian-era hotel in a conservation area, just a short walk from the town centre. Skilfully renovated, Newark Civic Trust gave it an award for how original features, such as a beautiful tiled floor in one of the entrance areas, have been retained. Public rooms include a bar called Potters (Potters Bar, perhaps), with framed illustrations of old crockery, and a residents' lounge. Beyond Potters is a stone-flagged patio shaded by tall yews and the immaculate landscaped garden, winner of a Newark in Bloom award. The bedrooms, some with four-posters, all feature newly designed bathrooms with bath and shower, co-ordinated soft furnishings, desk space with phone and computer access point, TV, radio alarm, beverage-making and ironing facilities, hair dryer, trouser press and, last but not least, a rubber duck for the very young (or perhaps the harassed business executive). High-ceilinged Cutlers restaurant, named after the antique cutlery on display, offers a frequently changing, à la carte menu, with main courses such as pan-fried fillet of pork; baked herb-crusted sea bass; and broccoli, cheese and potato bake. That it attracts non-residents as well as hotel guests says much about the restaurant's appeal. Weddings and business functions are expertly catered for.

Recommended in the area

Newark Castle and Gardens; Newark International Antiques Fair; Newark Air Museum

# The Nottingham Belfry

★★★★  81% ◉ HOTEL

| | |
|---|---|
| Address: | Mellor's Way,<br>Off Woodhouse Way,<br>NOTTINGHAM NG8 6PY |
| Tel: | 0115 973 9393 |
| Fax: | 0115 973 9494 |
| Email: | nottinghambelfry@qhotels.co.uk |
| Website: | www.qhotels.co.uk |
| Map ref: | 8, SK53 |

Directions: A610 towards Nottingham. A6002 to Stapleford/Strelley. 0.75m, last exit of rdbt
Rooms: 120 S £85–£134.5 D £120–£219 Facilities: ⓧ Sauna Jacuzzi  Gym STV Parking: 250
Notes: ⊗ in bedrooms ⊗ in restaurant

Recently opened, The Nottingham Belfry is a chic, stylish, ultra modern hotel and has already received two prestigious tourism awards. A contemporary feel and design runs throughout the hotel which is decorated with stunning original artwork depicting the area's rich culture. Guests are offered the choice of twin, double, executive or four-poster rooms, all beautifully fitted out. Each room has a flat screen TV or you can spoil yourself with a Suite that has a separate lounge, bedroom, lobby and even a TV to watch whilst relaxing in the bath. The hotel offers two restaurants – the Oaks Brasserie providing light meals, drinks and snacks throughout the day or the Lawrence Restaurant for more formal dining with a menu of varied, interesting and high quality dishes set to satisfy even the most experienced taste buds. There is also the chance to enjoy the excellent facilities of the Reflections Spa and Leisure Club for an invigorating swim, a workout in the gym, a relaxing steam or sauna or pampering Spa body/beauty treatments. Ideally located, offering easy routes into and out of the city, The Nottingham Belfry is a perfect venue from which to explore the area.

**Recommended in the area**

Lace Centre; Nottingham Castle; City of Caves

# Restaurant Sat Bains with Rooms

★★★ ◉◉◉◉ HOTEL

| | |
|---|---|
| Address: | Trentside, Lenton Lane, NOTTINGHAM NG7 2SA |
| Tel: | 0115 986 6566 |
| Fax: | 0115 986 0343 |
| Email: | info@restaurantsatbains.net |
| Website: | www.restaurantsatbains.com |
| Map ref: | 8, SK53 |

Directions: M1 junct 24 take A453 Nottingham S. Over River Trent in central lane to rdbt. Left then left again towards river. Hotel on left after bend

Rooms: 8, S £90–£100 D £100–£150 Parking: 22 Notes: ⊗ in bedrooms ⊘ in hotel

Chic boutique hotel, or restaurant with rooms? Take your pick. Named after the chef-patron, who runs it with his wife Amanda, this sympathetic conversion of farm buildings by the River Trent is close to the city's industrial area, yet manages to remain tucked away in idyllic seclusion. The individually designed bedrooms create a warmth and magic using quality soft furnishings and antique and period furniture; suites and four-poster rooms are also available. Cosy public rooms comprise the reception/lounge bar and two small linked dining rooms, whose outstanding cuisine earned the title of AA Restaurant of the Year for 2006-7. A delighted Sat Bains described this as "A great surprise and fantastic news for Nottingham". Behind this accolade is what he acknowledges as an obsession with quality and traceability of produce, declaring that everything from the lobster to the mackerel is worthy of the chef's time. A popular choice is the tasting menu, prepared for the whole table and designed to balance tastes, textures and temperatures. There's even a bespoke tasting menu tailored to individual preferences, although this requires 48 hours notice.

Recommended in the area

Trent Bridge Cricket Ground; Nottingham Castle; Nottingham Concert Arena

# OXFORDSHIRE

The Bridge of Sighs, Oxford

# The Bay Tree Hotel

★★★ 77% ◉ HOTEL

**Address:** Sheep Street, BURFORD OX18 4LW
**Tel:** 01993 822791
**Fax:** 01993 823008
**Email:** info@baytreehotel.info
**Website:** www.cotswold-inns-hotels.co.uk/bay-tree
**Map ref:** 3, SP21
**Directions:** From Burford High St turn into Sheep St, next to the old market square. Hotel is on right
**Rooms:** 21, S £60–£119 D £81–£175 **Parking:** 50
**Notes:** ⊗ in restaurant

Much of this delightful old inn's character comes from the flagstone floors, tapestries, high-raftered hall, galleried stairs and tastefully furnished oak-panelled bedrooms, some with four-poster or half-tester beds. Public areas consist of the country-style Woolsack Bar, a sophisticated airy restaurant with original leaded windows, a selection of meeting rooms and an attractive walled garden. An alternative to the restaurant's candle-lit atmosphere is the Woolsack's extensive menu of lighter meals.

**Recommended in the area**

Burford Wildlife Park; Blenheim Palace; Oxford

# The Lamb Inn

★★★ 78% ◉◉ HOTEL

**Address:** Sheep Street, BURFORD OX18 4LR
**Tel:** 01993 823155
**Fax:** 01993 822228
**Email:** info@lambinn-burford.co.uk
**Website:** www.cotswold-inns-hotels.co.uk
**Map ref:** 3, SP21
**Directions:** Off A40 into Burford, downhill, take 1st left
**Rooms:** 15, S £115 D £145–£235
**Notes:** ⊗ in restaurant

To quote the owners, "The phrase 'charming old inn' is used much too freely, but the Lamb has a genuine right to it". Indeed it has, with stone-flagged floors, log fires and many other time-worn features. The cosy lounges, warmed by those self-same fires, and with deep armchairs, are tranquillity itself. The en suite bedrooms contain fine furniture, much of it antique, in addition to all the usual amenities, including homemade cookies. All overlook leafy side streets, or the hotel courtyard. The light, airy restaurant serves traditional English cuisine with a modern twist.

**Recommended in the area**

Cotswold Wildlife Park; Blenheim Palace; City of Oxford

# The Mill House Hotel & Restaurant

★★★ 79% ◉◉ HOTEL

**Address:** KINGHAM OX7 6UH
**Tel:** 01608 658188
**Fax:** 01608 658492
**Email:** stay@millhousehotel.co.uk
**Website:** www.millhousehotel.co.uk
**Map ref:** 3, SP22
**Directions:** Off A44 onto B4450.
**Rooms:** 23, S £115–£125 D £180–£200 **Facilities:** STV Wi-fi available **Parking:** 60
**Notes:** ⊘ in restaurant

The stone construction of this 18th-century building is in harmony with the beautiful architectural style that distinguishes the Cotswolds. The former mill-house is in 10 acres of well kept grounds, with its own trout stream, and is a good base for visiting the villages of the Cotswolds. The individually furnished bedrooms have views over the surrounding countryside and all have en suite bathroom, satellite television, direct-dial telephone and hairdryer. The Mill Brook Room Restaurant serves British cuisine based on fresh local produce in season, including such products as freshly caught fish from Brixham, organic vegetables from the Vale of Evesham, and locally raised lamb and beef. There is an eight-course Menu Dégustation for the gourmet, and the wine list is extensive. Lighter meals can be taken under the low wood-beamed ceiling of the Mill Stream Bar. The Cotswold Lounge is the place to have light snacks or cream teas. The Mill House has a licence for civil wedding ceremonies and caters for up to 80 guests in the Cotswold Lounge. The hotel can accommodate private functions, including marquee wedding receptions for up to 180 guests. Special deals are available on breaks of two or more nights, and Christmas and New Year are always celebrated in style.

**Recommended in the area**

Blenheim Palace; Stratford-upon-Avon; Warwick Castle.

# The Oxford Belfry

★ ★ ★ ★   78%  HOTEL

| | |
|---|---|
| Address: | MILTON COMMON, |
| | Thame OX9 2JW |
| Tel: | 01844 279381 |
| Fax: | 01844 279624 |
| Email: | oxfordbelfry@marstonhotels.com |
| Website: | www.qhotels.co.uk |
| Map ref: | 3, SP60 |

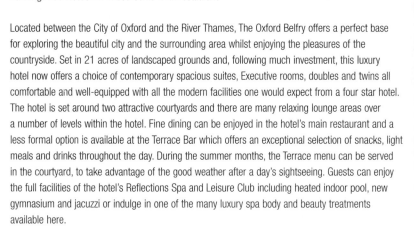

Directions: M40 junct 7 onto A329 to Thame. Left onto A40 by Three Pigeons pub. Hotel 300yds on right

Rooms: 130, S £132 D £171 Facilities: ⊗ Sauna Solarium Tennis Gym STV Wi-fi available

Parking: 250 Notes: ⊗ in bedrooms ⊘ in restaurant

Located between the City of Oxford and the River Thames, The Oxford Belfry offers a perfect base for exploring the beautiful city and the surrounding area whilst enjoying the pleasures of the countryside. Set in 21 acres of landscaped grounds and, following much investment, this luxury hotel now offers a choice of contemporary spacious suites, Executive rooms, doubles and twins all comfortable and well-equipped with all the modern facilities one would expect from a four star hotel. The hotel is set around two attractive courtyards and there are many relaxing lounge areas over a number of levels within the hotel. Fine dining can be enjoyed in the hotel's main restaurant and a less formal option is available at the Terrace Bar which offers an exceptional selection of snacks, light meals and drinks throughout the day. During the summer months, the Terrace menu can be served in the courtyard, to take advantage of the good weather after a day's sightseeing. Guests can enjoy the full facilities of the hotel's Reflections Spa and Leisure Club including heated indoor pool, new gymnasium and jacuzzi or indulge in one of the many luxury spa body and beauty treatments available here.

### Recommended in the area

Blenheim Palace; Oxford universities; Bicester Shopping Village

# Macdonald Randolph Hotel

★★★★★ 81% ◉◉ HOTEL

| | |
|---|---|
| Address: | Beaumont Street, |
| | OXFORD OX1 2LN |
| Tel: | 0870 400 8200 |
| Fax: | 01865 791678 |
| Email: | randolph@macdonald-hotels.co.uk |
| Website: | www.macdonaldhotels.co.uk |
| Map ref: | 3, SP50 |

Directions: M40 junct 8, A40 towards Oxford. Follow city centre signs, leading to St Giles, hotel on right
Rooms: 151, S £140–£180 D £150–£450
Facilities: Sauna Gym STV Wi-fi in bedrooms
Notes: ⊗ in restaurant

Oxford's landmark Macdonald Randolph Hotel is exceptionally well placed for visiting the many historic sights of the city and the busy shopping centre which is just a few minutes' walk away. The hotel was built in 1864 in a style known, somewhat confusingly, as Scottish Early English. Contrary to popular belief, it was named not after Randolph Churchill (who had local connections) but after the Randolph Gallery, part of the Ashmolean Museum which is situated opposite the hotel. A major refurbishment in 2003 ensured that it continues to provide guests with high levels of comfort and service in a traditional and welcoming atmosphere. The en suite bedrooms offer all the expected features, including satellite TV, CD player, mini-bar, beverage tray, and modem point. In addition, the de luxe suites have their own private sitting area, with crystal chandeliers and plush furnishings. Some suites have four-poster beds. Public areas

include the Morse Bar (that's right, named after Colin Dexter's famous local detective, who investigated an elderly lady's sudden demise in one of the bedrooms) which is an ideal place to relax with a drink after a long day sightseeing, and an award-winning restaurant, where fixed price and carte menus are available both at lunchtime and during the evening. Traditional afternoon tea is served in the Drawing Room. The Spa, in the old cellar, with vaulted ceilings and Italian tiling, has a thermal suite with four treatment rooms, hydrotherapy bath, bio-sauna and ice room. St John's and Worcester suites are ideal for meetings for up to 30 people, while the opulent Ballroom holds 300.

### Recommended in the area

The Oxford Story, Museum of Oxford; Blenheim Palace

All Souls College, Oxford.

# The Old Bank Hotel

★★★★ 78% ❀ HOTEL

**Address:** 92–94 High Street, OXFORD OX1 4BN
**Tel:** 01865 799599
**Fax:** 01865 799598
**Email:** info@oldbank-hotel.co.uk
**Website:** www.oldbank-hotel.co.uk
**Map ref:** 3, SP50
**Directions:** From Magdalen Bridge into High St, hotel 50yds on left
**Rooms:** 42, S £160–£305 D £165–£325
**Facilities:** STV **Parking:** 40 **Notes:** ✪ in bedrooms

Located on the High Street, The Old Bank Hotel sets the standard for stylish and comfortable accommodation with exceptional levels of personal service in central Oxford. Lying at the heart of the hotel is the perennially popular Quod Brasserie. This restaurant offers fresh modern British dishes from breakfast onwards, the emphasis here is on good quality seasonal produce, and an excellent atmosphere. Most of the rooms have spectacular views of Oxford's skyline of towers and spires.

**Recommended in the area**

Ashmolean Museum; Oxford Playhouse; University Botanic Garden

# Westwood Country Hotel

★★★ 77% HOTEL

**Address:** Hinksey Hilltop, Boars Hill, OXFORD OX1 5BG
**Tel:** 01865 735408
**Fax:** 01865 736536
**Email:** reservations@westwoodhotel.co.uk
**Website:** www.westwoodhotel.co.uk
**Map ref:** 3, SP50
**Directions:** Off Oxford ring road at Hinksey Hill junct towards Boars Hill & Wootton. At top of hill road bends to left. Hotel on right

**Rooms:** 23, S £75–£95 D £99–£145 **Facilities:** Wi-fi throughout **Parking:** 50
**Notes:** ⊗ in bedrooms ⊘ throughout

Proprietor Anthony Healy has realised his dream to create a peaceful retreat, free from the hustle and bustle of everyday living. Just two miles from the centre of the 'City of Dreaming Spires', and surrounded by 400 acres of ancient woodland and gardens, the Westwood was built by an Edwardian gentleman in 1910. Public areas include a contemporary bar, cosy lounge and restaurant overlooking the pretty garden. Many of the bedrooms have been recently refurbished, each individually styled to provide maximum comfort, with the help of an en suite bath and/or shower, fluffy cotton towels, TV, phone, and beverage tray. Different room shapes and sizes suit all needs; two have four-posters and many enjoy views over the gardens and woods. The general manager and head chef both come from AA-Rosette backgrounds and are building a formidable reputation for fine-dining here. Taken from a typical menu are slow-roasted salmon with carrots julienne, new potatoes and herb cream; roasted duck breast on spinach and basil mash; and penne pasta with Mediterranean vegetables. In the restaurant, or out on the terrace, order a fine wine from the world's most renowned vineyards. The hotel's location makes it ideal for weddings, meetings and conferences.

**Recommended in the area**

Ashmolean Museum; Bodleian Library; Blenheim Palace; Bicester Village Retail Outlet

# The Springs Hotel & Golf Club

★ ★ ★   78% ◉  HOTEL

| | |
|---|---|
| **Address:** | Wallingford Road, North Stoke, WALLINGFORD OX10 6BE |
| **Tel:** | 01491 836687 |
| **Fax:** | 01491 836877 |
| **Email:** | info@thespringshotel.com |
| **Website:** | www.thespringshotel.com |
| **Map ref:** | 3, SU68 |

**Directions:** Off A4074 (Oxford-Reading road) onto B4009 (Goring). Hotel approx 1m on right

**Rooms:** 32, S £95–£140 D £110–£155 **Facilities:** ↘ Sauna STV Wi-fi available **Parking:** 150

**Notes:** ⊘ in restaurant

The Springs, built in 1874, is a fine example of a Victorian country house, one of the first to be built in Mock-Tudor style. Standing in rolling parkland, possibly on the site of a Roman forum, it overlooks the Thames Valley and a lake fed by a million gallons of spring water daily. After several changes of ownership, it was bought in 1973 by Ian Gillan of rock group Deep Purple, who set about restoring its oak-panelled rooms and carved fireplaces and turning it into a luxury hotel. Its present owners acquired it in 2001, embarking on a continuing programme of further improvements, including luxury suites, heated outdoor pool, 18-hole golf course, croquet lawn and putting green. Public rooms include the beamed, richly carpeted lounge, and the Lord Nelson dining room, which has a decorative ceiling copied from a now-destroyed original in James I's Scottish hunting lodge. Among the variously sized en suite bedrooms are two bridal suites and one with a four-poster. The lattice-windowed Lakeside Restaurant offers an award-winning, daily changing menu of dishes such as grilled barramundi, fillet of beef Rossini, and pumpkin and oyster mushroom risotto.

### Recommended in the area

Ridgeway Path; Child Beale; Stonor Park

Sculpture on the shore of Rutland Water.

# Hambleton Hall

★★★★ ◎◎◎◎ COUNTRY HOUSE HOTEL

**Address:** Hambleton, OAKHAM LE15 8TH
**Tel:** 01572 756991
**Fax:** 01572 724721
**Email:** hotel@hambletonhall.com
**Website:** www.hambletonhall.com
**Map ref:** 3, SK90
**Directions:** 3m E off A606
**Rooms:** 17, S £165–£195 D £195–£360
**Facilities:** ↘ Tennis STV **Parking:** 40

This family-run hotel is a magnificent Victorian house, standing in its own beautiful gardens and enjoying fine views over Rutland Water, the largest man-made lake in Western Europe. Its rooms are highly individual in character, furnished with fine fabrics and sumptuous furniture, many having hand-stencilled walls. The Master rooms are the largest, and many of them overlook the lake. The smaller Standard rooms overlook the hotel's lawn and handsome cedar trees. The most luxurious rooms are in the two-bedroom Croquet Pavilion, a folly 50 yards from the main building. In the hotel's public areas there are open fireplaces in the cosy bar and sumptuous drawing-room. The restaurant serves outstanding cuisine, using local produce as far as possible. The food incorporates fresh and seasonal ingredients, and menus change frequently. Three private dining-rooms are available. Each month there is a Wine Dinner. Adventurous residents can participate in rock-climbing, windsurfing or canoeing in the local area. The hotel is a popular venue for business meetings, held in the ground floor of the main house. Full business support is available, including secretarial, fax, OHP, email and other services. The hotel is popular for prestigious private functions of all kinds, including wedding parties.

**Recommended in the area**

Burghley House; Rutland Water; Grimsthorpe Castle; Kelmarsh Hall Gardens

# SHROPSHIRE

Colemere Country Park.

# Rowton Castle Hotel

★★★ 88% ☺ HOTEL

**Address:** Halfway House,
SHREWSBURY SY5 9EP
**Tel:** 01743 884044
**Fax:** 01743 884949
**Email:** post@rowtoncastle.com
**Website:** www.rowtoncastle.com
**Map ref:** 2, SJ72
**Directions:** From A5 near Shrewsbury take A458
to Welshpool. Hotel 4m on right
**Rooms:** 19, S £74–£79 D £94 **Parking:** 100
**Notes:** ☒ in bedrooms ☺ in restaurant

Parts of this fine Grade II listed building date back to the 17th century, though it has been extensively rebuilt and refurbished in recent years. It stands in 17 acres of grounds, where croquet can be played in the shadow of a fine cedar of Lebanon, reputed to be the largest in Europe. Rooms are individually styled and furnished, six of them with four-poster beds, and range in quality from single rooms to suites. All have en suite bathrooms, television, direct-dial phone, free wireless Internet access, hairdryer, trouser press and facilities for making hot drinks. An intimate atmosphere is created by the oak panelling in the Cedar Restaurant, which is furnished with plush velvet armchairs. The restaurant offers fine dining with an emphasis on English cuisine, with some modern Continental features. The wine list is extensive. Private dining is available in the Georgian Dining Room. The grounds and lakes make ideal settings for private functions and especially wedding parties. The hotel can host business activities for up to 80 delegates in any of its three business meeting rooms, fully equipped with modern business technology. Team-building events can be arranged. The onveniently placed for the junction of the M5 and M6 motorways, providing easy access to Manchester and Birmingham.

**Recommended in the area**

Shrewsbury; Birmingham National Exhibition Centre; Ironbridge Gorge World Heritage Site

# Prince Rupert Hotel

★★★  82%  HOTEL

| | |
|---|---|
| Address: | Butcher Row, SHREWSBURY SY1 1UQ |
| Tel: | 01743 499955 |
| Fax: | 01743 357306 |
| Email: | post@prince-rupert-hotel.co.uk |
| Website: | www.prince-rupert-hotel.co.uk |
| Map ref: | 2, SJ41 |

**Directions:** Follow town centre signs, over English Bridge & Wyle Cop Hill. Right into Fish St, 200yds
**Rooms:** 70, S £85 D £105–£175 **Facilities:** Sauna Jacuzzi Gym **Parking:** 70 **Notes:** ⊗ in bedrooms ⊘ in restaurant

This ancient and elegant hotel in old Shrewsbury was once home to Prince Rupert, James I's grandson. The tasteful en suite bedrooms are equipped with modern facilities to suit business as well as leisure guests, and even more luxurious are the 12th-century Mansion House suites. Dining options include the Royalist Restaurant; innovative English food in the oak-panelled Chambers brasserie; and the hotel's own Italian restaurant, La Trattoria, in nearby Fish Street.

**Recommended in the area**

Shrewsbury Castle; Ironbridge Gorge World Heritage Site; Attingham Park (NT)

# Old Vicarage Hotel

★★★  ⚜⚜⚜  HOTEL

| | |
|---|---|
| Address: | Worfield, WORFIELD WV15 5JZ |
| Tel: | 01746 716497 |
| Fax: | 01746 716552 |
| Email: | admin@the-old-vicarage.demon.co.uk |
| Website: | www.oldvicarageworfield.com |
| Map ref: | 2, SO79 |

**Directions:** Off A454 Bridgnorth–Wolverhampton road, 5m S of Telford's southern business area
**Rooms:** 14, S £60–£110 D £80–£175 **Facilities:** Wi-fi in bedrooms **Parking:** 30 **Notes:** ⊘ restaurant

This small, privately owned hotel, formerly an Edwardian vicarage, offers individually styled rooms with antique furniture; one has a four-poster bed and those in the Coach House annexe have their own private gardens. In the Orangery Restaurant, with its fine country views, diners can enjoy a modern British treatment of seasonal local produce, with a fine wine list and cheeseboard. Conference capacity is up to 20, and the hotel and gardens provide unforgettable surroundings for wedding receptions.

**Recommended in the area**

Ironbridge Gorge (World Heritage Site); Severn Valley Railway; David Austin Roses

**173**

Glastonbury Abbey.

The Royal Crescent.

# Best Western The Cliffe Hotel

★★★ 85% ◉ HOTEL

| | |
|---|---|
| **Address:** | Cliffe Drive, Crowe Hill, Limpley Stoke, BATH BA2 7FY |
| **Tel:** | 01225 723226 |
| **Fax:** | 01225 723871 |
| **Email:** | cliffe@bestwestern.co.uk |
| **Website:** | www.bw-cliffehotel.co.uk |
| **Map ref:** | 2, ST76 |
| **Directions:** | From Bath take A36 S, turn left on B3108 Bradford-on-Avon rd, then rt before bridge, hotel on right |

**Rooms:** 11, S £97–£126 D £124–£166 **Facilities:** ⓧ STV Wi-fi **Parking:** 20 **Notes:** ⊘ in restaurant

The peace and tranquility here is not surprising, given its setting in over three acres of woodland, with spectacular views over the Avon Valley. Individually styled bedrooms include two with four-posters and one with whirlpool bath, and after a delicious meal in the AA Rosette-awarded restaurant, you can relax in the comfortable lounge. A small meeting room is available. A heated outdoor pool is open from June to September, weather permitting, and canal day boats and bikes can be hired locally.

**Recommended in the area**

World Heritage City of Bath; Lacock Abbey and Village (NT); Westwood Manor (NT)

# Dukes Hotel

★★★  82% ◉◉  SMALL HOTEL

**Address:**   Great Pulteney Street, BATH BA2 4DN
**Tel:**        01225 787960
**Fax:**        01225 787961
**Email:**      info@dukesbath.co.uk
**Website:**    www.dukesbath.co.uk
**Map ref:**    2, ST76
**Directions:** M4 junct 18 onto A46. At Bath turn left towards A36, right at next lights and right again onto Great Pulteney St
**Rooms:** 17, S £95–£115 D £125–£215
**Notes:** ⊗ in restaurant

An expertly restored, bow-fronted, Grade I-listed Georgian town house where the rooms are decorated with period furniture, fine fabrics, prints and portraits. Surviving original plasterwork includes delicate features such as Adams-style urns and floral swags. In winter a log fire in the lounge gives a warm welcome, while in summer the peaceful courtyard terrace, with a sparkling fountain, is perfect for a relaxing meal or drink. The en suite bedrooms and six suites (two with four-posters) have been restored to their original spacious dimensions. Many have enormous sash windows and splendid views over Great Pulteney Street, the Bath skyline or the surrounding countryside. Each differs in size and design, some Georgian themed, others more contemporary. All have bath and/or power shower, large fluffy towels and bathrobes, digital TV and hairdryers. The refurbished Cavendish Restaurant and Bar offers chef Richard Allen's modern British seasonal cooking, for which he sources locally grown and reared organic and free range produce. A fixed-price lunch menu offers two or three courses and the dinner menu is a la carte. The smaller, more intimate, of the two dining rooms can be reserved for receptions.

**Recommended in the area**

Thermae Bath Spa; Roman Baths; Royal Crescent and Circus

# The Queensberry Hotel

★★★ ◎◎  HOTEL

Address:   Russel Street, BATH BA1 2QF
Tel:          01225 447928
Fax:         01225 446065
Email:      reservations@thequeensberry.co.uk
Website:   www.thequeensberry.co.uk
Map ref:   2, ST76
Directions: 100mtrs from the Assembly Rooms
Rooms: 29, S £110–£300 D £110–£300 **Parking**: 6
Notes: ⊗ in bedrooms ⊘ in restaurant

Four Georgian townhouses form this charming, family-run hotel, in a quiet residential street near the city centre. It is the only contemporary boutique hotel in Bath, and has sumptuously furnished drawing rooms, a warm welcoming bar and secluded terraced gardens. Each of the spacious, individually designed bedrooms harmoniously combines up-to-date comfort with original features, plus marble bathrooms, deep armchairs, and plenty of other delights. The stylish Olive Tree restaurant specialises in fine, modestly priced contemporary British cuisine with Mediterranean influences.

**Recommended in the area**

Thermae Bath Spa; Beckford's Tower; Claverton Pumping Station

# Ash House Country Hotel

★★★  77% ◎  COUNTRY HOUSE HOTEL

Address:   41 Main Street, Ash, MARTOCK TA12 6PB
Tel:          01935 822036
Fax:         01935 822992
Email:      reception@ashhousecountryhotel.co.uk
Website:   www.ashhousecountryhotel.co.uk
Map ref:   2, ST41
Directions: Off A303 at Tintinhull Forts junct and left at top of slip road; 0.5m on right opposite recreation ground
Rooms: 9, S £60–£85 D £95–£105 **Facilities**: STV
**Parking**: 35 **Notes**: ⊗ in bedrooms ⊘ in restaurant

This listed Georgian country house, set in an acre and a half of beautiful mature gardens, has been carefully restored to provide individually furnished bedrooms which, while offering modern comforts, retain the grace and elegance of earlier times. Modern British cuisine is served in the light and airy Conservatory Restaurant overlooking the floodlit garden, or in the main dining room – particularly snug when its log fire blazes. Although small, Ash House is licensed to hold civil weddings.

**Recommended in the area**

Montacute House; East Lambrook Manor Gardens; Fleet Air Arm Museum

# The Oaks Hotel

★★★ ◉ HOTEL

Address:    PORLOCK TA24 8ES
Tel:        01643 862265
Fax:        01643 863131
Email:      info@oakshotel.co.uk
Website:    www.oakshotel.co.uk
Map ref:    2, SS84
Directions: On A39 Lynton rd, 5.7m W of Minehead
Rooms: 8, S £85 D £120 Parking: 12
Notes: ⊗ in bedrooms ⊘ in restaurant

Tim and Anne Riley have excelled in restoring this Edwardian country house setamong the majestic trees that gave it its name. From its lofty location, it has wonderful views of Exmoor and the Bristol Channel from bedrooms and the dining room. The lounge, with log fires in winter, is the place for afternoon tea and after-dinner coffee, or just to relax after a walk. Bedrooms have en suite baths and showers, fresh flowers, Egyptian cotton linen, TV and tea-making facilities. The dining room has a four-course, largely traditional menu, on which everything, from marmalade to after-dinner chocolates, is home made.

**Recommended in the area**

South West Coast Path; Watersmeet House (NT); Exmoor Bird Gardens

# Charlton House

★★★★ HOTEL

Address:    Charlton Road, SHEPTON MALLET
            Nr Bath BA4 4PR
Tel:        01749 342008
Fax:        01749 346362
Email:      enquiry@charltonhouse.com
Website:    www.charltonhouse.com
Map ref:    2, ST64
Directions: 1m from centre, on A361 Frome road
Rooms: 26, S £140–£260 D £180–£465
Facilities: Sauna Hydrotherapy pool  Gym STV Wi-fi in bedrooms Parking: 70 Notes: ⊘ in restaurant

Charlton House is just about as far away from the stuffy, uptight country house of old as you can get. So say owners Roger Saul, founder of the luxury Mulberry brand, and his wife, Monty. Fine fabrics and furnishings are a feature throughout, and the bedrooms, each equipped with the latest technology, are full of character. The highly regarded restaurant is backed by the Sauls' enthusiastically stocked wine cellar. Monty's spa offers treatments and therapies, while The Orangery is perfect for special events.

**Recommended in the area**

Cheddar Gorge; Stourhead; Wells Cathedral

# Lanes

★★★ 79% ◉ HOTEL

| | |
|---|---|
| Address: | West Coker, |
| | YEOVIL BA22 9AJ |
| Tel: | 01935 862555 |
| Fax: | 01935 864260 |
| Email: | stay@laneshotel.net |
| Website: | www.laneshotel.net. |
| Map ref: | 2, ST51 |

Directions: 2m SW of Yeovil on A30, in centre of village
Rooms: 27 S £88 D £110 Facilities: Sauna Jacuzzi
Gym Wi-fi available Parking: 40 Notes: ⊗ in bedrooms ⊘ in restaurant

At the heart of an attractive village of mellow hamstone cottages, within a conservation area, this fine former rectory is set in its own walled and landscaped gardens. The whole building has been recently refurbished with modern additions, but it retains its country-house elegance and style. The bedrooms are decorated in restful tones, and have contemporary furnishings of a high standard. Each room's facilities include an en suite bathroom, mini-bar, digital television, DVD player, and broadband Internet connection, and accommodation on offer includes a penthouse suite and an apartment. The hotel's brasserie-style restaurant is a modern addition to the building – bright, spacious and airy, with large windows and high ceilings, and with original paintings on the walls. The menu makes much use of local produce in season, and changes regularly according to what is best on the market. Guests and local people mingle in the Piano Bar, with its open fire and deep leather armchairs, where an extensive list of wines, spirits and beers is on offer. The hotel has its own leisure suite, available exclusively for residents, with a spa pool, sauna and gym. West Coker is well placed for excursions, with the historic towns of Yeovil and Sherborne close by, and within easy reach of the many attractions of Somerset, while the Dorset coast is only 20 miles away.

### Recommended in the area

Lyme Regis; Yeovilton Fleet Air Arm Museum; Montacute House and Gardens.

The view from Mow Cop Castle folly (NT).

Midland Railway Station, Burton upon Trent.

# Three Queens Hotel

★★★ 80% HOTEL

| | |
|---|---|
| **Address:** | One Bridge Street, |
| | BURTON UPON TRENT DE14 1SY |
| **Tel:** | 01283 523800 |
| **Fax:** | 01283 523823 |
| **Email:** | hotel@threequeenshotel.co.uk |
| **Website:** | www.threequeenshotel.co.uk |
| **Map ref:** | 3, SK22 |

**Directions:** At the junct Bridge St & High St
**Rooms:** 38, S £54.50–£69.50 D £64.50–£79.50
**Facilities:** STV Wi-fi in bedrooms **Parking:** 40
**Notes:** ⊗ in bedrooms ⊘ in restaurant

Parts of this historic hotel date back to the 16th century.
Bedrooms and suites have many facilities, including en
suite bathrooms, satellite TV, Internet access, and hot drinks supplies, and service extends to bringing
morning tea/coffee to rooms, and washing midweek guests' cars. The Grill Room offers English food.
**Recommended in the area**
Alton Towers; Staffordshire and Derbyshire Moorlands National Forest; Museum of Brewing

# SUFFOLK

River Blyth, Blythburgh.

# The Brudenell

★★★  85% ❀❀  HOTEL

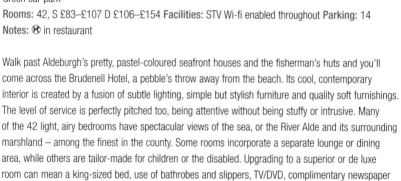

**Address:**    The Parade,
            ALDEBURGH IP15 5BU
**Tel:**        01728 452071
**Fax:**        01728 454082
**Email:**      info@brudenellhotel.co.uk
**Website:**    www.brudenellhotel.co.uk
**Map ref:**    4, TM45
**Directions:** A12/A1094, on reaching town, turn right
at junct into High St. Hotel on seafront adjoining Fort
Green car park
**Rooms:** 42, S £83–£107 D £106–£154 **Facilities:** STV Wi-fi enabled throughout **Parking:** 14
**Notes:** ⊗ in restaurant

Walk past Aldeburgh's pretty, pastel-coloured seafront houses and the fisherman's huts and you'll
come across the Brudenell Hotel, a pebble's throw away from the beach. Its cool, contemporary
interior is created by a fusion of subtle lighting, simple but stylish furniture and quality soft furnishings.
The level of service is perfectly pitched too, being attentive without being stuffy or intrusive. Many
of the 42 light, airy bedrooms have spectacular views of the sea, or the River Alde and its surrounding
marshland – among the finest in the county. Some rooms incorporate a separate lounge or dining
area, while others are tailor-made for children or the disabled. Upgrading to a superior or de luxe
room can mean a king-sized bed, use of bathrobes and slippers, TV/DVD, complimentary newspaper
and bottled water. In the warm and friendly restaurant constantly changing menus incorporating local
produce offer delicious grills, fish and seafood, including delectable oysters from nearby Orford. You
may also eat  al fresco out on the sea-facing terrace, while listening to the North Sea waves crashing
on the beach. Carefully selected wines complete the picture.

**Recommended in the area**

Snape Maltings; RSPB Minsmere; Suffolk Heritage Coast

# Wentworth Hotel

★★★  85% ◉◉  HOTEL

| | |
|---|---|
| Address: | Wentworth Road, |
| | ALDEBURGH IP15 5BD |
| Tel: | 01728 452312 |
| Fax: | 01728 454343 |
| Email: | stay@wentworth-aldeburgh.co.uk |
| Website: | www.wentworth-aldeburgh.com |
| Map ref: | 4, TM45 |

Directions:  Off A12 onto A1094, 7m to Aldeburgh,
with church on left and left at bottom of hill
Rooms: 35, S £61–£94 D £105–£211 Parking: 30 Notes: ⊗ in restaurant

This triple-gabled hotel has been managed by the Pritt family since 1920, and this continuous thread is responsible for the fact that the Wentworth is everything a seaside hotel should be. The attractive and well-maintained public rooms include three lounges furnished with comfortable chairs and sofas, which are sunny spots in summer and cosy places to relax by an open fire in winter. Outside are two sea-facing gardens in which to soak up the sun with a morning coffee, light lunch or cream tea. Many of the regularly refurbished en suite bedrooms have good views of the North Sea, for which the hotel thoughtfully provides binoculars. Seven rooms in Darfield House, just opposite the main building, are particularly spacious and well appointed. For those who find stairs difficult (there's no lift) there are five ground floor rooms. Room sizes and outlook do vary, and these differences are reflected in the tariff. All the rooms have a copy of Catherine Hale's *A Seaside Holiday*, about Orlando the cat and his holiday in Owlbarrow (Aldeburgh). You can start the day here with a locally smoked kipper, as part of your 'full-house' cooked breakfast. At lunchtime, the terrace bar menu offers a wide choice, from a fresh crab sandwich to traditional cod and chips, and the elegant candlelit restaurant has a daily changing dinner menu based on fresh local produce.

**Recommended in the area**

Minsmere (RSPB) Reserve; Snape Maltings (Aldeburgh Festival); Suffolk Heritage Coast

# The Bildeston Crown

★★★ 85% ◉◉ HOTEL

**Address:** 104 High Street,
BILDESTON, Ipswich IP7 7EB
**Tel:** 01449 740510
**Fax:** 01449 741843
**Email:** hayley@thebildestoncrown.co.uk
**Website:** www.thebildestoncrown.co.uk
**Map ref:** 4, TL94
**Directions:** N of Hadleigh on A1141
**Rooms:** 10 S from £70 D from £110 **Facilities:** STV
**Parking:** 30 **Notes:** ⊘ in restaurant

This small and intimate hotel is a coaching inn with its roots in the 15th century. Its public areas display its history in wooden beams, oak floors and exposed brickwork, but it has been refurbished to the highest modern standards. Its individually styled bedrooms have flat-screen satellite television, music system, hair-dryer, direct-dial telephone, wireless Internet and en suite bathroom (except for an economy single room that has shower only). The superior rooms include one with a four-poster bed, and another with a 16th-century fireplace. The restaurant, furnished with dark woods and leather furniture, offers both traditional and modern cuisine based on produce locally sourced in Suffolk and neighbouring counties. There is also a private dining-room. Guests can enjoy meals and drinks in the courtyard or patio in warm weather. Children can be accommodated, and dogs are welcome. Guests can arrange weekend breaks, which include full breakfast and dinner each day. The Bildeston Crown holds events throughout the year, including barbecues, dinner-dances and parties around Christmas and New Year. Sporting and leisure activities, including fishing, golf, riding and shooting, can be arranged in the area. A private room can provide a lovely setting for a wedding reception.

**Recommended in the area**

Kentwell Hall; Lavenham village; Christchurch Park, Ipswich

# The Swan

★★★★ 81% ◉◉ HOTEL

**Address:** High Street, LAVENHAM CO10 9QA
**Tel:** 01787 247477
**Fax:** 01787 248286
**Email:** info@theswanatlavenham.co.uk
**Website:** www.theswanatlavenham.co.uk
**Map ref:** 4, TL94
**Directions:** A12 onto A134, then B1071 to Lavenham
**Rooms:** 51, S £60–£80 D £120–£230
**Facilities:** STV **Parking:** 62 **Notes:** ⊘ on premises

This quintessential country hotel, situated in the heart of this historic town is fondly known as the jewel in Lavenham's crown. In the 1400s The Swan played a key role in Lavenham's thriving wool trade, and ancient beams, inglenook fireplaces and medieval wall paintings from that era have survived, blending seamlessly with modern furnishings. The Old Bar displays a fascinating collection of memorabilia, including a wall signed by British and American airmen stationed locally during World War II. Each of the en suite bedrooms is furnished and decorated in co-ordinating mellow colours, with pure linen sheets and feather pillows on the bed. Standard doubles, mezzanine suites and rooms with a four-poster are named after Suffolk villages and provided with TV and a turn-down service. The Swan is renowned for its culinary delights and offers a variety of dining options. From the characterful Old Bar and informal Garden Bar Lounge to the elegant two Rosette Gallery Restaurant, guests will find themselves spoilt for choice. In additional to the refreshing daily menus, the hotel also has an inspired Green Menu for vegetarians and its ever popular Kids Menyoo. Three newly refurbished meeting rooms are equipped with Wi-Fi and air conditioning. Licensed for Civil Wedding ceremonies, The Swan's medieval courtyard, garden and Minstrel's Gallery make the perfect backdrop for wedding photos and indeed a wide range of celebrations.

## Recommended in the area

Lavenham Guildhall; Melford Hall (NT); West Stow Anglo-Saxon Village

# The Westleton Crown

★★★ 79% ◉◉ HOTEL

| | |
|---|---|
| Address: | The Street, WESTLETON, |
| | Nr Southwold IP17 3AD |
| Tel: | 01728 648777 |
| Fax: | 01728 648239 |
| Email: | reception@westletoncrown.co.uk |
| Website: | www.westletoncrown.co.uk |
| Map ref: | 4, TM46 |

Directions: A12 N turn right for Westleton just after Yoxford. Hotel opposite on entering Westleton

Rooms: 25, S £85–£95 D £110–£170 Parking: 26 Notes: ⊘ in restaurant

So old is The Westleton Crown, that even its days as a coaching inn might with some justification be considered as modern history. Its origins actually lie back in the 12th century, yet it successfully presents contemporary comforts in the context of its ancient heritage. All the benefits of a true local can be found in the bar, where log fires crackle away on cold days. Refurbished in summer 2006, the bedrooms are graded Good, Better and Best, depending on the nature of indulgences provided, but all offer a contemporary en suite bathroom, crisp white Egyptian cotton linen, goose-down duvet, pocket-sprung mattress and flat-screen TV. Though they also contain tea- and coffee-making facilities, with fresh milk delivered to the room on request, drinks and snacks are available to residents at any time, day or night. The best-graded rooms are the largest, with a stylish roll-top bath that is big enough for two, a larger bed – maybe even a four-poster – and 20" flat-screen TV. The original, traditional style rooms are in the main inn, while the more contemporary ones are housed in newly converted stables and cottages. Meals may be enjoyed in the elegant dining room, cosy parlour, stylish conservatory and, in warmer weather, in the terraced gardens. The head chef and his skilled team produce imaginative and varied menus, using local suppliers wherever possible, but always the finest, freshest ingredients.

**Recommended in the area**

Suffolk Heritage Coast; Minsmere (RSPB); Southwold

Hampton Court.

# Macdonald Burford Bridge Hotel

★★★★ 81% ◉◉ HOTEL

| | |
|---|---|
| Address: | Burford Bridge, Box Hill, DORKING RH5 6BX |
| Tel: | 0870 400 8283 |
| Fax: | 01306 880386 |
| Email: | burfordbridge@macdonald-hotels.co.uk |
| Website: | www.macdonaldhotels.co.uk/burfordbridge |
| Map ref: | 3, TQ15 |
| Directions: | M25 junct 9 follow Dorking signs on A24 |

**Rooms:** 57, S £124–£139 D £138–£168 **Facilities:** ⳡ STV Wi-fi available **Parking:** 140
**Notes:** ⊘ in restaurant

Lord Nelson reputedly canoodled here with Lady Hamilton before heading off for his fatal engagement with Napoleon at Trafalgar. Whether the lovers knew, or cared, that the original inn was founded in 1254, history doesn't record. The inn obviously marketed itself well because John Keats, Jane Austen, William Wordsworth, Richard Brinsley Sheridan, Robert Louis Stevenson and Queen Victoria have all stayed here. Despite all the history, the hotel has an elegant, contemporary feel. It sits below the famous Box Hill, with the River Mole at the bottom of its extensive gardens. Guests in the beautifully appointed en suite bedrooms can enjoy satellite TV, iron and board, trouser press, tea and coffee making facilities, mini bar, complimentary mineral water and air-conditioning. The executive rooms have the extra luxury of an enclosed balcony with stunning views over the gardens as well as bathrobes and slippers plus a CD and DVD player. The restaurant is open for breakfast, lunch and dinner, with fixed price, seasonal menus offering English and international cuisine. Local wines feature among the extensive international selection. The nearest leisure centre is in Dorking and the hotel's outdoor heated pool is open in summer.

**Recommended in the area**

Polesdon Lacey (NT); RHS Garden Wisley; Denbies Wine Estate

# Lythe Hill Hotel & Spa

★★★★ 77% ◉◉ HOTEL

| | |
|---|---|
| **Address:** | Petworth Road, HASLEMERE GU27 3BQ |
| **Tel:** | 01428 651251 |
| **Fax:** | 01428 644131 |
| **Email:** | lythe@lythehill.co.uk |
| **Website:** | www.lythehill.co.uk |
| **Map ref:** | 3, SU93 |
| **Directions:** | Left from High St onto B2131 |

**Rooms:** 41, S £140–£275 D £140–£275 **Facilities:** ☏ Sauna Jacuzzi  Tennis Gym STV Wi-fi in bedrooms **Parking:** 200 **Notes:** ⊘ in restaurant

The hotel consists of several buildings, the earliest dating from the 15th century, set in 30 acres of attractive parkland. The bedrooms are all individually furnished in keeping with the building. Each bedroom is equipped with en suite bathrooms, television, and broadband wireless Internet access. Some have twin showers and jacuzzis. There are five luxury suites in the listed buildings, which retain their original oak beams and wood panelling. New for 2007 are 31 refurbished bedrooms as well as meeting rooms and public areas. The Auberge de France restaurant, in the 15th-century building, is an oak-panelled dining-room and includes a garden room that overlooks the lake and parkland. The cuisine is French-inspired, but uses the full range of local produce according to season. The wine list has over 200 wines. More informal dining is offered by the Italian Garden, the Pantry and the Dungeon. The Amarna Spa offers a a variety of treatment days and breaks and is available to guests together with a complete range of health and beauty treatments. The hotel can host business conferences, team-building events and private celebrations. It has a licence for civil wedding ceremonies, using the wedding rooms, the extensive gardens, and marquees as required.

### Recommended in the area

Haslemere; Petworth House (NT); Goodwood horse and motor racing; Lurgashall Winery.

# EAST SUSSEX

The Seven Sisters cliffs.

# Deans Place Hotel

★★★ 80% HOTEL

**Address:** Seaford Road, ALFRISTON,
Polegate BN26 5TW
**Tel:** 01323 870248
**Fax:** 01323 870918
**Email:** mail@deansplacehotel.co.uk
**Website:** www.deansplacehotel.co.uk
**Map ref:** 3, TQ50
**Directions:** Off A27, signed Alfriston & Drusillas Zoo
Park. Continue south through village
**Rooms:** 36, S £71–£88 D £88–£136 **Facilities:** ₹ STV **Parking:** 100 **Notes:** ⊘ in restaurant

Situated in the picturesque village of Alfriston, with its quaint buildings and narrow streets, privately owned 14th-century Deans Place Country Hotel is set in 4 acres of lovely gardens, with comfortable, well-appointed bedrooms, a public bar and lounges, an outdoor heated swimming pool, croquet lawn, mini-putting green and a large terrace for al fresco summer dining. Enjoy delicious food and attentive service in the locally renowned Harcourts Restaurant, or a drink, snack or cream tea in the Friston Bar.

**Recommended in the area**

Glyndebourne Opera; Drusillas Zoo; Beachy Head

# The Grand Hotel

★★★★★ 85% ⊛⊛ HOTEL

**Address:** King Edward's Parade,
EASTBOURNE BN21 4EQ
**Tel:** 01323 412345
**Fax:** 01323 412233
**Email:** reservations@grandeastbourne.com
**Website:** www.grandeastbourne.com
**Map ref:** 3, TV69
**Directions:** On seafront W of Eastbourne
**Rooms:** 152, S £150–£480 D £180–£510
**Facilities:** ⊗ ₹ Sauna Jacuzzi Solarium Gym STV **Parking:** 60 **Notes:** ⊘ in restaurant

Affectionately known as 'The White Palace', the 19th-century Grand stands at Eastbourne's classy Beachy Head end, across a green from the beach. There are 46 suites, including the Presidential, with a four-poster and luxurious lounge, and the Penthouse, which like many of the rooms has a panoramic view of the busy English Channel. The menus created for the Mirabelle and Garden Restaurants have won many awards. Seventeen conference and meeting rooms cater for all business needs.

**Recommended in the area**

Drusillas Zoo; Pevensey Castle; Battle Abbey

# Ashdown Park Hotel & Country Club

★★★★ ◉◉ HOTEL

| | |
|---|---|
| Address: | Wych Cross, FOREST ROW RH18 5JR |
| Tel: | 01342 824988 |
| Fax: | 01342 826206 |
| Email: | reservations@ashdownpark.com |
| Website: | www.ashdownpark.com |
| Map ref: | 3, TQ43 |

Directions: A264 to East Grinstead, then A22 to Eastbourne, 2m S of Forest Row at Wych Cross traffic lights. Left to Hartfield, hotel on right 0.75m
Rooms: 106, S £150–£370 D £180–£400 Facilities: ⊗ Sauna Steam Jacuzzi Solarium Tennis Golf Gym STV Wi-fi available Parking: 200 Notes: ⊗ in bedrooms ⊘ in restaurant

In the heart of Ashdown Forest, this magnificent hotel has evolved from an old country mansion. The bedrooms, all quite different in shape, style and decor, overlook the extensive grounds and each has modern facilities. The Anderida Restaurant sources ingredients locally or from London markets.

**Recommended in the area**

Hever Castle; Bluebell Railway; Wakehurst Place

# Newick Park Hotel & Country Estate

★★★ ◉◉ HOTEL

| | |
|---|---|
| Address: | NEWICK BN8 4SB |
| Tel: | 01825 723633 |
| Fax: | 01825 723969 |
| Email: | bookings@newickpark.co.uk |
| Website: | www.newickpark.co.uk |
| Map ref: | 3, TQ41 |

Directions: S off A272 in Newick between Haywards Heath and Uckfield. Pass church, left at junct and hotel 0.25m on right)
Rooms: 16, S £125 D £165–£285 Facilities: ⊾ Tennis STV Wi-fi available Notes: ⊘ in restaurant

It took five years to restore this beautiful Georgian country house, set in 250 acres of peaceful parkland. The house is full of antiques, many family heirlooms. Sleeping comfortably in your room is a requisite here, so expect a king-sized, four-poster or even an 8-foot bed. A typical dinner in the restaurant might be roast John Dory, or fillet of Angus beef. There is ample parking.

**Recommended in the area**

Glyndebourne Opera; Sheffield Park Gardens; Brighton's Lanes

# Best Western Flackley Ash Hotel

★★★ 78% HOTEL

| | |
|---|---|
| Address: | PEASMARSH TN31 6YH |
| Tel: | 01797 230651 |
| Fax: | 01797 230510 |
| Email: | enquiries@flackleyashhotel.co.uk |
| Website: | www.flackleyashhotel.co.uk |
| Map ref: | 4, TQ82 |
| Directions: | Between Newenden and Rye on A268 |

Rooms: 45, S £87–£127 D £144–£194 Facilities: ⊛ Sauna Jacuzzi  Gym STV Wi-fi in bedrooms
Parking: 80 Notes: ⊗ in restaurant

Five acres of beautifully kept grounds make a lovely backdrop to this elegant, privately-owned Georgian house hotel. The area is full of places to visit - mysterious Romney Marsh, and the ancient Cinque Ports of Rye and Winchelsea, for example. Feel very much at home in public areas such as the bar and lounge, or in one of the individually designed, en suite double rooms, twins or suites. Each has recently been given its own unique character with subtle, earthy colours, fabrics by top quality designers, such as Sanderson's, and quality beds, with soft, crisp white bedding. To this country house warmth add an LCD TV, DVD player, satellite channels and wireless broadband. In the Country Restaurant savour the delicious taste of expertly prepared traditional and international cuisine, such as homemade soups, roasts, perhaps rack of Romney lamb, and fresh local fish and seafood, including whole Rye Bay plaice. To unwind, visit the gym, sauna, steam room, spa bath or indoor swimming pool, or, to be pampered, head for the beauty suite. Entertain on special occasions or organise business events in one of two large function rooms, or five purpose-built syndicate rooms. Flackley Ash is also licensed for civil weddings.

Recommended in the area

Howletts Wild Animal Park; C M Booth Collection of Historic Vehicles, Rolvenden

West Dean College gardens.

# Bailiffscourt Hotel & Health Spa

★★★ 82% ◉◉ HOTEL

| | |
|---|---|
| Address: | Climbing Street, CLIMPING BN17 5RW |
| Tel: | 01903 723511 |
| Fax: | 01903 718987 |
| Email: | bailiffscourt@hshotels.co.uk |
| Website: | www.hshotels.co.uk |
| Map ref: | 3, SU90 |

Directions: A259, follow Climbing Beach signs. Hotel 0.5m on right

Rooms: 39, S £185–£455 D £205–£510 Facilities: ⊛ ⤢ Sauna Jacuzzi Tennis Gym STV Wi-fi in bedrooms Parking: 100 Notes: ⊗ in restaurant

This cluster of impressive 'medieval' buildings, in over 30 acres of grounds next to Climbing Beach, dates from 1927. A maze of narrow corridors connects the intimate lounges, with their open fires and antique furnishings. Rooms are well equipped and furnished either in period or modern style.

**Recommended in the area**

Arundel Castle; South Downs; Chichester Cathedral

# Gravetye Manor Hotel

★★★ ◉◉◉ HOTEL

| | |
|---|---|
| Address: | EAST GRINSTEAD RH19 4LJ |
| Tel: | 01342 810567 |
| Fax: | 01342 810080 |
| Email: | info@gravetyemanor.co.uk |
| Website: | www.gravetyemanor.co.uk |
| Map ref: | 3, TQ33 |

Directions: B2028 to Haywards Heath. 1m after Turners Hill fork left towards Sharpthorne, immediate 1st left into Vowels Lane

Rooms: 18, S £100–£170 D £155–£335 Facilities: Wi-fi in bedrooms Parking: 35 Notes: ⊗ in bedrooms ⊗ in restaurant

This Elizabethan mansion, built in 1598, still enjoys its tranquil setting in 35 acres of historic gardens, surrounded by a thousand acres of forest. Expect great country house hospitality in a timeless atmosphere – neither trendy, nor stuffy. Relax in oak-panelled day rooms with open fires and fresh flowers. Daily three-course menus make full use of fruit and vegetables from the kitchen garden.

**Recommended in the area**

Chartwell; Penshurst Place; Standen

# TYNE & WEAR

The Millennium and Tyne Bridges, Newcastle upon Tyne.

# Eslington Villa Hotel

★★★  77% ◉◉  HOTEL

| | |
|---|---|
| Address: | 8 Station Road, |
| | Low Fell, |
| | GATESHEAD NE9 6DR |
| Tel: | 0191 487 6017 |
| Fax: | 0191 420 0667 |
| Email: | home@eslingtonvilla.co.uk |
| Website: | www.eslingtonvilla.co.uk |
| Map ref: | 7, NZ26 |

Directions: Off A1 onto Team Valley Trading Est.
Right at 2nd rdbt along Eastern Av then left past Belle Vue Motors, hotel on left
Rooms: 17, S £69.50–£74.50 D £84.50–£89.50 Facilities: Wi-fi in bedrooms Parking: 28
Notes: ⊗ in bedrooms ⊜ in restaurant

In a quiet, leafy part of town and set within 2 acres of landscaped gardens with extensive views over the Team Valley, the Eslington Villa seems a long way from the hustle and bustle of downtown Newcastle or Gateshead. Yet it's not – both are just a short drive away. Neither is it far from the dramatic countryside and coastlines of Northumbria and County Durham. This smart hotel, ideal for both business and leisure guests, combines a bright contemporary atmosphere with the period style of a fine Victorian villa, which, of course, it once was (actually it was formerly two villas which were built around 1880 for prominent local businessmen). Nick and Melanie Tulip have run the hotel for the last 20 years and, with the help of their long-standing staff, they have brought it up to today's high standard. It retains many of its original features, yet has been tastefully extended without losing its charm. The overall ambience is relaxed and inviting. Chunky sofas fill the cocktail lounge. The award-

winning restaurant, ideal for both business lunches and intimate dinners, produces a delicious range of dishes which may be enjoyed in either the classical dining room or the modern conservatory, which overlooks landscaped gardens and beyond to the Team Valley. The individually decorated, en suite bedrooms range from the traditional – complete with four-poster bed – to the contemporary; all rooms are fully equipped with hairdryer, hospitality tray, trouser press, direct-dial telephone, satellite TV and free wireless Internet. Executive rooms benefit from panoramic views over the Team Valley. Weddings, special events, private dining and business events for up to 150 people are catered for.

**Recommended in the area**

Baltic Centre for Contemporary Art ;
Base Music centre; Millennium Bridge

# Vermont Hotel

★★★★ 79% ◉ HOTEL

| | |
|---|---|
| Address: | Castle Garth, |
| | NEWCASTLE UPON TYNE NE1 1RQ |
| Tel: | 0191 233 1010 |
| Fax: | 0191 233 1234 |
| Email: | info@vermont-hotel.co.uk |
| Website: | www.vermont-hotel.com |
| Map ref: | 7, NZ26 |

**Directions:** In centre by high level bridge and Castle
**Rooms:** 101 S £120–£185 D £120–£185 **Facilities:**
Solarium Gym STV Wi-fi in bedrooms **Parking:** 100

Adjacent to the castle and close to the buzzing Quayside area, this imposing, 12-storey, independently owned hotel enjoys fine views of the Tyne and Millennium Bridges. With an exterior style described as '1930s Manhattan tower', its plush interior is both traditional and contemporary. All bedrooms, including the grand suites, are equipped with three telephones, computer modem fax port, work desk, fully stocked mini-bar, satellite TV, and complimentary tea and coffee facilities. The elegant reception lounge encourages relaxation, while the Bridge Restaurant is open for breakfast, lunch and dinner. Through its windows, the Tyne Bridge looks close enough to reach out and pluck the suspension cables. The Blue Room provides the perfect setting for private dining in luxurious surroundings for up to 80 guests. The informal Redwood Bar is an intimate meeting place - which could explain its popularity - serving a large selection of wines and light meals until the early hours. Martha's Bar and Courtyard is popular too, particularly with the 20-somethings. Seven meeting and conference rooms cater as effortlessly for 300 people at a cocktail function as they do for a one-to-one meeting. The Health & Fitness Centre offers a selection of complimentary exercise equipment.

**Recommended in the area**

Newcastle Cathedral; Baltic Centre for Contemporary Art; Sage Centre, Gateshead

Warwick Castle.

# Best Western Peacock Hotel

★★★ 80% HOTEL

**Address:** 57 Warwick Road, KENILWORTH CV8 1HN
**Tel:** 01926 851156
**Fax:** 01926 864644
**Email:** reservations@peacockhotel.com
**Website:** www.peacockhotel.com
**Map ref:** 3, SP27
**Directions:** A46/A452 signed Kenilworth. Hotel 0.25m
on right after St John's Church
**Rooms:** 29, S £52–£80 D £65–£100 **Facilities:** STV
Wi-fi in bedrooms **Parking:** 30 **Notes:** ✪ in bedrooms

Established in 1998, this luxuriously appointed hotel in the heart of Warwickshire offers award-winning accommodation, facilities and cuisine, backed by outstanding service. All the en suite bedrooms have wireless internet, satellite TV, modem connection, direct-dial phone, CD player, radio-clock, beverage maker and air conditioning. Club bedrooms are decorated in 1920s colonial style with chandeliers, wooden floors, sepia prints, Persian rugs and Javanese furniture. The attached en suites are tiled with roman mosaic and have an oval bath, large separate shower cubicle, anti-mist mirrors, bathroom speaker and telephone. Laundry and dry-cleaning facilities are available, as is a comprehensive room service menu. Breakfast, a wide selection of English and Continental choices, may be taken in The Malabar Room where, in the evening, European-style dinner is served. Those preferring the tastes of the East have to make a tough decision – to opt for cuisines of Kerala, Karnataka, Andhra Pradesh or Goa in the vibrant and colourful, highly regarded Coconut Lagoon; or to walk the short distance to Raffles, a Malay restaurant, where meals are served in an appropriately designed colonial ballroom setting. The Peacock is able to host a wide range of corporate events, private entertaining, weddings and other functions.

**Recommended in the area**

Warwick Castle; Stratford-upon-Avon; NEC Birmingham

# Best Western Lea Marston Hotel & Leisure Complex

★★★★ 75% HOTEL

| | |
|---|---|
| Address: | Haunch Lane, LEA MARSTON, Sutton Coldfield B76 0BY |
| Tel: | 01675 470468 |
| Email: | info@leamarstonhotel.co.uk |
| Website: | www.leamarstonhotel.co.uk |
| Map ref: | 3, SP29 |
| Directions: | M42 junct 9, A4097 to Kingsbury. Hotel signed 1.5m on right |

Rooms: 80, S £75–£125 D £95–£145 Facilities: ⓧ Sauna Jacuzzi Solarium Tennis Gym STV Wi-fi available Notes: ⊗ in bedrooms ⊘ in restaurant

The Lea Marston is a modern hotel within easy reach of motorway, rail and air links. Lounges are spacious, airy and comfortable, while all bedrooms and the larger suites come with all the expected facilites. Enjoy fine dining in the Adderley Restaurant, or the bistro-style menu in Hathaways gastropub.

**Recommended in the area**

Twycross Zoo; Lichfield Cathedral; Staffordshire Regimental Museum

# Billesley Manor Hotel

★★★★ 77% ⦾⦾ HOTEL

| | |
|---|---|
| Address: | Billesley, Alcester, STRATFORD-UPON-AVON B49 6NF |
| Tel: | 01789 279955 |
| Fax: | 01789 764145 |
| Email: | enquiries@billesleymanor.co.uk |
| Website: | www.billesleymanor.co.uk |
| Map ref: | 3, SP15 |
| Directions: | A46 towards Evesham. Over 3 rdbts, right for Billesley after 2m |

Rooms: 72 Facilities: ⓧ Sauna Solarium Tennis Gym STV Wi-fi available Parking: 100 Notes: ⊘ in restaurant

This 16th-century manor has oak panelling, big fireplaces, exposed stone and other original features in the public areas. The spacious, country house-style bedrooms and suites are well equipped, and three have four-posters. Most of the standard doubles are in the main building, overlooking courtyards or a quiet lane. The award-winning Stuart Restaurant, Spa bistro and bar mean there's no need to eat out.

**Recommended in the area**

Cadbury World; Warwick Castle; Heritage Motor Centre

# Stratford Manor

★★★★  80% ◉  HOTEL

| | |
|---|---|
| Address: | Warwick Road, |
| | STRATFORD-UPON-AVON CV37 0PY |
| Tel: | 01789 731173 |
| Fax: | 01789 731131 |
| Email: | stratfordmanor@qhotels.co.uk |
| Website: | www.qhotels.co.uk |
| Map ref: | 3, SP25 |

Directions: M40 junct 15, take A439 towards
Straford-upon-Avon, hotel 2m on left
Rooms: 104, S £32.50 D £171 Facilities: ⓧ Sauna
Solarium Tennis Gym STV Parking: 250
Notes: ⊗ in bedrooms ⊘ in restaurant

Superbly situated within 21 acres of peaceful Warwickshire countryside in the heart of England and just 3 miles from Stratford-upon-Avon, Stratford Manor is a perfect base for exploring the delights of Shakespeare country. Warwick, a small historic town with a formidable14th-century castle and a good selection of small individual shops, is also nearby. The spacious, smartly-appointed and well-equipped bedrooms have generously sized beds, and a range of useful facilities including a full compliment of quality toiletries, tea- and-coffee making equipment, trouser press, hairdryer, direct-dial phone and satellite television. Several rooms interconnect, making them ideal for families. The new bright and contemporary award-winning restaurant offers good food with great wines and attentive service whilse the bar/lounge provides quiet corners on one level and plenty of space on others for teas, coffees or lunch in a more informal style. Natural light through the conservatory creates a peaceful air that permeates the hotel. For relaxation, the Reflections Leisure Club invites guests to indulge in a sauna, swim in the indoor pool, enjoy the plunge pool, a work out in the gym or use of the all-weather tennis courts.

### Recommended in the area

Hatton Country Park; Warwick Castle; Royal Shakespeare Theatre

# Stratford Victoria

★★★★ 76% ◉ HOTEL

| | |
|---|---|
| **Address:** | Arden Street, |
| | STRATFORD-UPON-AVON CV37 6QQ |
| **Tel:** | 01789 271000 |
| **Fax:** | 01789 271001 |
| **Email:** | stratfordvictoria@qhotels.co.uk |
| **Website:** | www.qhotels.co.uk |
| **Map ref:** | 3, SP15 |

**Directions:** A439 into Stratford. In town follow A3400/Birmingham, at lights left into Arden Street, hotel 150yds on right

**Rooms:** 102, S £103 D £171 **Facilities:** Gym STV Wi-fi available **Parking:** 100 **Notes:** ⊘ in restaurant

Set in mature gardens and just minutes from the historic town of Stratford-upon-Avon the Stratford Victoria is within easy walking distance of many local attractions. The bedrooms are tastefully decorated and many enjoy the peaceful view of the hotel's gardens and include Executive, intern-connecting rooms for families, four-poster beds as well as a luxury suite. All are well-equipped with toiletries, tea and coffee making facilities, trouser press, hairdryer, direct dial phone and satellite television. The restaurant offers the very best of British cuisine with a continental twist and seasonal menus using only the finest of local produce, which has ensured it an AA Rosette for culinary excellence. Known for its fine service and welcoming atmosphere, you can enjoy the comfort of leather chesterfield sofas in the lounge area which offers an attractive informal alternative for a light lunch or dinner or an ideal place to meet friends for a traditional cream tea, frothy cappucino or a chilled glass of wine. As well as a whirlpool spa and mini fitness gym on site, guests have free access to the leisure facilities at the Victoria's sister hotel, the Stratford Manor – just five minutes' drive away.

**Recommended in the area**

William Shakespeare's birthplace; Anne Hathaway's Cottage; river trips on the Avon.

Warwick Castle.

# Ardencote Manor Hotel, Country Club & Spa

★★★★ 79% ◉◉ HOTEL

**Address:** Claverdon, nr. WARWICK CV35 8LT
**Tel:** 01926 843111
**Fax:** 01926 842646
**Email:** hotel@ardencote.com
**Website:** www.ardencote.com
**Map ref:** 3, SP16
**Directions:** In Claverdon centre follow Shrewley signs off A4189. Hotel 0.5m on right
**Rooms:** 76, S £90–£110 D £130–£165 **Facilities:** ⊗
Sauna Jacuzzi Solarium Tennis Gym STV Wi-fi **Parking:** 150 **Notes:** ⊗ in bedrooms ⊘ on premises

This beautiful hotel and spa is set in 42 acres of landscaped grounds. Public rooms include lounge areas, a cocktail bar and conservatory breakfast room. Main meals, selected from a menu of modern English dishes with international influences, are served in the award-winning Lodge Restaurant.
**Recommended in the area**
Warwick Castle; Stratford-upon-Avon; Cadbury World

The City of Birmingham Council House.

# Best Western The Fairlawns at Aldridge

★★★  85% ◉◉  HOTEL

**Address:**  178 Little Aston Road, Aldridge,
WALSALL WS9 0NU
**Tel:**  01922 455122
**Fax:**  01922 743148
**Email:**  reception@fairlawns.co.uk
**Website:**  www.fairlawns.co.uk
**Map ref:**  3, SK00
**Directions:**  Off A452 towards Aldridge at x-roads with A454. Hotel 600yds on right
**Rooms:** 59, S £65–£165 D £89.5–£225 **Facilities:** ⊗ Sauna Solarium Tennis Gym STV
Wi-fi in bedrooms **Parking:** 150 **Notes:** ⊗ in restaurant

The hotel stands in 9 acres of landscaped grounds in a rural location, yet is only 8 miles from central Birmingham. Some of the rooms are furnished and decorated in a traditional manner, others are in a more modern style. All have en suite bathroom, direct-dial telephone, high-speed Internet access, multi-channel television, hairdryer, facilities for making tea and coffee, and ironing-boards; many have comfort cooling. Room grades range from Budget Single to Four-Poster Room. There are also family rooms and suites with lounge/study areas. The Fairlawns Restaurant has a wide range of menus, and imaginative seafood dishes are a feature of the restaurant. The Say it with Seafood speciality menu can be reserved 24 hours in advance for lunch or dinner from Tuesday to Friday. There are five private dining-rooms. Guests can enjoy the benefits of the newly redeveloped adult fitness club. Residential offers at the Fairlawns include Romantic Evenings, Honeymooners overnight stays, and relaxation breaks. A golf package includes access to the exclusive Little Aston Golf Club, 2 miles away. Conferences and meetings of up to 100 representatives can be accommodated.

**Recommended in the area**

Walsall Art Gallery; Lichfield Cathedral; Cannock Chase Area of Outstanding Natural Beauty

The Orangery at Bowood House.

# Lucknam Park

★★★★★ ◉◉◉ COUNTRY HOUSE HOTEL

| | |
|---|---|
| Address: | COLERNE, Chippenham SN14 8AZ |
| Tel: | 01225 742777 |
| Fax: | 01225 743536 |
| Email: | reservations@lucknampark.co.uk |
| Website: | www.lucknampark.co.uk |
| Map ref: | 2, ST87 |

Directions: M4 junct 17, A350 to Chippenham, then A420 to Bristol for 3m. At Ford village, left to Colerne
Rooms: 41, S £245–£840 D £245–£840 Facilities: ⊗
Sauna Jacuzzi Tennis Gym STV Wi-fi in bedrooms Parking: 70 Notes: ⊗ in bedrooms ⊘ in restaurant

During World War II Spitfires and Hurricanes were hidden from enemy aircraft beneath the foliage of the one-mile, tree-lined approach to this handsome mansion. With no fear of aerial attack today, visitors experience only mounting anticipation – just how special is Lucknam Park? It was built in 1720 by a wealthy Bristol merchant following a lucrative tobacco deal. The war years apart, it was used continuously as a family home until 1987, when it opened as a country house hotel. Set in 500 acres of parkland, its 41 bedrooms include 13 suites, many with four-posters, and five with separate sitting rooms. The Park Restaurant (Head Chef Hywel Jones) has won many awards including a Michelin star. For more leisurely dining, try the Pavilion Restaurant. Only the best local ingredients, organic where possible, are used to produce seasonal dishes, old favourites and new ideas for guests who want the finest fine-dining. Dinner for one costs what elsewhere might treat the whole family, but such mouth-watering menu descriptions as 'pan-fried gilt-head sea bream, tomato and Alsace bacon risotto, provençal vegetables, calamari and tapenade', show that this is no ordinary restaurant. In the walled garden, the Roman villa-styled Spa offers a world of health, beauty and relaxation. Lucknam also has an equestrian centre. Private rooms are available for meetings, private dining and receptions.

**Recommended in the area**

Thermae Bath Spa; Jane Austen Centre; Lacock Village (NT)

# Cricklade Hotel

★★★ 77% HOTEL

**Address:** Common Hill, CRICKLADE SN6 6HA
**Tel:** 01793 750751
**Fax:** 01793 751767
**Email:** reception@crickladehotel.co.uk
**Website:** www.crickladehotel.co.uk
**Map ref:** 3, SU09
**Directions:** Off A419 onto B4040. Turn left at clock tower. Right at rdbt. Hotel 0.5m up hill on left)
**Rooms:** 46, S £115–£120 D £155–£158 **Facilities:** ⊗
Jacuzzi Solarium Tennis Gym STV Wi-fi available **Parking:** 100 **Notes:** ⊗ in bedrooms ⊗ in bedrooms

A warm welcome awaits guests in this country house hotel on the edge of the Cotswolds with glorious views across the Vale of Cricklade. Built at the turn of the last century, it has been tastefully restored and extended, perhaps most impressively in the magnificent Victorian-style conservatory. All bedrooms and suites are furnished with typical comforts such as hairdryer and courtesy tray. Dine on skilfully presented fresh, local produce in candlelit Doves Restaurant, the conservatory, or the cosy Snug.
**Recommended in the area**
Bowood House and Gardens; Swindon Steam railway Museum; Lacock Abbey

# Old Bell Hotel

★★★ 81% ⊛⊛ HOTEL

**Address:** Abbey Row, MALMESBURY SN16 0BW
**Tel:** 01666 822344
**Fax:** 01666 825145
**Email:** info@oldbellhotel.com
**Website:** www.oldbellhotel.com
**Map ref:** 2, ST98
**Directions:** M4 junct 17, follow A429 north. Left at first rdbt. Left at T-junct. Hotel next to Abbey
**Rooms:** 31, S £95 D £125 **Facilities:** STV Wi-fi available
**Parking:** 31 **Notes:** ⊗ in restaurant

Dating from around 1220, the Old Bell stands alongside Malmesbury Abbey, once an important seat of learning. Medieval features include the Great Hall's stone fireplace, discovered in 1986. Public rooms include the library, two lounges and the bar. Bedrooms are split between the main building, where some are furnished with antiques, and the Coach House, where a simpler style prevails. The elegant restaurant serves award-winning cuisine prepared from mainly local produce.
**Recommended in the area**
Westonbirt Arboretum; Castle Combe; World Heritage City of Bath

Worcester Cathedral.

# Brockencote Hall Country House Hotel

★★★ ◉◉ HOTEL

**Address:** CHADDESLEY CORBETT DY10 4PY
**Tel:** 01562 777876
**Fax:** 01562 777872
**Email:** info@brockencotehall.com
**Website:** www.brockencotehall.com
**Map ref:** 2, SO87
**Directions:** 0.5m W, off A448, opp St Cassians Church
**Rooms:** 17, S £96–£150 D £120–£190 **Facilities:** Tennis  Wi-fi in bedrooms **Parking:** 45
**Notes:** ⊗ in bedrooms ⊘ in restaurant and lounges

This fine mansion stands in 70 acres of landscaped grounds containing a lake and splendid trees, beyond which the Worcestershire countryside extends to the Malvern Hills. Sheep graze within sight of the residents taking tea in the conservatory. The high-ceilinged rooms are furnished in elegant fabrics and furnishings with many period features. Some bedrooms have a four-poster bed and a whirlpool bath. All rooms have en suite facilities, a restful view, satellite television, a telephone and wireless Internet access. There are two conference rooms, able to accommodate 20 and 30 delegates respectively. The public rooms are light and airy, and warmed by log fires in the winter. In the elegant chandelier-lit restaurant the outstanding cuisine bears the stamp of the owner's and the head chef's French origins. The cooking also offers a choice of lighter dishes and occasional local specialities, and is supported by an extensive wine cellar. The hotel is licensed for civil wedding ceremonies and is well equipped to host wedding receptions, with the beautiful surroundings ideal for photography. Brockencote Hall is only 30 minutes from Birmingham, with its international airport and the National Exhibition Centre.

**Recommended in the area**

Ironbridge Gorge; Severn Valley Steam Railway; West Midlands Safari Park

# The Granary Hotel & Restaurant

★ ★ ★  75% ⊛  HOTEL

| | |
|---|---|
| Address: | Heath Lane, Shenstone, |
| | KIDDERMINSTER DY10 4BS |
| Tel: | 01562 777535 |
| Fax: | 01562 777722 |
| Email: | info@granary-hotel.co.uk |
| Website: | www.granary-hotel.co.uk |
| Map ref: | 2, SO87 |

Directions: On A450, 0.5m from junct with A448

Rooms: 18, S £75–£90 D £90–£140 Parking: 96 Notes: ⊗ in restaurant

This modern, independent hotel offers comfortable accommodation in pretty countryside not far from Kidderminster. All bedrooms have a bathroom with shower and the expected facilites. The redesigned restaurant serves contemporary English food, a carvery operates on Sundays and snacks are served in the bar lounge. Patios and secluded gardens make a perfect backdrop for wedding photographs.

**Recommended in the area**

Malvern Hills; Severn Valley Railway; West Midland Safari Park

# Colwall Park

★ ★ ★  80% ⊛⊛  HOTEL

| | |
|---|---|
| Address: | Walwyn Road, Colwall, |
| | MALVERN WR13 6QG |
| Tel: | 01684 540000 |
| Fax: | 01684 540847 |
| Email: | hotel@colwall.com |
| Website: | www.colwall.com |
| Map ref: | 2, SO74 |

Directions: Between Malvern & Ledbury in centre of Colwall on B4218

Rooms: 22, S £79–£89 D £120–£140 Facilities: STV Wi-fi in bedrooms Parking: 40

Notes: ⊗ in restaurant

This hotel boasts 2 acres of gardens in the heart of the village of Colwall, at the foot of the Malvern Hills. The individually decorated bedrooms are decorated in country-house style and have en suite facilities. They range from small single rooms with showers to de luxe doubles and family suites with full bathrooms. The Seasons Restaurant offers gourmet dining in oak-panelled surroundings.

**Recommended in the area**

Ledbury; Eastnor Castle; Hereford; Royal Worcester porcelain factory; Gloucester

Bromsgrove.

# Best Western Abbey Hotel Golf & Country Club

★★★★ 80% HOTEL

| | |
|---|---|
| **Address:** | Hither Green Lane, Dagnell End Road, Bordesley, REDDITCH B98 9BE |
| **Tel:** | 01527 406600 |
| **Email:** | info@theabbeyhotel.co.uk |
| **Website:** | www.theabbeyhotel.co.uk |
| **Map ref:** | 2, SP06 |

**Directions:** M42 junct 2, A441 to Redditch. Left at rbt (A441), Dagnell End Rd on left. Hotel 600yds on right

**Rooms:** 100, S £75–£165 D £95–£185 **Facilities:** ⊗ Sauna Jacuzzi Solarium Gym STV Wi-fi in bedrooms **Parking:** 200 **Notes:** ⊗ in bedrooms ⊗ in restaurant

A £2 million investment programme has resulted in the creation of stylish and well-appointed bedrooms and two penthouses. Bramblings Restaurant offers a choice of freshly prepared dishes; Tawny's is more bistro style. Along with the golf course there's a beauty salon and health club.

**Recommended in the area**

Coughton Court (NT); Severn Valley Railway; Anne Hathaway's Cottage

# NORTH YORKSHIRE

Staithes harbour, North Yorkshire Moors National Park.

# Aldwark Manor

★★★★  85% ⊛⊛  HOTEL

Address:     ALDWARK, York YO61 1UF
Tel:         01347 838146
Fax:         01347 838867
Email:       aldwarkmanor@qhotels.co.uk
Website:     www.qhotels.co.uk
Map ref:     8, SE46
Directions:  A1/A59 towards Green Hammerton, then
B6265 Little Ouseburn. Follow signs for Aldwark
Bridge/Manor. A19 through Linton-on-Ouse

Rooms: 55, S £132.50 D £171 Facilities: ⊗ Sauna Jacuzzi Solarium Gym STV Parking: 150
Notes: ⊗ in bedrooms ⊘ in restaurant

Set amidst 100 acres of beautiful Yorkshire countryside, this lovely historical house has been sympathetically extended and offers 55 en suite rooms in classical or contemporary style as well as four-poster and executive suites. The majority of bedrooms have superb views over the golf course and surrounding countryside. For relaxation and pampering, guests can enjoy the facilities of the Reflections Spa and Leisure Club which includes indoor swimming pool, gymnasium, steam room and sanarium, spa pool, state of the art gymnasium and power sports fitness suite as well as fun showers with tropical mist drench. There is an impressive choice of body/beauty treatments, including alternative therapies, available from qualified staff. For the golf lover, Aldwark Manor is utopia, with every hole bordered by ancient oak and beech trees and the River Ure coming into play on a number of holes providing the player with an exciting challenge. Guests are offered the finest cuisine from a varied and exciting menu in the two Rosette restaurant. For a more informal meal, there is The Terrace offering a good selection of snacks and light meals. For a peaceful break, with all modern facilities, close to York and Harrogate, this is the place to stay.

**Recommended in the area**

Castle Howard; James Herriot Museum, Harewood House

# Grants Hotel

★★★ 78% HOTEL

| | |
|---|---|
| Address: | 3–13 Swan Road, HARROGATE HG1 2SS |
| Tel: | 01423 560666 |
| Fax: | 01423 502550 |
| Email: | enquiries@grantshotel-harrogate.com |
| Website: | www.grantshotel-harrogate.com |
| Map ref: | 7, SE25 |
| Directions: | Off A61 |

**Rooms:** 42 **Facilities:** STV **Parking:** 26
**Notes:** ⊘ in restaurant

All bedrooms in this family-run hotel in the centre of Harrogate offer TV, radio, direct-dial telephone, facilities for making hot drinks and modem point. Some of the rooms have four-poster beds. Meals are served in the informal surroundings of the Chimney Pots bistro, where the cuisine is traditional English together with some Oriental dishes; puddings are home-made. Light meals are available in the cocktail bar and lounge.

**Recommended in the area**

Royal Pump Room Museum; Harlow Carr Gardens; Yorkshire Dales; Fountains Abbey; City of York

# Rudding Park Hotel & Golf

★★★★ ◉◉ HOTEL

| | |
|---|---|
| Address: | Rudding Park, Follifoot, |
| | HARROGATE HG3 1JH |
| Tel: | 01423 871350 |
| Fax: | 01423 872286 |
| Email: | reservations@ruddingpark.com |
| Website: | www.ruddingpark.com |
| Map ref: | 7, SE35 |
| Directions: | From A61 at rdbt with A658 take York exit |

and follow signs to Rudding Park

**Rooms:** 49, S £150–£350 D £180–£350 **Facilities:** STV Wi-fi in bedrooms **Parking:** 150
**Notes:** ⊘ in restaurant

Since opening as a hotel in 1997, Rudding Park has rapidly won widespread acclaim. Often called Yorkshire's Premier Hotel and Golf Resort', it certainly looks the part. Guests can unwind with a drink, a newspaper, or even a board game in the luxurious Mackaness Room. Cuisine ranges from gourmet to alfresco barbecue, depending on location – the Clocktower restaurant, bar, conservatory or the terrace.

**Recommended in the area**

Harewood House; Castle Howard; Jorvik Viking Centre

# Pheasant Hotel

★★★  78% SMALL HOTEL

Address:     Harome,
             HELMSLEY YO62 5JG
Tel:         01439 771241
Fax:         01439 771744
Map ref:     8, SE68
Directions:  2.5m SE, leave A170 after 0.25m. Right
signed Harome for further 2m)
Rooms: 14, S £75.5–£82 D £151–£165
Facilities: ⓢ STV Parking: 20 Notes: ⊘ in restaurant

The horse's loss is the modern traveller's gain at this country hotel, converted from two old blacksmith's cottages. Inside is a small oak-beamed bar with a log fire, and a large drawing room and conservatory dining room, both of which open on to the stone-flagged terrace and mill stream. Spacious, comfortable bedrooms, all with private bath, face either the village pond, or overlook the courtyard and pretty walled garden. In her kitchen, Tricia Binks produces the best of English dishes, wherever possible using local produce, such as Whitby fish, Yorkshire lamb and Helmsley beef.

**Recommended in the area**

North Yorks Moors National Park; Rievaulx Abbey; North Yorkshire Moors Railway

# Hob Green Hotel

★★★  80% HOTEL

Address:     MARKINGTON HG3 3PJ
Tel:         01423 770031
Fax:         01423 771589
Email:       info@hobgreen.com
Website:     www.hobgreen.com
Map ref:     7, SE26
Directions:  From A61, 4m N of Harrogate, left at
Wormald Green, follow hotel signs
Rooms: 12, S £90–£95 D £115–£125 Facilities: Wi-fi
in bedrooms Parking: 40 Notes: ⊘ on premises

A small country-house hotel in rolling countryside halfway between Harrogate and Ripon, Hob Green stands in beautiful award-winning gardens. The rooms are individually furnished in traditional English style, and are fully equipped with television, facilities for making hot drinks, mini-bar, hairdryer, trouser press and ironing board. The restaurant makes much use of seasonal local produce, including fruit and vegetable from the hotel's own gardens. The Yorkshire Dales and the North York Moors are nearby.

**Recommended in the area**

Ripon racecourse; Harrogate; Fountains Abbey; Studley Royal Water Garden

# Hazlewood Castle

★★★ 83% ◉◉ HOTEL

| | |
|---|---|
| Address: | Paradise Lane, Hazlewood, |
| | TADCASTER, York LS24 9NJ |
| Tel: | 01937 535353 |
| Fax: | 01937 530630 |
| Email: | info@hazlewood-castle.co.uk |
| Website: | www.hazlewood-castle.co.uk |
| Map ref: | 7, SE43 |

Directions: Signed off A64, W of Tadcaster & before A1/M1 link road
Rooms: 21, S £140–£280 D £155–£295 Facilities: STV Wi-fi in bedrooms Parking: 150
Notes: ⊗ in bedrooms ⊘ in restaurant

Set in 77 acres of tranquil parkland, this former monastery and retreat offers tastefully and individually designed bedrooms split between the main house and other buildings in the picturesque courtyard. The award-winning Restaurant Anise serves Mediterranean cuisine in intimate surrounds. The Castle is the perfect backdrop for both business events and family celebrations.
**Recommended in the area**
York Racecourse; Hazlewood House; The Royal Armouries Museum (Leeds)

# Judges Country House Hotel

★★★ ◉◉ HOTEL

| | |
|---|---|
| Address: | Kirklevington Hall, YARM, |
| | Tees Valley TS15 9LW |
| Tel: | 01642 789000 |
| Fax: | 01642 782878 |
| Email: | enquiries@judgeshotel.co.uk |
| Website: | www.judgeshotel.co.uk |
| Map ref: | 8, NZ41 |

Directions: 1.5m from A19. At A67 junct, follow Yarm road, hotel on left
Rooms: 21, S £142–£155 D £175–£185 Facilities: Gym STV Free Wi-fi in bedrooms
Parking: 102 Notes: ⊗ in bedrooms ⊘ in restaurant

Formerly a lodging for local circuit judges, this country house hotel is tucked away in 22 acres of landscaped grounds. Within, all is Victorian charm. The individually furnished bedrooms, fresh from extensive restoration, include three with four-posters and two suites. The Conservatory Restaurant serves award-winning cuisine, and the genuinely caring and attentive service is equally memorable.
**Recommended in the area**
North Yorks Moors National Park; Rosedale Abbey; Whitby

# Best Western Dean Court Hotel

★★★ 85% ◉◉ HOTEL

**Address:** Duncombe Place, YORK YO1 7EF
**Tel:** 01904 625082
**Fax:** 01904 620305
**Email:** info@deancourt-york.co.uk
**Website:** www.deancourt-york.co.uk
**Map ref:** 8, SE65
**Directions:** City centre opposite York Minster
**Rooms:** 37, S £80–£120 D £125–£205 **Facilities:** Wi-fi in available throughout **Parking:** 30
**Notes:** ⊗ in bedrooms ⊛ in hotel

This hotel, located in the very centre of York next to the Minster, has been recently refurbished. The rooms are individually furnished, some in traditional and some in modern styles. The room grades range from Single up to Deluxe Double and Four-Poster Deluxe, as well as suites. All rooms have en suite bathrooms, 20-channel television, clock radio/alarm, CD/DVD player, a writing-desk, direct-dial telephone, trouser press, hair dryer and facilities for making tea and coffee. The DCH Restaurant, looking out onto the Minster, offers fine dining, based on fresh local produce. The Court café-bistro and bar offers a more informal all day menu, including sandwiches and snacks, and a clotted-cream and champagne tea. The hotel offers a variety of imaginative add-ons to its normal service, such as "PS – I Love You!" (romantic additions to a night's stay) and "It's Show Time!" (meal, cocktail, etc, added when you book a visit to the nearby Theatre Royal). Other special offers include a two-night short break, a three-day Christmas in York package, and a New Year's Eve dinner-dance. From late November until early January there are disco-dinners and murder-mystery dinners. There are two conference rooms, the larger able to accommodate up to 50 people in a theatre-style format, or 28 in boardroom format.

**Recommended in the area**

National Railway Museum; the Yorkshire Wheel; Jorvik Viking Centre; Castle Museum.

The River Ouse, York.

# The Grange Hotel

★★★ ◉◉ HOTEL

| | |
|---|---|
| **Address:** | 1 Clifton, YORK YO30 6AA |
| **Tel:** | 01904 644744 |
| **Fax:** | 01904 612453 |
| **Email:** | info@grangehotel.co.uk |
| **Website:** | www.grangehotel.co.uk |
| **Map ref:** | 8, SE55 |

**Directions:** On A19 approx 500yds from city centre
**Rooms:** 30, S £115–£185 D £139–£265 **Facilities:** STV Wi-fi in bedrooms **Parking:** 26 **Notes:** ⊘ in restaurant

This superbly restored Regency townhouse is in the city but feels just like a warm country house. Top priority is given to attention to detail and efficient room service in the luxuriously appointed en suite bedrooms, including two with four-posters. The newly refurbished award-winning Ivy Brasserie complements the hotel's stylish character, with modern British and European cuisine making good use of local produce, while the charming Cellar Bar also serves lunches and snacks. First class facilities for business meetings, private dining, weddings and receptions are available.

**Recommended in the area**

York Minster; National Railway Museum; Castle Howard

# SOUTH YORKSHIRE

Langsett, Peak District National Park.

Damflask Reservoir, near Sheffield.

# Best Western Mosborough Hall Hotel

★★★ 77% HOTEL

| | |
|---|---|
| Address: | High Street, Mosborough, SHEFFIELD S20 5EA |
| Tel: | 0114 248 4353 |
| Fax: | 0114 247 9759 |
| Email: | hotel@mosboroughhall.co.uk |
| Website: | www.mosboroughhall.co.uk |
| Map ref: | 8, SK49 |

Directions: M1 junct 30, A6135 towards Sheffield. Follow Eckington/Mosborough signs 2m. Sharp bend at top of hill, hotel on right

Rooms: 47, S £75–£120 D £75–£120 Facilities: Wi-fi in bedrooms Notes: ⊗ in restaurant

This imposing 16th-century manor house set in four acres of grounds has some feature bedrooms and others have been recently renovated in contemporary fashion. All have tea and coffee facilities, TV, hairdryer, phone and Internet. The John D'Arcy restaurant offers well-presented classic dishes.

**Recommended in the area**

Peak District National Park; Sheffield Arena; Meadowhall Shopping Centre; Magna

# Tankersley Manor

★★★★ 75%  HOTEL

| | |
|---|---|
| Address: | Church Lane, TANKERSLEY |
| | S75 3DQ |
| Tel: | 01226 744700 |
| Fax: | 01226 745405 |
| Email: | tankersleymanor@qhotels.co.uk |
| Website: | www.qhotels.co.uk |
| Map ref: | 8, SK39 |

Directions: M1 junct 36 take A61 (Sheffield road). Hotel 0.5m on left

Rooms: 99, S £132 D £171 Facilities: ⓢ Sauna Gym STV Wi-fi available
Parking: 200 Notes: ⊗ in bedrooms ⊘ in restaurant

Sensitively incorporating a 17th-century building with a modern hotel, retaining many original features, this stunning manor house hotel combines four star luxury with the attributes of a real country pub. Open fires and exposed beams create a relaxing ambience and a warm welcome in one of South Yorkshire's leading hotels. Guests can choose from the beautifully appointed bedrooms including suites, executive rooms and a four-poster suite which caters for every comfort. The extensively refurbished "Onward Arms", a traditional pub at the heart of the hotel, offers a delicious and varied range of meals. The charming, more formal Manor Restaurant is also available serving excellent cuisine from around the world as well as offering many fine wines. For relaxation, guests can enjoy the superb facilities of the Reflections Spa and Leisure Club with heated indoor pool, spa, steam room, sauna and well-equipped gymnasium as well as a range of luxurious Spa body/beauty treatments by trained therapists. Backing onto woodland and the accessible Trans Pennine Trail, the hotel is ideally situated to explore the delights of South Yorkshire and the surrounding, picturesque moorland scenery.

### Recommended in the area

The Royal Armouries; York Dungeons; Meadowhall Shopping Centre

Ilkley'a packhorse bridge.

# Best Western Rombalds Hotel & Restaurant

★★★ 82% ◉◉ HOTEL

| | |
|---|---|
| Address: | 11 West View, Wells Road, |
| | ILKLEY LS29 9JG |
| Tel: | 01943 603201 |
| Fax: | 01943 816586 |
| Email: | reception@rombalds.demon.co.uk |
| Website: | www.rombalds.co.uk |
| Map ref: | 7, SE14 |

Directions: A65 from Leeds. Left at 3rd main lights, follow Ilkley Moor signs. Right at HSBC Bank onto Wells Rd. Hotel 600yds on left

Rooms: 15, S £75–£109 D £95–£128 Facilities: STV Parking: 28 Notes: ⊘ in restaurant

Following Colin and Jo Clarkson's caring, extensive refurbishment Rombalds is a gracefully furnished, classic country house hotel. Day rooms include delightful lounges and a much commended restaurant, offering a pleasing selection of local and international cuisine, and wines from around the world.

**Recommended in the area**

Ilkley Moor; Yorkshire Dales National Park; Harewood House

# Queens Hotel

★★★★ 78% HOTEL

| | |
|---|---|
| Address: | City Square, LEEDS LS1 1PL |
| Tel: | 0113 243 1323 |
| Fax: | 0113 242 5154 |
| Email: | queensreservations@qhotels.co.uk |
| Website: | www.qhotels.co.uk |
| Map ref: | 7, SE23 |

Directions: M621 junct 3. Follow signs for city centre, under railway bridge. Left at 2nd lights, hotel on left

Rooms: 217, S £139 D £139 Facilities: STV Wi-fi

Fresh from a £10 million refit that has restored its art deco splendour, this landmark hotel occupies a prime location in the city. More than 200 spacious, air conditioned bedrooms on eight floors are provided with tea and coffee making facilities, wireless broadband and games consoles, and many have superb views across Leeds and beyond. The Queens Grill offers a range of contemporary and traditional dishes. Sixteen conference and event rooms cater for up to 700 delegates. Complimentary health and leisure facilities are available a short walk away at LA Fitness.

**Recommended in the area**

Royal Armouries; Harewood House; Kirkstall Abbey

Pontefract Castle.

# Wentbridge House Hotel

★★★ 79% ◉ HOTEL

| | |
|---|---|
| **Address:** | Wentbridge, PONTEFRACT WF8 3JJ |
| **Tel:** | 01977 620444 |
| **Fax:** | 01977 620148 |
| **Email:** | info@wentbridgehouse.co.uk |
| **Website:** | www.wentbridgehouse.co.uk |
| **Map ref:** | 8, SE41 |
| **Directions:** | 0.5m off A1 & 4m S of M62 junct 33 onto A1 south |

**Rooms:** 18, S £90–£130 D £120–£160 **Facilities:** Wi-fi in bedrooms **Parking:** 100 **Notes:** ⊗ in bedrooms

This ivy-covered hotel dating from 1700 stands in 20 acres of landscaped gardens in the beautiful Went Valley. Bedrooms are individually designed, with sizes and styles to suit all, from standard doubles to some with traditional English four-posters. Classic and contemporary lunch and dinner dishes, prepared by an award-winning kitchen team, are served in the elegant Fleur de Lys Restaurant, or the more contemporary brasserie and bar. A popular venue for wedding receptions.

**Recommended in the area**

Noskell Priory; Bradsworth Hall and gardens; Leeds city centre

# CHANNEL ISLANDS

Moulin Huet Bay, near St Martin, Guernsey.

# La Barbarie Hotel

★★★ 77% ◉ HOTEL

**Address:** Saints Road, Saints Bay, ST MARTIN, Guernsey GY4 6ES
**Tel:** 01481 235217
**Fax:** 01481 235208
**Email:** reservations@labarbariehotel.com
**Website:** www.labarbariehotel.com
**Map ref:** 13
**Directions:** Off road between St Peter Port and the airport; follow signs for Saints Bay
**Rooms:** 22, S £50–£68 D £60–£96 **Facilities:**⚲ **Parking:** 50 **Notes:** ⊗ ⊘ on premises

This fine hotel was named after Barbary Coast pirates who kidnapped and held to ransom the house's owner in the 17th century. A hotel since 1950, it lies in a quiet green valley close to some of the lovely bays, coves and cliffs in the south of the island, and retains all of its historic charm, not least in the lovely residents' lounge, with its old beams and open fireplace. Bedrooms have private bath or shower rooms, TV, radio, trouser press, iron, tea and coffee facilities and hair dryer. Two-room suites with inter-connecting doors are ideal for families with children. Some self-catering apartments are also available, most of which overlook the heated swimming pool and its surrounding patio. Dining at La Barbarie is serious but far from pretentious, and accolades include one from the producer of one of celebrity chef Rick Stein's TV series, who is quoted as saying that the lobster he had here was the best he had ever tasted in all his 15 years of travelling the world making food programmes. The fixed-price four-course dinner menu, with four choices in each course, is very good value. There is also a bar and poolside menu, which includes 'old favourites', pastas, fish, salads and sandwiches. The warm patio is the ideal secluded spot for a lazy lunch or quiet aperitif before dinner. The hotel is ideally placed for walkers, cyclists, horse riders and even those who fancy a jog with the MD, if they 'offer to buy refreshments'.

**Recommended in the area**

Saumarez Manor; Castle Cornet; South Coast Cliff Path

# Best Western Hotel de Havelet

★★★ 77% HOTEL

| | |
|---|---|
| Address: | Havelet, ST PETER PORT, Guernsey GY1 1BA |
| Tel: | 01481 722199 |
| Fax: | 01481 714057 |
| Email: | havelet@sarniahotels.com |
| Website: | www.havelet.sarniahotels.com |
| Map ref: | 13 |

Directions: From airport follow signs for St Peter Port through St. Martins. At bottom of 'Val de Terres' hill turn left into Havelet

Rooms: 34, S £48–£105 D £82–£132 Facilities: ⊗ Sauna Jacuzzi STV Wi-fi in bedrooms

Parking: 40 Notes: ⊗ in bedrooms ⊘ in restaurant

A handsome Georgian house surrounded by sheltered gardens and flower-filled terraces on the outskirts of the island's capital. From its elevated position there are magnificent views over the harbour to Herm and other neighbouring islands. Many of the comfortable, well-equipped bedrooms are set around a pretty colonial-style courtyard. The elegant drawing room, one of several locations for afternoon tea, is always welcoming, but particularly so on chilly evenings and wintry days when warmed by a blazing log fire. Two of the island's most popular restaurants are within the hotel, in the converted coach house. The Wellington Boot offers an extensive four-course dinner menu featuring Guernsey fish, seafood and flambée dishes, while the Havelet Grill, where charcoal grills and fresh fish are served, has a more relaxed environment. The coach house is also home to the Saddle Room Bar, which offers hot and cold buffet lunches and afternoon tea. Hotel guests on half board terms may take advantage of a dinner exchange scheme with other Sarnia hotels in Guernsey.

**Recommended in the area**

Hauteville House; Castle Cornet; Sark; South Coast Cliff Path

# Somerville Hotel

★★★ 83% ◉◉ HOTEL

**Address:** Mont du Boulevard, ST AUBIN, Jersey JE3 8AD
**Tel:** 01534 741226
**Fax:** 01534 746621
**Email:** somerville@dolanhotels.com
**Website:** www.dolanhotels.com
**Map ref:** 13
**Directions:** From village, follow harbour then take Mont du Boulevard and 2nd right bend
**Rooms:** 56, S £70–£126 D £88–£158
**Facilities:** ⟋ STV Wi-fi in all public areas **Parking:** 26
**Notes:** ⊗ in bedrooms ⊘ in restaurant

Nestling on the hillside, overlooking the yachting harbour, the village of St Aubin and the bay beyond, the views from the Somerville Hotel are breathtaking. As one of the island's finest hotels, it is well known for its warm welcome and excellent reputation and most of the comfortable and tastefully furnished bedrooms, enjoy spectacular sea views. Jersey has earned a worldwide reputation for the quality of its restaurants and Tides Restaurant at the Somerville Hotel is no exception. Recently awarded two AA Rosettes for its food, coupled with the restaurants panoramic views over the harbour, the Somerville offers a memorable dining experience. Lunch on the terrace is a particular favourite. Before and after a meal enjoy a drink in the cocktail bar, or simply relax and unwind with coffee in the lounge. Following the completion of a two year refurbishment in 2007, including the addition of conference and banqueting facilities, the hotel will offer a choice of three meeting rooms, two of which will benefit from natural light and have spectacular views as a perfect backdrop. The hotel is just five minutes walk from the sandy expanse of St. Aubin's Bay and the sheltered cove of Belcroute Beach.

**Recommended in the area**

Durrell Wildlife Conservation trust; Elizabeth Castle; Jersey War Tunnels

# The Atlantic Hotel

★★★★ ◎◎◎ HOTEL

**Address:** Le Mont de la Pulente, ST BRELADE,
Jersey JE3 8HE
**Tel:** 01534 744101
**Fax:** 01534 744102
**Email:** info@theatlantichotel.com
**Website:** www.theatlantichotel.com
**Map ref:** 13
**Directions:** From Petit Port turn right into Rue de la
Sergente & right again, hotel signed
**Rooms:** 50 **Facilities:** ◔ ↘ Sauna Jacuzzi Solarium
Tennis Gym STV **Parking:** 60 **Notes:** ✪ in bedrooms
✪ in restaurant and public areas

Family owned since 1970, this luxury hotel occupies six acres adjoining the manicured fairways of La Moye championship golf course. It is a peaceful setting, with breathtaking views over St Ouen's Bay, an internationally significant conservation area. Recently remodelled, its crisp, clean exterior is reminiscent of 1930s seaside architecture, and an air of understated luxury pervades throughout, with attentive service achieving a balance of friendliness with professionalism. In the public areas fine antiques, a wrought-iron staircase and balustrade, urns, fountains and specially commissioned furniture in richly upholstered fabrics contribute to the timeless elegance. Bedrooms decorated in pale, cool colours, and with custom-designed furniture, look out over the golf course or the sea, and bathrooms make good use of marble. The elegant, award-winning Ocean restaurant is the setting for accomplished innovative cooking that makes use of the finest and freshest produce from Jersey's coastal waters and countryside. Light lunches and salads are served on the terrace or by the pool. Business facilities include a private dining room.

## Recommended in the area

Durrell Wildlife Conservation Trust; Jersey War Tunnels; La Mere Vineyards

St Ouen's Bay and La Rocco Tower.

# Longueville Manor Hotel

★★★★ ◉◉◉ HOTEL

| | |
|---|---|
| Address: | ST SAVIOUR, Jersey JE2 7WF |
| Tel: | 01534 725501 |
| Fax: | 01534 731613 |
| Email: | info@longuevillemanor.com |
| Website: | www.longuevillemanor.com |
| Map ref: | 13 |
| Directions: | A3 E from St Helier towards Gorey |

Rooms: 30, S £190–£205 D £230–£260 Facilities: ⚲
Tennis STV Wi-fi in bedrooms Parking: 40 Notes:

This 13th-century manor house in its own wooded valley has been for the last 50-odd years a charming family-run hotel. Decorated in warm colours, and furnished with fine antiques, it invites complete relaxation. The en suite bedrooms, each named after a type of rose, come with chaise longue, Egyptian cotton sheets, satellite TV and homemade biscuits, while those on the ground floor have a garden-facing private patio. In the Oak and Garden Room restaurants the Master Sommelier will advise on wines. The hotel's Victorian glasshouses provide fresh out-of-season produce.

**Recommended in the area**

Royal Jersey Golf Club, Mont Orgueil Castle, Durrell Wildlife Conservation Trust

# Water's Edge Hotel

★★★ 77% ◉◉ HOTEL

Address: Bouley Bay, TRINITY, Jersey JE3 5AS
Tel: 01534 862777
Fax: 01534 863645
Email: mail@watersedgehotel.co.je
Website: www.watersedgehotel.co.je
Map ref: 13
Directions: From St Helier, go N on A8, then follow signs for Bouley Bay
Rooms: 50 S £40–£90 D £80–£130 Facilities: ⚲
Parking: 20 Notes: ⊗ in bedrooms ⊘ in restaurant

Jersey's north coast can be hilly, but guests here need ascend only a few gently rising feet to reach the hotel after a day on the beach. As its name implies, Water's Edge could hardly be closer to the shoreline of pretty Bouley Bay, and many of the rooms and luxury suites face the ocean, while the rest have southward views over the garden. All the bedrooms are decorated in contemporary style and have en suite bathrooms, tea- and coffee-making facilities, telephone and TV. Through the huge picture windows of the Waterside Restaurant, the Cotentin Peninsula of France, about 11 miles distant, can usually be seen. The menu is modern British with hints of classical, and choices might include starters such as Royal Grouville Bay oysters or ham and foie gras terrine, followed by seafood and meat main courses, or a steak from the flambée trolley, the Waterside's signature dish. The well-balanced wine list guarantees something suitable as an accompaniment. On warm days, meals can also be enjoyed on the large deck overlooking the harbour, or in the Black Dog Bar, full of character and well known to locals for its delicious food, enjoyed in the cosy warmth of a real fire in winter. The heated outdoor kidney-shaped pool is on a delightful terrace overlooking the bay. There are spectacular cliffpath walks leading both east and west from the hotel, and a five-star dive centre not far away.

### Recommended in the area

Durrell Wildlife Conservation Trust; Mont Orgueil Castle; Jersey Living Legend Village

# SCOTLAND

Loch an Eilean.

# Marcliffe Hotel & Spa

★★★★ 86% ◉ HOTEL

**Address:** North Deeside Road,
CITY OF ABERDEEN AB15 9YA
**Tel:** 01224 861000
**Fax:** 01224 868860
**Email:** enquiries@marcliffe.com
**Website:** www.marcliffe.com
**Map ref:** 10, NJ90
**Directions:** A90 onto A93 signed Braemar. 1m on right after turn at lights
**Rooms:** 42, S £140–£295 D £140–£295
**Facilities:** Gym STV Wi-fi in bedrooms **Parking:** 220
**Notes:** ⊘ on premises

The Spence family won the AA Hotel of the Year for Scotland Award for their impressive establishment situated in 11 acres of wooded grounds west of the city. It was opened in 1993 by then Soviet premier Mikhail Gorbachev. Its location is ideal for visiting Scotland's celebrated castle and whisky country. Many of the beautifully appointed rooms have antique furniture and paintings; all have goose-down pillows, satellite TV, direct-dial phone, mini-bar and iron and ironing board. The split-level Conservatory Restaurant, terraces and courtyards all help to give a sense of the Mediterranean, while the sophisticated cocktail lounge is classical in style. Breakfast, lunch and dinner are served in the restaurant, which specialises in local Grampian produce, such as Aberdeen Angus beef, game from the estates, fish and shellfish from local rivers and ports. The wine cellar holds more than 400 wines and the Drawing Room bar is stocked with over 100 malt whiskies. A huge range of outdoor pursuits are on hand, including golf, salmon fishing, stalking and grouse and pheasant shooting – just ask hotel staff to arrange whatever you want to do.

**Recommended in the area**

Balmoral Castle, Glenfiddich Distillery, Royal Aberdeen Golf Club

# Banchory Lodge Hotel

★★★ 81% COUNTRY HOUSE HOTEL

**Address:** BANCHORY AB31 5HS
ABERDEENSHIRE
**Tel:** 01330 822625
**Fax:** 01330 825019
**Email:** enquiries@banchorylodge.co.uk
**Website:** www.banchorylodge.co.uk
**Map ref:** 10, NO79
**Directions:** Off A93, 13m W of Aberdeen, hotel off
Dee Street
**Rooms:** 22, S £85 D from £150 **Parking:** 50 **Notes:** ⊘ on premises

This privately-owned former coaching inn stands in richly wooded grounds alongside the Dee, one of Scotland's premier salmon rivers, and offers superior accommodation and high standards of service. Long ago, the old Deeside road passed this way and the mail coach would halt here for a change of horses. The hotel's homely atmosphere owes much to its traditional decor, fresh flowers, open fires and collection of original paintings. The 22 en suite bedrooms, among which are three with four-posters and several spacious family rooms, are all luxuriously furnished and comprehensively equipped. Many have river views. The hotel bar features an ornately carved oak counter and a selection of over 50 malt whiskies. Guests can choose one of the two public lounges in which to relax over morning coffee or afternoon tea with a newspaper, or watch anglers trying their skill. The Riverview Dining Room, overlooking the confluence of the Feugh and Dee, offers a daily menu of imaginative dishes including Scottish salmon, local lamb and Aberdeen Angus beef, all personally supervised by the owner. Breakfast is served in a smaller room, which is also available for private functions. Fishing (from 1st February to 30th September) and shooting can be arranged through the hotel.

**Recommended in the area**

Crathes Castle; Balmoral Castle; Lochnagar Whisky Distillery

# The Falls of Lora Hotel

★★★ 75% HOTEL

**Address:** CONNEL PA37 1PB ARGYLL & BUTE
**Tel:** 01631 710483
**Fax:** 01631 710694
**Email:** enquiries@fallsoflora.com
**Website:** www.fallsoflora.com
**Map ref:** 9, NM93
**Directions:** Hotel set back from A85 from Glasgow, 0.5m past Connel sign, 5m before Oban
**Rooms:** 30, S £41–£69 D £49–£119 **Parking:** 40

This Victorian owner-run hotel enjoys views over the hotel gardens (across the road), Loch Etive and the Connel Bridge. The ground floor includes a comfortable traditional lounge and cocktail bar with open log fires, offering more than 100 whiskies. Well-equipped bedrooms come in a variety of styles, ranging from cosy standard doubles to high quality luxury suite-type rooms. Although not all have views, the one that does has a king-size bed and bay windows overlooking the Loch. Guests may eat in the comfortable and attractive Bistro and in the evening there is an exciting and varied menu

**Recommended in the area**

Oban Distillery, Iona Abbey, Ben Nevis

# The Lodge on Loch Lomond Hotel & Restaurant

★★★ 79% ◉◉ HOTEL

**Address:** LUSS G83 8PA ARGYLL & BUTE
**Tel:** 01436 860201
**Fax:** 01436 860203
**Email:** res@loch-lomond.co.uk
**Website:** www.loch-lomond.co.uk
**Map ref:** 9, NS39
**Directions:** Off A82, follow sign for hotel
**Rooms:** 47, S £70–£269 D £90–£379 **Facilities:** ⊗
Sauna Steam Room 16m Swimming Pool Jacuzzi STV **Parking:** 120 **Notes:** ⊘ on premises

The Lodge on Loch Lomond stands among some of Scotland's most idyllic, unspoilt scenery. The bedrooms and suites are contemporary in style and provide private sauna and massaging shower as well as the usual comforts and facilities. There are also Conference facilities. Colquhoun's, the hotels' award-winning restaurant, serves traditional and contemporary dishes from a changing menu.

**Recommended in the area**

Loch Lomond Aquarium; Queen Elizabeth Forest Park; City of Glasgow

# Highland Cottage

★ ★ ★ ◉◉ SMALL HOTEL

| | |
|---|---|
| **Address:** | Breadalbane Street, TOBERMORY, |
| | Isle of Mull PA75 6PD ARGYLL & BUTE |
| **Tel:** | 01688 302030 |
| **Email:** | davidandjo@highlandcottage.co.uk |
| **Website:** | www.highlandcottage.co.uk |
| **Map ref:** | 9, NM55 |

**Directions:** A848 Craignure/Fishnish ferry terminal, pass Tobermory signs, straight on at mini rdbt across narrow bridge, turn right. Hotel opposite fire station

**Rooms:** 6 S £100 D £140–£175 **Facilities:** STV Wi-fi available **Parking:** 6

**Notes:** ⊗ on premises

David and Jo Currie designed and built this small hotel. Both are career hoteliers and bring to it many years of experience. The hotel stands above Tobermory, the Isle of Mull's pretty 'capital', in the town's quiet conservation area, yet only minutes from the hustle and bustle of Main Street and Fisherman's Pier. With just six individually-designed bedrooms, staff rarely need to ask guests for their room number. This relaxed policy continues in the rooms themselves, where the Curries have deliberately avoided decor that screams 'Hotel!' All are provided with a video TV, music centre, and an en suite bathroom with full-size bath and thermostatic shower, while some have four-posters. There are two inviting lounges - the Sitting Room upstairs, with an honesty bar and views across the bay to the mainland; and downstairs the Sun Lounge, an extension of the Dining Room and the ideal place for pre- or after-dinner drinks. Breakfasts are described as 'memorable', dinners as 'splendid'. Whenever feasible, the kitchen uses only the freshest of locally-sourced ingredients, such as scallops from Tobermory Bay, crabs from Croig on the island's west coast, mussels farmed at Inverlussa on Loch Spelve, and venison reared at Ardnamurchan.

**Recommended in the area**

Duart Castle; Fingal's Cave (Staffa); Whale-watching

# The Balmoral

★★★★★ 86% ◉◉◉ HOTEL

**Address:** 1 Princes Street, CITY OF EDINBURGH EH2 2EQ
**Tel:** 0131 556 2414
**Fax:** 0131 557 3747
**Email:** reservations.balmoral@roccofortehotels.com
**Website:** www.roccofortehotels.com
**Map ref:** 10, NT27
**Directions:** Follow city centre signs. Hotel at E end of Princes St, adjacent to Waverley Station
**Rooms:** 188, S £270–£1500 D £320–£1500 **Facilities:** ⊗ Sauna Solarium Gym STV Wi-fi in bedrooms **Notes:** ⊗ in bedrooms ⊘ on premises

The Balmoral is more than a hotel, it's an Edinburgh landmark, thanks to the majestic clocktower that has been a feature of the city skyline for a century or so. Built as a traditional railway hotel, its public areas, conference and banqueting suites, and stylish bedrooms have been beautifully refurbished to designs by Rocco Forte's sister, Olga Polizzi. Although given individual treatment, each room is decorated in the muted hues of Scottish moors, mists and heathers. All are equipped with two phone lines, fax-modem, broadband, interactive national and satellite TV, in-room refreshments, air conditioning, and spacious marble and ceramic bathroom with fluffy towels, robes and other luxuries. Some look towards Edinburgh Castle, some the Old Town, and some over the courtyard. When it comes to fine dining, guests can choose to match the mood of the moment: attentive but non-intrusive service in Number One, with outstanding cuisine by chef, Jeff Bland; Hadrian's Brasserie for chic and informal dining; The Bollinger Bar at Palm Court for cocktails or afternoon tea, or NB's Bar for a relaxing drink. Enjoy the facilities in the Spa - the Finnish sauna, Turkish steam room, 15-metre crystal-clear pool, air conditioned fully equipped gymnasium, and exercise room.

**Recommended in the area**

Palace of Holyrood; St Giles Cathedral; Royal Mile

The view from Calton Hill, Edinburgh.

# Best Western Bruntsfield Hotel

★★★ 81% ◎ HOTEL

| | |
|---|---|
| **Address:** | 69 Bruntsfield Place, |
| | CITY OF EDINBURGH EH10 4HH |
| **Tel:** | 0131 229 1393 |
| **Fax:** | 0131 229 5634 |
| **Email:** | sales@thebruntsfield.co.uk |
| **Website:** | www.bw-bruntsfieldhotel.co.uk |
| **Map ref:** | 10, NT27 |

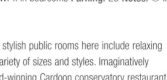

**Directions:** From S into Edinburgh on A702. Hotel 1m S of west end of Princes Street)

**Rooms:** 71, S £95–£140 D £180–£250 **Facilities:** STV Wi-fi in bedrooms **Parking:** 25 **Notes:** ⊗ in bedrooms ⊘ on premises

Close to the city centre, overlooking Bruntsfield Links, the stylish public rooms here include relaxing lounge areas and a lively pub. The bedrooms come in a variety of sizes and styles. Imaginatively created evening meals and are served in the bright, award-winning Cardoon conservatory restaurant.

**Recommended in the area**

Edinburgh Castle and Royal Mile; Edinburgh Old Town; Royal Yacht *Britannia*

# Prestonfield

★★★★★ ◉◉ TOWN HOUSE HOTEL

**Address:** Priestfield Road,
CITY OF EDINBURGH EH16 5UT
**Tel:** 0131 225 7800
**Fax:** 0131 220 4392
**Email:** reservations@prestonfield.com
**Website:** www.prestonfield.com
**Map ref:** 10, NT27
**Directions:** A7 towards Cameron Toll. 200mtrs beyond
Royal Commonwealth Pool, into Priestfield Rd
**Rooms:** 24 **Facilities:** STV **Parking:** 250 ⊘ on premises

To the many AA and other awards this 17th-century
mansion has gained should be added this plaudit from
Tatler magazine: "Divine decadence. Rich, ripe and
dangerously close to dissolute". Other commentators have sprinkled their reviews of this celebrated
city centre hotel with words such as 'opulent', 'indulgent' and 'Baroque extravaganza'. So when James
Thomson, the creative force behind Prestonfield and other prestigious Scottish restaurants, calls it the
'ultimate retort to minimalism', a picture begins to take shape. Interiors are gilded, brocaded and
velvet-covered, and to the fine art and antique furnishings Thomson has added a quixotic assortment
of finds from European auction rooms. Bedrooms and suites have discreet technology, including air
conditioning, high-speed internet, Bose sound system and flat-screen TV. Bed linen is by Frette and
there are luxurious bathrobes, fresh flowers and exclusive toiletries. The unusually named Rhubarb
restaurant is split between a pair of grand oval Regency rooms. Here, exceptional cooking might
include smoked salmon with Beluga caviar, fillet of Black gold beef, and Lindisfarne oysters, not
to mention the famed rhubarb desserts, and a choice of wines from the much-praised cellars.

**Recommended in the area**

Museum of Scotland; Scottish Parliament (Palace of Holyrood); Edinburgh Castle

# ABode Hotel Glasgow

★★★★ 76% ◉◉ HOTEL

**Address:** 129 Bath Street, CITY OF GLASGOW G2 2SZ
**Tel:** 0141 221 6789
**Fax:** 0141 221 6777
**Email:** reservationsglasgow@abodehotels.co.uk
**Website:** www.abodehotels.co.uk/glasgow
**Map ref:** 9, NS66
**Directions:** Centre of Glasgow, south of Sauchiehall St
**Rooms:** 60, S £125–£225 D £115–£225
**Notes:** ⊘ on premises

No, it's not a mistake. The typographically quirky 'ABode' is an example of how this concept hotel seeks to stand out in a city generously endowed with chic establishments. The building, situated in Glasgow's historic art district, has been transformed from offices occupied by the Department of Education, which mercifully left untouched many of the original grand Edwardian features. Meticulous attention to detail is evident in the contemporarily designed rooms, each is decorated in subtle tones, and offering practicalities like a hand-built bed with cashmere throw, LCD TV, DVD player, comfort cooling, secondary glazing and a tuck box of regional produce. At street level is Michael Caines' hugely popular restaurant. Caines, one of Britain's most talented and respected chefs, and awarded an MBE in 2006 for services to the hospitality industry, works closely with local suppliers to ensure that all his menus showcase the best regional produce. MC Café Bar serves breakfast, elevenses, lunch and full evening meals. ABode Glasgow is also home to the first MC Vibe Bar, a stylish and relaxed late-night lounge with funky lighting and furniture and all the latest cocktails, and champagne by the glass or bottle. Finally, there's MC Boutique for fine oils, pasta, chocolate and other gourmet products as used in the hotel kitchens. ABode Glasgow is the perfect venue for weddings, private parties and business meetings.

**Recommended in the area**

Burrell Collection; Glasgow Cathedral; Museum of Transport

The Clyde Auditorium, Glasgow.

# Langs Hotel

★★★★ 77% ◉◉ HOTEL

| | |
|---|---|
| **Address:** | 2 Port Dundas Place, GLASGOW |
| | G2 3LD CITY OF GLASGOW |
| **Tel:** | 0141 333 1500 |
| **Fax:** | 0141 333 5700 |
| **Email:** | reservations@langshotels.co.uk |
| **Website:** | www.langshotels.co.uk |
| **Map ref:** | 9, NS66 |

**Directions:** M8 junct 16, follow signs for George Sq. Hotel immediately left after Concert Square car park

**Rooms:** 100, S £90 D £100 **Facilities:** Gym STV Wi-fi in bedrooms **Notes:** ⊗ on premises

A sharply styled, modern hotel slap-bang in the city centre. The rooms all have remarkable bathrooms with jet showers; satellite TV, Sony PlayStation and CD player, WiFi, a great bed and efficient room service. There are a range of suites too. Dinner might be Euro-fusion style in Oshi; the Aurora's award-winning food in more formal surroundings; or a drink and maybe a sirloin steak baguette in BBar. State-of-the-art spa facilities ensure guests can unwind fast.

**Recommended in the area**

Burrell Collection; Gallery of Modern Art; Glasgow Science Centre and Tower

# Balcary Bay Hotel

★★★ 85% ◉◉ HOTEL

| | |
|---|---|
| **Address:** | AUCHENCAIRN, Castle Douglas |
| | DG7 1QZ DUMFRIES & GALLOWAY |
| **Tel:** | 01556 640217 |
| **Fax:** | 01556 640272 |
| **Email:** | reservations@balcary-bay-hotel.co.uk |
| **Website:** | www.balcary-bay-hotel.co.uk |
| **Map ref:** | 5, NX75 |
| **Directions:** | On the A711 between Dalbeattie and |

Kirkcudbright, hotel on Shore road, 2m from village

**Rooms:** 20, S £67 D £120–£150 **Parking:** 50 **Notes:** ⊘ on premises

The hotel lawns run down to the edge of the beautiful bay from which it takes its name. Just offshore is Heston Isle, hideout of 17th-century smugglers who used to store contraband in the house's secret underground passages. Nowadays, while modernised and tastefully decorated, the hotel still retains much of its old character (without the smuggling, of course). Public rooms include the cocktail bar and log fire-warmed lounges. There are twenty well-appointed en suite bedrooms, all with TV, radio, phone, tea and coffee tray, and hairdryer. Other facilities at the Balcary are available on request. From many rooms there are magnificent views across the Solway Firth to the beautiful peaks of the Lake District. Three superior ground floor rooms have their own patio overlooking the bay, leaving the remaining rooms to look over the gardens. In the restaurant award-winning cuisine is based on local Scottish fare, often given a Gallic twist. Local delicacies such as prime Galloway beef, lamb, lobsters, prawns and, of course, Balcary Bay salmon are likely to appear on the carte and fixed price menus. A bistro-style lunch menu is available seven days a week. The wine list is extensive and draws from both the Old and New Worlds, and even includes examples from Lebanon.

### Recommended in the area

East Stewartry Coast; Threave Garden (NT); Loch Ken

The Forth Rail Bridge.

# Greywalls Hotel

★ ★ ★ ◎◎◎ HOTEL

| | |
|---|---|
| **Address:** | Muirfield, GULLANE |
| | EH31 2EG EAST LOTHIAN |
| **Tel:** | 01620 842144 |
| **Fax:** | 01620 842241 |
| **Email:** | hotel@greywalls.co.uk |
| **Website:** | www.greywalls.co.uk |
| **Map ref:** | 10, NT48 |

**Directions:** A198, hotel signposted at E end of village
**Rooms:** 23, S £140–£280 D £240–£300
**Facilities:** Tennis STV Wi-fi available **Parking:** 40 **Notes:** ⊘ on premises

A dignified and relaxing Edwardian country house designed by Sir Edwin Lutyens, with a garden by Gertrude Jekyll, overlooking the famous Muirfield golf course. The hotel has a firm reputation for excellent service and cuisine, and its style and comfort are, perhaps, best exemplified by the panelled, log fire-warmed library. The chefs use only fresh local ingredients to produce a short, regularly changing menu. There are stylish bedrooms within the grounds, and more in the Colonel's House nearby.

**Recommended in the area**

Edinburgh Castle; Museum of Flight; Tantallon Castle

# Best Western Keavil House Hotel

★★★ 79% ⑳ HOTEL

| | |
|---|---|
| **Address:** | Crossford, DUNFERMLINE KY12 8QW FIFE |
| **Tel:** | 01383 736258 |
| **Fax:** | 01383 621600 |
| **Email:** | reservations@keavilhouse.co.uk |
| **Website:** | www.keavilhouse.co.uk |
| **Map ref:** | 10, NT08 |
| **Directions:** | 2m W of Dunfermline on A994 |

**Rooms:** 47 **Facilities:** ⓡ Sauna Jacuzzi Solarium Gym STV Wi-fi in bedrooms
**Parking:** 150 **Notes:** ⊗ in bedrooms ⊘ on premises

This former manor house, dating from the 16th century, is set in gardens and parkland 30 minutes from Edinburgh. Well-furnished and equipped bedrooms and inter-linked family suites come in a variety of sizes; some have four-posters. Cardoons conservatory restaurant serves breakfast, an extensive daily lunch buffet, and dinner from the carte menu. There is a wide choice of function rooms.
**Recommended in the area**
Dunfermline Abbey; St Andrews; Andrew Carnegie Museum

St Andrews Castle.

# St Andrews Golf Hotel

★★★ ◉◉ HOTEL

| | |
|---|---|
| **Address:** | 40 The Scores, |
| | ST ANDREWS KY16 9AS FIFE |
| **Tel:** | 01334 472611 |
| **Fax:** | 01334 472188 |
| **Email:** | reception@standrews-golf.co.uk |
| **Website:** | www.standrews-golf.co.uk |
| **Map ref:** | 10, NO51 |

**Directions:** Follow signs 'Golf Course' into Golf Place
and in 200yds turn right into The Scores

**Rooms:** 21, S £100–£130 D £200–£240 **Facilities:** STV Wi-fi available **Parking:** 6
**Notes:** ⊘ on premises

From its inviting day rooms, the hotel's superb location is clear, with the beach, coastline and golf links all in view. Bedrooms and suites come in several configurations, and with different views. All have private en suite facilities with top-brand toiletries, bathrobes, TV, phone, hairdryer and beverages. The award-winning restaurant produces a daily mouth-watering menu using the freshest local produce.

**Recommended in the area**

St Andrews Cathedral, Scotland's Secret Bunker, Falkland Palace

# Inverlochy Castle Hotel

★★★★★ ◎◎◎ COUNTRY HOUSE HOTEL

| | |
|---|---|
| **Address:** | Torlundy, FORT WILLIAM |
| | PH33 6SN HIGHLAND |
| **Tel:** | 01397 702177 |
| **Fax:** | 01397 702953 |
| **Email:** | info@inverlochy.co.uk |
| **Website:** | www.inverlochycastlehotel.com |
| **Map ref:** | 12, NN17 |

**Directions:** (accessible from either A82 Glasgow-Fort William or A9 Edinburgh-Dalwhinnie. Hotel 3m N of Fort William on A82, in Torlundy)

**Rooms:** 17, S £250–£350 D £390–£490 **Facilities:** Tennis STV Wi-fi in bedrooms
**Parking:** 17 **Notes:** ⊘ on premises

At the foot of mighty Ben Nevis, this imposing, mid-19th-century castle stands in 500 acres of landscaped gardens and grounds, incorporating its own small loch. After staying at the castle in 1873, when she dabbled at sketching and painting, Queen Victoria wrote in her diary 'I never saw a lovelier or more romantic spot'. Lavishly appointed in classic country-house style, the 17 spacious bedrooms are extremely comfortable and although each is individually designed, they all have large bathrooms, flat-screen TVs, laptops with internet access, an iron and ironing board and, it goes without saying, stunning views. Dinner is an experience to savour in any of its three dining rooms, each decorated with period and elaborate furniture presented as gifts by the King of Norway. The menu features modern British cuisine using the finest and freshest local ingredients. Watching the sun setting over the loch through the restaurant windows is one of those sights you will never forget. Cherubs at play adorn the painted ceiling of the sumptuous Great Hall and lounge, where afternoon tea or a pre-dinner cocktail is an essential part of this Scottish castle experience.

**Recommended in the area**

Loch Ness; Ben Nevis Distillery; Glenfinnan Monument

# Moorings Hotel

★★★ 79% ◉ HOTEL

| | |
|---|---|
| Address: | Banavie, FORT WILLIAM |
| | PH33 7LY HIGHLAND |
| Tel: | 01397 772797 |
| Fax: | 01397 772441 |
| Email: | reservations@moorings-fortwilliam.co.uk |
| Website: | www.moorings-fortwilliam.co.uk |
| Map ref: | 12, NN17 |

Directions: Take A380 (N from Fort William), cross Caledonian Canal, 1st right

Rooms: 27, S £39–£94 D £78–£118 Facilities: STV Parking: 60 Notes: ⊗ on premises

You will receive a true Highland welcome from the friendly staff at this extensively upgraded hotel standing next to a famous series of canal locks known as Neptune's Staircase. In either the comfortable Jacobean Restaurant, or the less formal Upper Deck Bar, dine on award-winning West Coast seafood, salmon and game, as well as other Scottish fare. On summer evenings the pub-like atmosphere of Mariners cellar bar is popular with both guests and locals.

**Recommended in the area**

Ben Nevis; Aonoch Mor; Caledonian Canal

# Kincraig House Hotel

★★★ 79% HOTEL

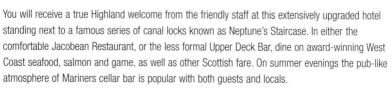

| | |
|---|---|
| Address: | INVERGORDON, |
| | IV18 0LF HIGHLAND |
| Tel: | 01349 852587 |
| Fax: | 01349 852193 |
| Email: | info@kincraig-house-hotel.co.uk |
| Website: | www.kincraig-house-hotel.co.uk |
| Map ref: | 12, NH76 |

Directions: Off A9 past Alness towards Tain. Hotel on left 0.25m past Rosskeen Church

Rooms: 15, S £70–£80 D £120–£190 Facilities: Wi-fi in bedrooms Parking: 30
Notes: ⊗ on premises

Moulded ceilings, fireplaces and oak panelling create a warm, inviting atmosphere at this hotel overlooking the Cromarty Firth. The tasteful Premier bedrooms overlook the gardens, while the similarly finished Executive rooms are slightly smaller. A massive fireplace dominates the restaurant where dishes feature seafood, game and other local produce. The small bar serves lighter meals.

**Recommended in the area**

Dunrobin Castle; Falls of Shin; Tain and Dornoch golf courses

# Glenmoriston House Hotel

★ ★ ★   85% ◉◉◉   HOTEL

| | |
|---|---|
| **Address:** | 20 Ness Bank, INVERNESS |
| | IV2 4SF HIGHLAND |
| **Tel:** | 01463 223777 |
| **Fax:** | 01463 712378 |
| **Email:** | reservations@glenmoristontownhouse.com |
| **Website:** | www.glenmoristontownhouse.com |
| **Map ref:** | 12, NH64 |
| **Directions:** | On riverside opposite theatre |

**Rooms:** 30, S £95–£115 D £130–£170 **Facilities:** STV
Wi-fi in bedrooms **Parking:** 40 **Notes:** ⊗ in bedrooms ⊘ on premises

The stylish Town House is close to Inverness city centre and enjoys charming views of the River Ness. The hotel's bold contemporary designs blend seamlessly with its original classical architecture. The smart, well-proportioned bedrooms have all the latest technology you are likely to want, including a CD and DVD player, flat-screen TV and fax and modem dataport facilities. Many of the rooms look out over towards the river. Both dining areas – the French-style Abstract, again overlooking the Ness, and the more relaxed Contrast Brasserie – give priority to Scottish produce prepared by French chefs, their experience in top restaurants in Europe and the USA locally unmatched, so it's no surprise to discover that they keep winning prestigious awards. Choose from their sumptuous carte menu featuring Scottish spring lamb, North Sea turbot and West Coast scallops, or watch them at work at the Chef's Table preparing an eight-course tasting menu. Enjoy before and after dinner drinks in the stylish and cosy Piano bar, maybe by sampling some of the 180 Scottish malt, Irish and Japanese whiskies kept in stock. Live music is played every Friday and Saturday night from 9pm. The Hotel has conference and meetings facilities with a full range of equipment, and is also a popular venue for couples wanting a Highland wedding.

**Recommended in the area**

Culloden Battlefield; Loch Ness; Cawdor Castle

# The New Drumossie Hotel

★★★★ 80% ◉◉ HOTEL

| | |
|---|---|
| **Address:** | Old Perth Road, INVERNESS |
| | IV2 5BE HIGHLAND |
| **Tel:** | 01463 236451 |
| **Fax:** | 01463 712858 |
| **Email:** | stay@drumossiehotel.co.uk |
| **Website:** | www.drumossiehotel.co.uk |
| **Map ref:** | 12, NH64 |

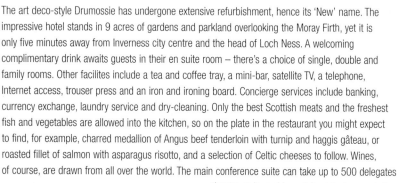

**Directions:** From A9 follow signs for Culloden
Battlefield, hotel on left after 1m
**Rooms:** 44, S £95–£180 D £150–£200 **Facilities:** STV **Parking:** 200 **Notes:** ⊗ in bedrooms
⊘ on premises

The art deco-style Drumossie has undergone extensive refurbishment, hence its 'New' name. The impressive hotel stands in 9 acres of gardens and parkland overlooking the Moray Firth, yet it is only five minutes away from Inverness city centre and the head of Loch Ness. A welcoming complimentary drink awaits guests in their en suite room – there's a choice of single, double and family rooms. Other facilites include a tea and coffee tray, a mini-bar, satellite TV, a telephone, Internet access, trouser press and an iron and ironing board. Concierge services include banking, currency exchange, laundry service and dry-cleaning. Only the best Scottish meats and the freshest fish and vegetables are allowed into the kitchen, so on the plate in the restaurant you might expect to find, for example, charred medallion of Angus beef tenderloin with turnip and haggis gâteau, or roasted fillet of salmon with asparagus risotto, and a selection of Celtic cheeses to follow. Wines, of course, are drawn from all over the world. The main conference suite can take up to 500 delegates

theatre-style, and has all the latest presentation and communications kit. Additional meeting rooms are ideal for smaller gatherings. An extensive range of outdoor pursuits and attractions awaits in the surrounding Highlands, including hiking and rambling, pony trekking; mountain biking; golf, mountaineering, skiing, traditional fishing and game shooting. Drumossie is also an ideal base for touring the Scottish Highlands. A magnificent new ballroom, with floor to ceiling windows with views over the lawns, is proving a popular venue with wedding parties.

### Recommended in the area

Cawdor Castle; Culloden Battlefield and Visitor Centre (NTS); Loch Ness; Urquhart Castle; Caledonian Canal; Great Glen Way; Cairngorms National Park: Fort George Military Museum; Tomatin Whisky Distillery

# Inver Lodge Hotel

★★★★ ◉ HOTEL

**Address:** LOCHINVER IV27 4LU HIGHLAND
**Tel:** 01571 844496
**Fax:** 01571 844395
**Email:** stay@inverlodge.com
**Website:** www.inverlodge.com
**Map ref:** 12, NC12
**Directions:** A835 to Lochinver, through village, left after village hall, follow private road for 0.5m
**Rooms:** 20, S £155 D £200 **Facilities:** Sauna Solarium STV Wi-fi available **Parking:** 30 **Notes:** ⊗ on premises

The Inver Lodge offers a tranquil retreat in spectacular surroundings. A blazing log fire warms the Residents' Lounge during afternoon tea, a card game, or the inevitable 'post mortem' following a day's fishing. The kitchen takes full advantage of abundant local produce, preparing such topographically named dishes as Kyle of Tongue scallops, Lochinver-landed sea bass or Morayshire black pudding. Head for bed in one of the comfortably equipped rooms, all named after local mountains and lochs.

**Recommended in the area**

Eas Caul Aulin Waterfall; Handa Island (RSPB); Knockan Cliff Nature Trail

# Onich Hotel

★★★ 81% ◉ HOTEL

**Address:** ONICH, Nr Fort William
PH33 6RY HIGHLAND
**Tel:** 01855 821214
**Fax:** 01855 821484
**Email:** enquiries@onich-fortwilliam.co.uk
**Website:** www.onich-fortwilliam.co.uk
**Map ref:** 9, NN06
**Directions:** Beside A82, 2m N of Ballachulish Bridge
**Rooms:** 26, S £39–£90 D £78–£118 **Facilities:** Jacuzzi STV **Parking:** 50 **Notes:** ⊗ on premises

The gardens of the Onich Hotel, beautifully situated overlooking Loch Linnhe, extend to the water's edge. Look east and see the mountains of Glencoe, look west to the Isle of Mull. Many of the tastefully decorated and furnished en suite bedrooms overlook the loch, although the best views are from three more luxurious balcony rooms. The award-winning restaurant offers excellent service and mouthwatering meals, including West Coast seafood and Highland game. The bar serves tasty meals all day.

**Recommended in the area**

Ice Factor; Ben Nevis; Glencoe Ski Resort

Portree harbour.

# Cuillin Hills Hotel

★★★  81% ◎◎  HOTEL

| | |
|---|---|
| Address: | PORTREE, Isle of Skye |
| | IV51 9QU HIGHLAND |
| Tel: | 01478 612003 |
| Fax: | 01478 613092 |
| Email: | info@cuillinhills-hotel-skye.co.uk |
| Website: | www.cuillinhills-hotel-skye.co.uk |
| Map ref: | 11, NG44 |
| Directions: | turn right 0.25m N of Portree off A855. |

Follow hotel signs

**Rooms:** 27, S £70–£90 D £120–£250 **Facilities:** STV **Parking:** 56

**Notes:** ⊗ in bedrooms ⊘ on premises

In a truly outstanding location overlooking Portree Bay and the Cuillin mountains of Skye, this former hunting lodge stands in 15 acres of grounds. The generally spacious, well-equipped en suite rooms include seven in a neighbouring building. Diners are offered plenty of choice with Highland game, locally caught seafood and home-made breads among the specialities. Service is friendly and unobtrusive.

**Recommended in the area**

Dunvegan Castle; Talisker Distillery (Skye); Bella Jane boat trips

# The Torridon

★★★ ◉◉  COUNTRY HOUSE HOTEL

| | |
|---|---|
| Address: | By Achnasheen, Wester Ross, |
| | TORRIDON IV22 2EY |
| | HIGHLAND |
| Tel: | 01445 791242 |
| Fax: | 01445 712253 |
| Email: | infoe@thetorridon.com |
| Website: | www.thetorridon.com |
| Map ref: | 11, NG95 |

**Directions:** from A832 at Kinlochewe, take A896 towards Torridon. Do not turn into village, continue 1m, hotel on right

**Rooms:** 19 S £115 D £175–£440 STV Wi-fi in bedrooms **Parking:** 20 **Notes:** ⊘ in hotel

Delightfully set in one of the most impressive coastal positions in the Highlands, this grand late-Victorian shooting lodge stands among 58 acres of private mature trees and parkland at the foot of Ben Damph, on Upper Loch Torridon. Walk round the loch shore, then look back to see just how amazing the location is. A brilliant restoration has brought out the best of its original features. The attractive bedrooms are all individually styled and furnished, with huge Victorian baths, and many with superb views across to the loch and mountains. The former stable block has been converted to the Torridon Inn, all with en suite bath and shower. Sumptuous day rooms feature fine wood panelling, and roaring fires when temperatures demand. The large restaurant offers excellent, simply created menus, frequently commended by top cookery writers. Fish may come from the loch, vegetables, fruit and herbs from the kitchen garden. Outdoor activities nearby include walking and kayaking.

### Recommended in the area

Inverewe Gardens; Beinn Eighe Nature Reserve; Glen Ord and Talisker distilleries

River Tay, Dunkeld

# Ballathie House Hotel

★★★ ◉◉ COUNTRY HOUSE HOTEL

| | |
|---|---|
| **Address:** | KINCLAVEN, Stanley |
| | PH1 4QN PERTH & KINROSS |
| **Tel:** | 01250 883268 |
| **Fax:** | 01250 883396 |
| **Email:** | email@ballathiehousehotel.com |
| **Website:** | www.ballathiehousehotel.com |
| **Map ref:** | 10, NO13 |

**Directions:** From A9 2m N of Perth, B9099 through Stanley & signed, or off A93 at Beech Hedge follow signs for Ballathie 2.5m

**Rooms:** 41, S £85–£130 D £170–£240 **Facilities: Parking:** 50 **Notes:** ⊗ on premises

Ballathie dates from the 17th century and great care has been taken to preserve its beauty, with many original features to give it an extremely classy air. Bedrooms range from well-proportioned master rooms to modern standards, many with antique furniture and art deco bathrooms. Menus change daily and use fresh local produce to create traditional Scottish cuisine with a modern twist.

**Recommended in the area**

Scone Palace; Pitlochry; Glamis Castle

# Pine Trees Hotel

★★★ 85% ⊛ COUNTRY HOUSE HOTEL

**Address:** Strathview Terrace,
PITLOCHRY PH16 5QR
PERTH & KINROSS
**Tel:** 01796 472121
**Fax:** 01796 472460
**Email:** info@pinetreeshotel.co.uk
**Website:** www.pinetreeshotel.co.uk
**Map ref:** 10, NN95
**Directions:** Along main street (Atholl Rd), into
Larchwood Rd, follow hotel signs
**Rooms:** 20, S £56–£84 D £112–£168 **Parking:** 40 **Notes:** ⊘ on premises

A fine country house hotel within a classic Victorian mansion, set in 10 acres of elevated private grounds and woodland on the edge of this famous Highland resort. It has a tranquillity that belies its closeness to Pitlochry's busy, if admittedly hardly noisy, town centre. Many original features have been retained, including wood panelling, ornate ceilings and an impressive marble staircase. The public rooms look out over the well-kept lawns. Nineteen individually decorated bedrooms and one suite - the crimson-painted Molyneux (with a four-poster) - all have a private bathroom and feature the comprehensive range of useful extras that hotel guests expect. The Garden Restaurant, which benefits from plenty of natural daylight, has acquired a worthy reputation for sourcing and serving the best local fish, game and meat. Follow a delicious meal with a wee dram or two, ideally settled comfortably in an armchair or sofa in the Lounge Bar. The Fire Lounge, with an impressive fireplace that stretches to the ceiling, is another possibility. Loch and river fishing, hill walking, Munro-bagging (climbing Scottish mountains over 3000 feet), cycling and golf can all be arranged with the assistance of friendly hotel staff. There is ample private parking in the grounds.

**Recommended in the area**

Blair Castle; House and Falls of Bruar; Pitlochry Festival Theatre

# The Four Seasons Hotel

★★★  82% ◉◉  HOTEL

| | |
|---|---|
| **Address:** | Loch Earn, |
| | ST FILLANS PH6 2NF |
| | PERTH & KINROSS |
| **Tel:** | 01764 685333 |
| **Fax:** | 01764 685444 |
| **Email:** | info@thefourseasonshotel.co.uk |
| **Website:** | www.thefourseasonshotel.co.uk |
| **Map ref:** | 10, NN62 |
| **Directions:** | On A85, towards W of village facing Loch |

**Rooms:** 18, S £53–£78 D £106–£126 **Parking:** 40 **Notes:** ⊘ on premises

Of countless highly desirable hotel settings in Scotland, this is unquestionably in the upper echelons. Looking south west down beautiful Loch Earn, the views are almost too good to be true – they include spectacular sunsets, morning mists and snow-covered mountains. Built in the 1800s for the manager of the local limekilns, the house has been extended over the years to become today's small but exceedingly comfortable hotel, with several individual sitting rooms, a choice of bedrooms and, out on the wooded hillside at the rear, six comfortable and well-equipped chalets. All bedrooms are spacious, most with bath and shower, and many have uninterrupted views down the loch. The chalets have a double or twin room and a bunk room making them ideal for family use. When eating, choose between the more formal Meall Reamhar Room or the Tarken Room. Both offer the same high standard of contemporary Scottish cuisine, with much, as you might expect, coming from local sources and suppliers – Loch Fyne mussels, Tweed Valley partridge, East Coast halibut, and Orkney scallops, for example. A large selection of malts is stocked in the bar. Dog owners will be gratified to know that resident canine Sham welcomes his cousins; he'll even tolerate cats, parrots and gerbils, depending on his humour at the time.

### Recommended in the area

Tartans Museum; Stirling Castle; Doune Motor Museum

Leithen Water, Innerleithin.

# Castle Venlaw Hotel

★★★ 83% ◉◉ COUNTRY HOUSE HOTEL

| | |
|---|---|
| **Address:** | Edinburgh Road, PEEBLES |
| | EH45 8QG SCOTTISH BORDERS |
| **Tel:** | 01721 720384 |
| **Fax:** | 01721 724066 |
| **Email:** | stay@venlaw.co.uk |
| **Website:** | www.venlaw.co.uk |
| **Map ref:** | 10, NT24 |
| **Directions:** | Off A703 Peebles/Edinburgh road, 0.75m |
| | from Peebles |

**Rooms:** 12, £120–£230 **Facilities:** STV Wi-fi in bedrooms **Parking:** 30 **Notes:** ⊘ on premises

This is a family-owned, 18th-century, Scottish baronial-style castle in its own grounds overlooking the ancient town of Peebles. At its heart, in the distinctive tower, is the informal oak-panelled Library Bar and Lounge, with book alcoves and glowing winter log fire. The light, spacious restaurant is the perfect place to enjoy fine Scottish salmon, Borders lamb and local game. The charming bedrooms range from doubles to a family suite at the top of the tower, complete with children's den.

**Recommended in the area**

City of Edinburgh; Traquair House; Abbotsford

# Macdonald Cardrona Hotel Golf & Country Club

★★★★ 77% ◉ HOTEL

**Address:** Cardrona Mains, PEEBLES
EH45 6LZ SCOTTISH BORDERS
**Tel:** 0870 1942114
**Fax:** 01896 831166
**Email:** general.cardrona@macdonald-hotels.co.uk
**Website:** www.macdonald-hotels.co.uk
**Map ref:** 10, NT64
**Directions:** 20m south of Edinburgh on A72, 3m south of Peebles

**Rooms:** 99 **Facilities:** ⓢ Sauna Solarium Gym STV Wi-fi in bedrooms **Parking:** 200
**Notes:** ⊘ on premises

Standing on the banks of the River Tweed, with the rolling hills of the Scottish Borders as a stunning backdrop, this modern hotel is part of the newly built village of Cardrona. The jewel in its crown is the 18-hole, par 72 championship golf course designed by Dave Thomas, who was also responsible for the Ryder Cup course at The Belfry in Warwickshire. Some of the five different styles of bedroom are named after the world's great golfers. All are equipped with a range of extras, such as ironing board, shoe cleaning kit, Sky TV, ISDN lines, direct-dial modem, tea/coffee tray, soft bathrobes and trouser press. From most rooms the Tweed Valley or the golf course can be seen. Renwick's Restaurant offers dishes such as grilled lemon sole, seared venison steak, breast of guinea fowl, and woodland mushroom and leek cassoulet. Leisure facilities include an 18-metre indoor pool and a gym. On the hotel's behalf, Go Forth Partnership arranges mountain biking, fly-fishing, off-road driving and safaris, climbing, abseiling and archery. The function suite can accommodate up to 180 guests.

**Recommended in the area**

Melrose Abbey; Traquair House; Kailzie Gardens

Glen Trool, Dumfries.

# Glenapp Castle

★★★★ ◉◉◉ HOTEL

| | |
|---|---|
| **Address:** | BALLANTRAE KA26 0NZ SOUTH AYRSHIRE |
| **Tel:** | 01465 831212 |
| **Fax:** | 01465 831000 |
| **Email:** | enquiries@glenappcastle.com |
| **Website:** | www.glenappcastle.com |
| **Map ref:** | 5, NX08 |

**Directions:** 1m from A77 near Ballantrae
**Rooms:** 17, S £255–£455 D £375–£575
**Facilities:** Tennis STV Wi-fi in bedrooms **Parking:** 20
**Notes:** ⊘ on premises

Glenapp Castle is a magnificent Victorian castellated mansion set in its own 36 acres of beautiful grounds. The perfect romantic hideaway, Glenapp enjoys breathtaking views to the islands of Arran and Ailsa Craig and is decorated throughout in an opulent traditional style, with fine antique furnishings and art. Gourmet cuisine is served in the gracious dining rooms and the hotel can arrange many sporting activities including world class golf, and salmon and trout fishing.

**Recommended in the area**

Logan Botanical Garden; Culzean Castle and Country Park; Galloway Forest Park

# Scotland

# Macdonald Houstoun House

★★★★ 77% ◉ HOTEL

**Address:** UPHALL EH52 6JS WEST LOTHIAN
**Tel:** 0870 1942107
**Fax:** 01506 854220
**Email:** houstoun@macdonald-hotels.co.uk
**Website:** www.macdonaldhotels.co.uk
**Map ref:** 10, NT07
**Directions:** M8 junct 3 follow Broxburn signs, straight over rdbt then at mini-rdbt turn right towards Uphall, hotel 1m on right

**Rooms:** 71 S £85 D £85 **Facilities:** ⓣ Sauna Solarium Gym STV Wi-fi in bedrooms **Parking:** 250
**Notes:** ⊗ in bedrooms ⊘ on premises

Set in 20 acres of beautifully landscaped grounds and mature woodland, this historic hotel is actually three houses in one: an elegant, white-painted country manor, a 16th-century tower and the steading, or farmstead. This characterful combination gives most rooms benefit views across the gardens to the Ecclesmachan Hills. Each luxurious bedroom is elegantly furnished and comes with a wide range of modern facilities. Executive rooms in the tower come are supplied with bathrobes, slippers, a choice of fresh fruit or hand-made chocolates, and a Houstoun House Bear to take home. The Superior four-poster rooms in the main house upstage the Executives by providing fruit and chocolates, as well as wine. Dinner is available nightly in the award-winning House Restaurant; try the relaxing Steakhouse for chargrilled beef from grass-fed Aberdeen Anguses; or the Tower Restaurant for a menu that might offer pan-fried breast of duck on red cabbage with hazelnuts, and grilled monkfish with braised pak choi, and tomato and chorizo risotto. The Tower is also suitable for private family celebrations. The vaulted House Bar offers an impressive selection of malt whiskies. Leisure facilities include an 18-metre pool, a toning and cardiovascular technogym and a beauty spa and outdoor tennis court.

## Recommended in the area

Linlithgow Palace; Edinburgh Old and New Towns (World Heritage Site); City of Glasgow

Lady Gifford's Well in West Linton.

# WALES

Morfa Nefyn, Gwynedd.

# Park Plaza Cardiff

★★★★ 80% ◉ HOTEL

**Address:** Greyfriars Road, CARDIFF CF10 3AL
**Tel:** 029 2011 1111
**Fax:** 029 2011 1112
**Email:** ppcres@parkplazahotels.co.uk
**Website:** www.parkplazacardiff.com
**Map ref:** 2, ST17
**Directions:** M4 onto A470 to city centre, Turn left into Boulevard de Nantes then immediate right across traffic into Greyfriars Road, Hotel situated on left by New Theatre
**Rooms:** 129, S £95–£200 D £110–£320 **Facilities:** ⓧ Jacuzzi Steam Room 8 Massage & Beauty Rooms Gym STV Wi-fi in bedrooms **Notes:** ⊘ in restaurant **AA Hotel of the Year, Wales 2007**

The Park Plaza is a modern building in the city centre, with impressive contemporary styling. The bedrooms are sumptuously furnished and have full facilities, including a mini-bar and safe. Free wireless Internet access is available throughout the Hotel. There are facilities for wedding receptions and other functions. The Laguna Kitchen and Bar offers international and Welsh cuisine.

**Recommended in the area**

Cardiff Castle; Millennium Stadium; National Museum of Wales

# The St David's Hotel & Spa

★★★★★ 84% ◉◉ HOTEL

**Address:** Havannah Street,
CARDIFF CF10 5SD CARDIFF
**Tel:** 029 2045 4045
**Fax:** 029 2048 7056
**Email:** reservations@thestdavidshotel.com
**Website:** www.roccofortehotels.com
**Map ref:** 2, ST17
**Directions:** M4 junct 33/A4232 for 9m, for Techniquest, at top exit slip road, 1st left at rdbt, 1st right
**Rooms:** 132, D from £130 **Facilities:** ⓧ Sauna Jacuzzi Gym STV **Parking:** 80 **Notes:** ⊗ in bedrooms ⊘ in restaurant

This striking hotel on the Cardiff Bay waterfront is next to Mermaid Quay, with its wide range of restaurants and bars. Inside, a dramatic glass-fronted atrium rises the full seven storeys of the building. All rooms and suites have private balconies, giving views across the bay while bathrooms feature stylish mosaic designs. The award-winning Tides Grill serves tempting and delicious dishes.

**Recommended in the area**

Cardiff Castle; Wales Millennium Centre; Techniquest

# Ivy Bush Royal Hotel

★★★ 75% HOTEL

| | |
|---|---|
| **Address:** | Spilman Street, CARMARTHEN |
| | SA31 1LG CARMARTHENSHIRE |
| **Tel:** | 01267 235111 |
| **Fax:** | 01267 234914 |
| **Email:** | reception@ivybushroyal.co.uk |
| **Website:** | www.ivybushroyal.co.uk |
| **Map ref:** | 1, SN42 |

**Directions:** M4 onto A48 W, over 1st rdbt, 2nd rdbt turn right. Straight over next 2 rdbts. Left at lights. Hotel on right at top of hill

**Rooms:** 70, S £55–£95 D £75–£130 **Facilities:** Sauna Gym STV Wi-fi available **Parking:** 80
**Notes:** ⊗ in bedrooms ⊗ in restaurant

This friendly, family-run hotel has been tastefully refurbished to offer spacious, well-equipped bedrooms and bathrooms, including family and executive rooms, and private suites. In the restaurant seasonal menus make extensive use of fresh local produce, such as Welsh Black beef.

**Recommended in the area**

National Botanic Garden of Wales; Aberglasney House and Gardens; Oakwood Theme Park

# Best Western Falcondale Mansion

★★★ 80% ⊛ HOTEL

| | |
|---|---|
| **Address:** | LAMPETER SA48 7RX CEREDIGION |
| **Tel:** | 01570 422910 |
| **Fax:** | 01570 423559 |
| **Email:** | info@falcondalehotel.com |
| **Website:** | www.falcondalehotel.com |
| **Map ref:** | 1, SN54 |

**Directions:** 800yds W of High St A475 or 1.5m NW of Lampeter A482

**Rooms:** 20, S £95–£168 D £130–£168 **Facilities:** Wi-fi in bedrooms **Parking:** 60 **Notes:** ⊗ in restaurant

Built in the Italianate style, this charming Victorian property is set in 14 acres of beautiful parkland. Bedrooms are generally spacious, well equipped and tastefully decorated, and from most there are delightful valley views. Bars and lounges are well appointed and diners have a choice of either the restaurant or the less formal brasserie, both with daily changing menus. No mobile phone signal here.

**Recommended in the area**

Llanerchaeron House; National Botanic Garden of Wales; Aberaeron

# Craig-y-Dderwen Riverside Hotel

★★★ 77% ❀ COUNTRY HOUSE HOTEL

| | |
|---|---|
| Address: | BETWS-Y-COED LL24 0AS CONWY |
| Tel: | 01690 710293 |
| Fax: | 01690 710362 |
| Email: | craig-y-dderwen@betws-y-coed.co.uk |
| Website: | www.snowdonia-hotel.com |
| Map ref: | 5, SH75 |
| Directions: | A5 to town, cross Waterloo Bridge, 1st left |

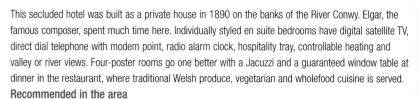

**Rooms:** 16, S £70–£130 D £80–£140 **Facilities:** Jacuzzi STV **Parking:** 50 **Notes:** ⊘ in restaurant

This secluded hotel was built as a private house in 1890 on the banks of the River Conwy. Elgar, the famous composer, spent much time here. Individually styled en suite bedrooms have digital satellite TV, direct dial telephone with modem point, radio alarm clock, hospitality tray, controllable heating and valley or river views. Four-poster rooms go one better with a Jacuzzi and a guaranteed window table at dinner in the restaurant, where traditional Welsh produce, vegetarian and wholefood cuisine is served.

**Recommended in the area**

Snowdon; Portmeirion; Bodnant Gardens

# Castle Hotel Conwy

★★★ 78% ❀❀ HOTEL

| | |
|---|---|
| Address: | High Street, CONWY LL32 8DB CONWY |
| Tel: | 01492 582800 |
| Fax: | 01492 582300 |
| Email: | mail@castlewales.co.uk |
| Website: | www.castlewales.co.uk |
| Map ref: | 5, SH77 |
| Directions: | A55 junct 18, follow town centre signs, |

cross estuary (castle on left). Right then left at mini-rdbts onto one-way system. Right at Town Wall Gate, right onto Berry St then along High St on left

**Rooms:** 28, S £75–£85 D £110–£135 **Facilities:** STV Wi-fi available **Parking:** 34 **Notes:** ⊘ in restaurant

Many of the bedrooms at this 16th-century former coaching inn have been recently upgraded. One of the luxury suites has a Jacuzzi, while another has an ornately carved four-poster. Eat in Shakespeare's, the award-winning restaurant, or alternatively try the wide-ranging bistro menu in Dawsons Bar.

**Recommended in the area**

Conwy Castle; Caernarfon Castle; Snowdon

# Dunoon Hotel

★★★ 78% HOTEL

| | |
|---|---|
| **Address:** | Gloddaeth Street, |
| | LLANDUDNO LL30 2DW CONWY |
| **Tel:** | 01492 860787 |
| **Fax:** | 01492 860031 |
| **Email:** | reservations@dunoonhotel.co.uk |
| **Website:** | www.dunoonhotel.co.uk |
| **Map ref:** | 5, SH78 |

**Directions:** Exit Promenade at war memorial by pier onto wide avenue. 200yds on right

**Rooms:** 49 S £55–£85 D £96

**Parking:** 24 **Notes:** ⊗ in restaurant

Close to the promenade in this well preserved Victorian seaside resort, the Dunoon has a certain old world grace about it. Hushed and stuffy it isn't, though. In fact, the Williams family, who have been here a good while, make sure that it offers a happy antidote to what they regard as anodyne modern living. For example, they treat returning guests like old friends, and first-time customers as new ones. Their approach is evident too in the way they have styled the bedrooms, with no two alike, and in their attention to detail, with crisp Egyptian cotton bedlinen, and Molton Brown toiletries in every bathroom. It is evident too in the restaurant, where silver rings contain freshly pressed linen napkins, and white porcelain is used on the tables. Food and wine are their abiding passions. Cooking is unpretentious, using fresh ingredients sourced locally as far as the seasons allow, with specialities such as terrine of game, medley of local fish, ragout of Welsh lamb with mint dumplings and asparagus mousse. Their taste in wines is adventurous, with a wine list that, in their words, 'offers more than you would expect from a modest hotel in the sleepy outer reaches of Britain'.

**Recommended in the area**

Great Orme; Bodnant Gardens; Snowdonia National Park

Llandudno Bay from Great Orme.

# Empire Hotel

★★★ 81% ◉ HOTEL

| | |
|---|---|
| **Address:** | Church Walks, |
| | LLANDUDNO LL30 2HE CONWY |
| **Tel:** | 01492 860555 |
| **Fax:** | 01492 860791 |
| **Email:** | reservations@empirehotel.co.uk |
| **Website:** | www.empirehotel.co.uk |
| **Map ref:** | 5, SH78 |

**Directions:** From Chester, A55 junct 19 for Llandudno. Follow town centre signs. Hotel at end facing main street

**Rooms:** 57, S £70–£100 D £100–£130 **Facilities:** ⓧ ↖ Sauna STV Wi-fi in bedrooms **Parking:** 40

**Notes:** ⊗ in bedrooms ⊘ in restaurant

Run by the same family for nearly 60 years, this beautifully furnished hotel stands at the foot of the Great Orme headland. The luxurious bedrooms all have cast-iron beds, marble bathrooms and many thoughtful accessories. Eight superior rooms are in a carefully renovated Victorian bank next door. The Watkins restaurant offers a fixed-price menu, and snacks are served in the lounge.

**Recommended in the area**

Conwy Castle; Caernarfon Castle; Portmeirion Italianate village

# Osborne House

★★★★ ⊛ TOWN HOUSE HOTEL

**Address:** 17 North House,
LLANDUDNO LL30 2LP CONWY
**Tel:** 01492 860330
**Fax:** 01492 860791
**Email:** sales@osbornehouse.com
**Website:** www.osbornehouse.com
**Map ref:** 5, SH78
**Directions:** Exit A55 junct 19. Follow signs for
Llandudno then Promenade. Continue to junct, turn right.
Hotel on left opposite pier entrance
**Rooms:** 6, S £145–£200 D £145–£200 **Facilities:** STV Wi-fi in bedrooms **Parking:** 6
**Notes:** ⊗ in bedrooms ⊘ in restaurant

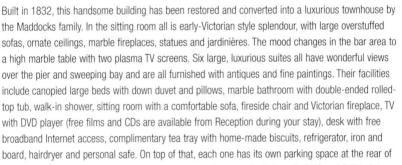

Built in 1832, this handsome building has been restored and converted into a luxurious townhouse by the Maddocks family. In the sitting room all is early-Victorian style splendour, with large overstuffed sofas, ornate ceilings, marble fireplaces, statues and jardinières. The mood changes in the bar area to a high marble table with two plasma TV screens. Six large, luxurious suites all have wonderful views over the pier and sweeping bay and are all furnished with antiques and fine paintings. Their facilities include canopied large beds with down duvet and pillows, marble bathroom with double-ended rolled-top tub, walk-in shower, sitting room with a comfortable sofa, fireside chair and Victorian fireplace, TV with DVD player (free films and CDs are available from Reception during your stay), desk with free broadband Internet access, complimentary tea tray with home-made biscuits, refrigerator, iron and board, hairdryer and personal safe. On top of that, each one has its own parking space at the rear of the property. Osborne's Café and Grill is lit by a

multitude of candles, with opulent drapes and dazzling chandeliers, gilt-edge mirrors and original art. Open throughout the day, it offers a carte menu of high quality brasserie style meat, fish and vegetarian dishes, as well as light bites. There are aslo excellent restaurants and lively bars within walking distance of the hotel. Llandudno, North Wales' largest resort, has sandy beaches and good shopping, and is within easy reach of many attractions. The Snowdonia National Park attracts walkers and other outdoor enthusiasts while on the Llyn Peninsula there are quaint coastal towns to discover and some of the best sailing and surfing in Wales.

### Recommended in the area

Mostyn Art Gallery, Llandudno; Great Orme Heritage Coast; Medieval castles; Bodelwyddan; Bodnant Garden (NT)

# St Tudno Hotel & Restaurant

★★ ◉◉ HOTEL

| | |
|---|---|
| **Address:** | The Promenade, |
| | LLANDUDNO LL30 2LP CONWY |
| **Tel:** | 01492 874411 |
| **Fax:** | 01492 860407 |
| **Email:** | sttudnohotel@btinternet.com |
| **Website:** | www.st-tudno.co.uk |
| **Map ref:** | 5, SH78 |
| **Directions:** | On Promenade towards pier, hotel opposite |

pier entrance

**Rooms:** 18, S £75–£85 D £94–£220 **Facilities:** ⓧ STV **Parking:** 5 **Notes:** ⊘ in restaurant

With many awards for excellence, this delightful seafront hotel has been furnished most elegantly. Richly decorated public areas include the coffee and bar lounges, and a sitting room looking over the sea. There's also a small indoor pool. The individually designed bedrooms are all equipped with robes, satellite TV and mini-bar. The newly redesigned Terrace Restaurant offers modern British seasonal cuisine. Typical, from daily-changing menus, are Welsh Black beef fillet and line-caught sea bass.

**Recommended in the area**

Great Orme Tramway; Conwy Castle; Snowdonia National Park

# Palé Hall Country House Hotel

★★★ 85% ◉ COUNTRY HOUSE HOTEL

| | |
|---|---|
| **Address:** | Palé Estate, Llandderfel, |
| | BALA LL23 7PS GWYNEDD |
| **Tel:** | 01678 530285 |
| **Fax:** | 01678 530220 |
| **Email:** | enquiries@palehall.co.uk |
| **Website:** | www.palehall.co.uk |
| **Map ref:** | 5, SH93 |
| **Directions:** | Off B4401 (Corwen/Bala road) 4m from Llandrillo |

**Rooms:** 17, S £85–£150 D £115–£200 **Parking:** 40 **Notes:** ⊗ on premises ⊘ on premises

This enchanting mansion was built in 1870 and is surrounded by extensive grounds and beautiful woodland scenery. The spacious guest rooms contain an extraordinary selection of beds and bathing facilities, including the half-tester occupied by Queen Victoria in 1889. Dining is stylish and restful, with regularly changing menus bringing out the best of fresh, natural ingredients.

**Recommended in the area**

Snowdonia National Park; Llechwedd Slate Caverns; Penmachno Woollen Mill

Meolfre Bay, Anglesey.

# Tre-Ysgawen Hall Country House Hotel & Spa

★★★ 78% HOTEL

| | |
|---|---|
| **Address:** | Capel Coch, LLANGEFNI LL77 7UR |
| | ISLE OF ANGLESEY |
| **Tel:** | 01248 750750 |
| **Email:** | enquiries@treysgawen-hall.co.uk |
| **Website:** | www.treysgawen-hall.co.uk |
| **Map ref:** | 2, SH47 |

**Directions:** From A55 take A5114, then B5111. After Rhosmerch right to Capel Coch. Hotel 1.5m on left

**Rooms:** 29, S £82–£107 D £132–£169 **Facilities:** ⊗ Sauna Jacuzzi Gym STV Spa Breaks available throughout the year **Parking:** 140 **Notes:** ⊗ in bedrooms ⊘ in restaurant

A few miles inland from the breathtaking east coast of Anglesey with individually designed bedrooms, two four-poster suites both with a jacuzzi and state of the art Spa and Beauty Therapy Suite. Superb cuisine from the best seasonal, local and regional produce while the wine list leans towards France.

**Recommended in the area**

Beaumaris Castle; Plas Newydd; Anglesey Sea Zoo

# Llansantffraed Court Hotel

★★★ 77% ◉◉ COUNTRY HOUSE HOTEL

**Address:** Llanvihangel Gobion,
ABERGAVENNY NP7 9BA MONMOUTHSHIRE
**Tel:** 01873 840678
**Fax:** 01873 840674
**Email:** reception@llch.co.uk
**Website:** www.llch.co.uk
**Map ref:** 2, SO21
**Directions:** At A465/A40 Abergavenny junct take B4598 signed Usk (do not join A40). Continue towards Raglan, hotel on left in 4.5m
**Rooms:** 21, S £86–£115 D £115–£175
**Facilities:** Tennis STV Wi-fi available **Parking:** 250
**Notes:** ⊘ in restaurant

The site of Llansantffraed Court dates from the 12th century, although the present imposing, William and Mary-style house has been a hotel since only the 1920s. Grade II-listed, it is set in 20 acres of landscaped parkland, complete with ornamental trout lake. Inside, the bedrooms, some with oak beams and dormer windows, offer magnificent panoramic views. In the lounge, open fires await on cold days and in warmer weather guests take afternoon tea on the terrace. The multi-award-winning Court Restaurant team produces outstanding modern Welsh cuisine to an internationally recognised standard. Enjoy a light brunch or full candlelit dinner knowing that the daily changing menus take full advantage of local bounty and tempting examples include Llansantffraed rabbit and hazelnut terrine wrapped in smoked bacon and a local goat's cheese, spinach and laverbread ravioli. The fine dining is complemented by an impressive wine cellar. Outdoors, there's plenty to do, either in the grounds or nearby, such as archery, go-karting and fishing. Weddings and conferences cater for up to 200.

**Recommended in the area**

Big Pit Blaenavon; Tintern Abbey; Black Mountains

# The Celtic Manor Resort

★★★★★ 85% ◉◉ HOTEL

**Address:** Coldra Woods, NEWPORT
NP18 1HQ NEWPORT

**Tel:** 01633 413000

**Fax:** 01633 412910

**Email:** postbox@celtic-manor.com

**Website:** www.celtic-manor.com

**Map ref:** 1, ST28

**Directions:** M4 junct 24, take B4237 towards Newport

**Rooms:** 400, S £225 D £225 **Facilities:** ⓡ Sauna
Jacuzzi Spa Tennis Gym STV Wi-fi available **Parking:** 1000 **Notes:** No pets (except guide dogs)

The Celtic Manor Resort is two hotels, one old, one new, that stand together in 1400 acres of parkland in the beautiful Usk Valley. The 19th-century Manor House was where the Resort's owner, Sir Terence Matthews, was born when it was a maternity hospital. Original character is all around – admire, for example, the leaded windows, wood-panelled walls and sweeping wooden staircase. Recently refurbished, traditionally styled bedrooms include three with four-posters. There's a choice of places to eat or drink: The Patio Restaurant, serving Italian-style dishes, the Cellar Bar and the Manor Lounge. The separate Resort Hotel was opened in 1999, with a soaring atrium and 330 individually decorated and beautifully appointed bedrooms. One of the two Presidential Suites even has a baby grand piano. Guests in both hotels may make complimentary phone calls to national landlines. Dining choices are the boldly stylish, fine-dining Owens, with awards to prove it; the informal Olive Tree offering contemporary Mediterranean cuisine; Merlins piano bar serving afternoon teas; and the Forum Café providing light refreshments. The Resort also contains a convention centre and exhibition hall, 31 function rooms, a top golf academy, two health clubs and two spas. Quite a venue for the 2010 Ryder Cup.

### Recommended in the area

Caerleon Roman Town; Tintern Abbey; Raglan Castle

# Beggars Reach Hotel

★★★ 79% HOTEL

| | |
|---|---|
| Address: | PEMBROKE, Milford Haven |
| | SA73 1PD PEMBROKESHIRE |
| Tel: | 01646 600700 |
| Fax: | 01646 600560 |
| Email: | stay@beggars-reach.com |
| Website: | www.beggars-reach.com |
| Map ref: | 1, SM90 |
| Directions: | 8m S of Haverfordwest, 6m N of Pembroke, off A477 |

**Rooms:** 30 en suite S £69.5–£89.5 D £100–£130 **Facilities:** STV Wi-fi available
**Parking:** 80 **Notes:** ⊗ in bedrooms ⊘ in restaurant

A privately owned hotel in a tranquil spot, run by experienced hoteliers, William and Gillian Smallman. "Beggars Reach is our long term future," they say, "and we intend to channel all our energies into fulfilling our dream". Formerly the village rectory, and retaining much of its Victorian character, it stands in three acres of grounds, surrounded by farmland. Comfortable, high-standard accommodation is provided in individually designed, en suite bedrooms with tea- and coffee-making facilities, phones and satellite TV; some have views over the garden and Pembrokeshire countryside. Guests can enjoy a morning coffee or pre-dinner drink in the cosy lounge before a typical meal of rack of Welsh lamb, perhaps, or pan-fried fresh marlin steak in the bright and airy Garden Restaurant, whose french windows open on to the terrace. The cuisine is traditional, with the menu written afresh daily, and food sourced largely from local suppliers. An alternative is to have a drink in Harry's Bar, followed by anything from a snack to a three-course meal in the smaller, less formal Anna's Restaurant. Wines from around the world may be enjoyed in both. Conference facilities cater for up to 80 delegates and wedding breakfasts for up to 140 guests.

**Recommended in the area**

Pembrokeshire Coast National Park; Pembroke Castle; Milford Haven Waterway

# Warpool Court Hotel

★★★ 79% ⚘⚘ COUNTRY HOUSE HOTEL

**Address:** ST DAVID'S SA62 6BN PEMBROKESHIRE
**Tel:** 01437 720300
**Fax:** 01437 720676
**Email:** info@warpoolcourthotel.com
**Website:** www.warpoolcourthotel.com
**Map ref:** 1, SM72
**Directions:** At Cross Square left by Cartref Restaurant (Goat St). Pass Farmers Arms pub, after 400mtrs left, follow hotel signs, entrance on right

**Rooms:** 25, S £95–£110 D £160–£220 **Facilities:** ⊗ Tennis **Parking:** 100 **Notes:** ⊘ in restaurant

A privately-owned hotel in large grounds on St David's peninsula, overlooking the gentle sweep of St Bride's Bay and the offshore islands. Attractively furnished bedrooms have direct-dial phone, radio, hairdryer, TV, and tea- and coffee-making facilities. The spacious restaurant, with sea views, offers an extensive menu, with fish much in evidence. A heated swimming pool opens from Easter to the end of October and there is an all-weather tennis court.

**Recommended in the area**

Pembrokeshire Coast National Park; St David's Cathedral; Pembroke Castle

# Heywood Mount Hotel & Spa Leisure Suite

★★★ 77% HOTEL

**Address:** Heywood Lane, TENBY
SA70 8DA PEMBROKESHIRE
**Tel:** 01834 842087
**Email:** reception@heywoodmount.co.uk
**Website:** www.heywoodmount.co.uk
**Map ref:** 1, SN10
**Directions:** A478 to Tenby, follow Heywood Mount signs, right into Serpentine Road, right at T-junct into Heywood Lane, 3rd hotel on left

**Rooms:** 28, S £45–£65 D £90–£170 **Facilities:** ⊗ Sauna Jacuzzi Solarium Gym **Parking:** 28 **Notes:** ⊗ in bedrooms ⊘ in restaurant

The hotel stands in an acre of grounds, close to the centre of picturesque Tenby and its beaches. All bedrooms are en suite and have been recently upgraded and modernised. First-class cuisine offers a generous choice, with locally caught seafood a speciality. The bar is a popular local watering hole.

**Recommended in the area**

Caldey Island; Pembrokeshire Coast National Park; Oakwood Adventure and Leisure Park

# Peterstone Court Hotel

★★★ 79% ◉◉ COUNTRY HOUSE HOTEL

**Address:** Llanhamlach,
BRECON LD3 7YB
POWYS
**Tel:** 01874 665387
**Fax:** 01874 665376
**Email:** info@peterstone-court.com
**Website:** www.peterstone-court.com
**Map ref:** 2, SO02
**Directions:** From Brecon take A40 towards
Abergavenny, hotel approx 4m, on right
**Rooms:** 12, S £90–£130 D £110–£170 **Facilities:** ⚐ Sauna Jacuzzi Gym **Parking:** 50
**Notes:** ⊘ in restaurant

This beautiful early Georgian manor, elegant in design, is completely at ease in its setting on the edge of the Brecon Beacons overlooking the River Usk. The style here is friendly, informal and unfussy. Eight of the bedrooms are in the main house and there are four split-level rooms in the stable block. No two are alike, but all share comparable levels of comfort and quality, with tasteful furnishings, soft linens and, naturally, comfortable beds. Public areas reflect similar standards, eclectically styled with a blend of contemporary and traditional. The restaurant, once the ballroom, added in 1901, is the heart of the Peterstone. From simple Welsh breakfasts to classic dinners, chef Lee Evans uses only the freshest of ingredients, including locally sourced quality produce that includes meat and poultry from the hotel's own organic hill farm at Glaisfer Uchaf 7 miles away. Fresh fish and seafood is delivered daily. After a day's caving, painting or cycling return to a glowing log fire, leave your boots by the front door, and settle back with a fine brandy in the library. Or you could work out in the fully equipped gym, relax in the Jacuzzi and pamper yourself with one of many available treatments on offer.

**Recommended in the area**

Llanthony Abbey; Black Mountains; Hay-on-Wye (Town of Books)

# Bear Hotel

★★★ 78% ◉◉ HOTEL

| | |
|---|---|
| **Address:** | CRICKHOWELL |
| | NP8 1BW POWYS |
| **Tel:** | 01873 810408 |
| **Fax:** | 01873 811696 |
| **Email:** | bearhotel@aol.com |
| **Website:** | www.bearhotel.co.uk |
| **Map ref:** | 2, SO21 |
| **Directions:** | On A40 between Abergavenny & Brecon |

**Rooms:** 34, S £65–£115 D £80–£150 **Parking:** 45

Travellers look forward to stopping at the Bear for all sorts of reasons, not least for its great antiquity, convivial surroundings, welcoming atmosphere, comfortable rooms and good food. A cobbled forecourt, an archway into the inner courtyard – ablaze with floral colour in summer – and a low-beamed, award-winning bar with a 19th-century stagecoach timetable are all reminders of its erstwhile role. Room types, all individually furnished with carefully chosen fabrics, begin with the perfectly adequate, if not overly large, Standards; then come more spacious Superiors, with en suite bath and/or shower; followed by the more modern de luxe rooms, situated mainly in the courtyard area, again en suite, and with a Jacuzzi; and finally there are the Executives, featuring armchairs, desks and double whirlpool baths and separate showers. The bar menu offers bistro-style meals, while the management even acknowledges that the small candlelit restaurant's regularly changing menu 'surpasses the high standard set by the bistro'. Typically on offer might be loin of local venison, fillet of beef, and tournedos of monkfish. Look at the website for details of members of staff and some of the regulars, including Pepper, a Jack Russell who magnanimously "allows other well behaved dogs into 'her' bar". Frequented by both visitors and locals alike, the Bear is a popular meeting place in the pretty little town of Crickhowell.

**Recommended in the area**

Blaenavon Big Pit; Brecon Beacons National Park; Offa's Dyke Path

The canal and towpath, Llangattock.

# Gliffaes Country House Hotel

★★★  80% ❀ HOTEL

| | |
|---|---|
| Address: | CRICKHOWELL NP8 1RH POWYS |
| Tel: | 01874 730371 |
| Fax: | 01874 730463 |
| Email: | calls@gliffaeshotel.com |
| Website: | www.gliffaeshotel.com |
| Map ref: | 2, SO21 |

Directions: 1m off A40, 2.5m W of Crickhowell

Rooms: 22, S £75–£0 D £85–£200 Facilities: Tennis Wi-fi available Parking: 34 Notes: ⊗ in bedrooms ⊗ in restaurant

Off the beaten track between the Brecon Beacons and the Black Mountains, hidden among trees in 33 acres, and owned by the same family since 1948. The Gliffaes has a great view of the Usk, and actually owns 2.5 miles of this prime wild brown trout river. Elegant public rooms include a balcony and conservatory. The 23 individually decorated and furnished bedrooms, priced according to size and view, all have private bathrooms. The restaurant uses local produce and the freshest of ingredients.

**Recommended in the area**

Brecon Beacons National Park; The Big Pit; Tretower Court

# Lake Country House Hotel & Spa

★★★ ◎◎  COUNTRY HOUSE HOTEL

**Address:** LLANGAMMARCH WELLS LD4 4BS POWYS
**Tel:** 01591 620202
**Fax:** 01591 620457
**Email:** info@lakecountryhouse.co.uk
**Website:** www.lakecountryhouse.co.uk
**Map ref:** 2, SN94
**Directions:** W from Builth Wells on A483 to Garth (approx 6m). Left for Llangammarch Wells, follow hotel signs
**Rooms:** 30, S £110–£175 D £160–£240
**Facilities:** ⓢ Tennis STV Conferencing for up to 40 **Parking:** 70 **Notes:** ⊘ in restaurant

Standing serenely in 50 acres of parkland, with sweeping lawns, rhododendron-lined pathways and riverside walks, this magnificent former hunting and fishing lodge is grandeur epitomised. Begun in 1840 and remodelled 60 years later, the house is an architectural confusion, with half-timbering declaring mock-Tudor, but with the verandahs and french windows giving it a colonial air. From the turn of the 20th century until World War II it was the only barium spa resort outside Germany. Everywhere you look are beautiful paintings, fascinating features and fine furnishings. Bedrooms, some in an annexe, are individually styled and provide many extra comforts. Dining in the spacious and elegant restaurant is an experience to savour, with fresh local ingredients creatively combined to create an award-winning, modern Celtic style of cuisine. The owners are justifiably proud of their 350-bin wine list, one of the finest in Wales. A newly developed spa has an indoor pool, ground floor treatment rooms and a hot tub on the balcony overlooking the shoreline of the lake. Guests can fish the lake and river free of charge (angling tuition can be arranged) and use the 9-hole, par 3 golf course and tennis courts.

**Recommended in the area**

Dolaucothi Gold Mines; Brecon Beacons National Park; Black Mountains

# Llangoed Hall

★★★★  86% ◉◉  HOTEL

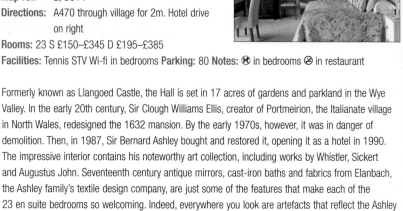

| | |
|---|---|
| **Address:** | LLYSWEN, Nr Brecon LD3 0YP POWYS |
| **Tel:** | 01874 754525 |
| **Fax:** | 01874 754545 |
| **Email:** | enquiries@llangoedhall.com |
| **Website:** | www.llangoedhall.com |
| **Map ref:** | 2, SO14 |
| **Directions:** | A470 through village for 2m. Hotel drive on right |

**Rooms:** 23 S £150–£345 D £195–£385
**Facilities:** Tennis STV Wi-fi in bedrooms **Parking:** 80 **Notes:** ⊗ in bedrooms ⊘ in restaurant

Formerly known as Llangoed Castle, the Hall is set in 17 acres of gardens and parkland in the Wye Valley. In the early 20th century, Sir Clough Williams Ellis, creator of Portmeirion, the Italianate village in North Wales, redesigned the 1632 mansion. By the early 1970s, however, it was in danger of demolition. Then, in 1987, Sir Bernard Ashley bought and restored it, opening it as a hotel in 1990. The impressive interior contains his noteworthy art collection, including works by Whistler, Sickert and Augustus John. Seventeenth century antique mirrors, cast-iron baths and fabrics from Elanbach, the Ashley family's textile design company, are just some of the features that make each of the 23 en suite bedrooms so welcoming. Indeed, everywhere you look are artefacts that reflect the Ashley family's interests, from Sir Bernard's models of boats and aircraft to Regine Ashley's rare wine labels. Head Chef, Sean Ballington, winner of two AA rosettes, is a firm believer in fresh, local produce. From Welsh lamb, and Black beef to local salmon, his signature dishes are best described as classic with a twist. Regine, an acknowledged oenophile, chooses the wines. Llangoed Hall makes a stimulating setting for conferences and board meetings.

**Recommended in the area**

Elan Valley Dam and Reservoir; Brecon Beacons; Black Mountains

# Fairyhill

★★★ ◉◉ COUNTRY HOUSE HOTEL

| | |
|---|---|
| **Address:** | REYNOLDSTON, Swansea |
| | SA3 1BS SWANSEA |
| **Tel:** | 01792 390139 |
| **Fax:** | 01792 391358 |
| **Email:** | postbox@fairyhill.net |
| **Website:** | www.fairyhill.net |
| **Map ref:** | 2, SS48 |

**Directions:** Just outside Reynoldston off A4118
**Rooms:** 8, S £145–£250 D £165–£275 **Facilities:** Wi-fi
available **Parking:** 50 **Notes:** ⊗ in bedrooms ⊘ in restaurant

A distinctive, creeper-covered 18th-century house in 24 acres of mature woodland, with a trout stream and lake. A relaxed, casual air runs through the public areas, including the warming bar and splendid lounge. Lighting and furnishings in the bedrooms were thoughtfully designed and all rooms have a modern, private bathroom, TV, and CD player. Restaurant menus make good use of local fish and shellfish, beef, lamb and cheeses. The boldly designed bar and brasserie serves tasty food all day.

**Recommended in the area**

Worms Head (NT); National Botanic Garden of Wales; National Waterfront Museum, Swansea

# The Grand Hotel

★★★★ 76% ◉◉ HOTEL

| | |
|---|---|
| **Address:** | Ivey Place, High Street, |
| | SWANSEA SA1 1NE SWANSEA |
| **Tel:** | 01792 645898 |
| **Email:** | info@thegrandhotelswansea.co.uk |
| **Website:** | www.thegrandhotelswansea.co.uk |
| **Map ref:** | 2, SS69 |

**Directions:** M4 junct 42, follow rail station signs
**Rooms:** 31, S £95–£250 D £95–£250 **Facilities:** Sauna
Jacuzzi Solarium Gym STV **Notes:** ⊗ in bedrooms ⊘ in
restaurant

Located in the city centre, close to the railway station, the Grand Hotel has been renovated and restored to its original elegance. Its rooms and public areas are air-conditioned and decorated in modern styles. Bedrooms have full en suite facilities and are equipped with TVs, DVD players and power showers. The highest grades of rooms, the Executive and Penthouse rooms have balconies and Jacuzzis. Beeches Restaurant provides fine dining, while the bistro offers more informal meals.

**Recommended in the area**

The Mumbles; The National Waterfront Museum; The Dylan Thomas Centre

Barry harbour.

# Vale Hotel Golf & Spa Resort

★★★★ 79% HOTEL

| | |
|---|---|
| **Address:** | Hensol Park, HENSOL, Cardiff CF72 8JY |
| | VALE OF GLAMORGAN |
| **Tel:** | 01443 667800 |
| **Fax:** | 01443 665850 |
| **Email:** | reservations@vale-hotel.com |
| **Website:** | www.vale-hotel.com |
| **Map ref:** | 2, ST07 |
| **Directions:** | M4 junct 34 towards Pendoylan, hotel |

signed approx 3 mins' drive from junct

**Rooms:** 143, S £80–£350 D £90–£370 **Facilities:** ⊗ Sauna Jacuzzi Solarium Tennis Gym STV Wi-fi in bedrooms **Parking:** 300 **Notes:** ⊗ in bedrooms ⊗ in restaurant

This large resort stands in over 600 acres of parkland. Its rooms are furnished in modern style, and have all the expected modern facilities. The Lakes Restaurant offers breakfast and dinner – the menus are based on Welsh and international cuisine, while Mediterranean-style cooking is on offer in La Cucin. There are two championship-standard golf courses. a driving range and a gym.

## Recommended in the area

Cardiff; Museum of Welsh Life, St Fagan's; Rhondda Heritage Park

# West Arms Hotel

★ ★ ★  83% ◉◉  HOTEL

**Address:**    LLANARMON DYFFRYN CEIRIOG, Ceiriog
Valley Nr Llangollen LL20 7LD WREXHAM
**Tel:**    01691 600665
**Fax:**    01691 600622
**Email:**    gowestarms@aol.com
**Website:**    www.thewestarms.co.uk
**Map ref:**    5, SJ13
**Directions:**  Off A483/A5 at Chirk, take B4500 to
Ceiriog Valley. Llanarmon 11m at end of B4500)
**Rooms:** 15 **Parking:** 20 **Notes:** ⊗ in restaurant

In the beautiful Ceiriog Valley, this delightful old drovers' inn oozes warmth and character, with 17th-century timberwork, period furniture, undulating floors and blazing inglenook fires. Centuries ago, cattle drovers down from the hills rested and refreshed their cattle here on their slow journeys to Oswestry and Wrexham markets. Today, a comfortable lounge, a room for private dining and two bars, as well as an award-winning restaurant, await travellers. The hotel has seven 'character' bedrooms, plus a further eight, all with bath and hand shower facilities. Furnished in a mix of modern and period styles, many still feature their original exposed beams. The Howard Room has a four-poster bed, and overlooks the village. In the restaurant, chef Grant Williams has won many accolades for his set-price menus of freshly cooked dishes for which he makes extensive use of local produce. He has worked here for 14 years after travelling the kitchens of the world, and has even cooked for HRH Prince Charles. Lunch and dinner can also be taken round the log fire in the cosy bar. The hotel will arrange a range of activities for guests such as pony-trekking, quad-biking and even white water rafting. Alternatively, there are always the riverside gardens in which to wander and relax.

**Recommended in the area**

Chirk Castle; Llangollen Viaduct; Erddig Hall (NT)

Llangollen Station and the River Dee.

# MAPS

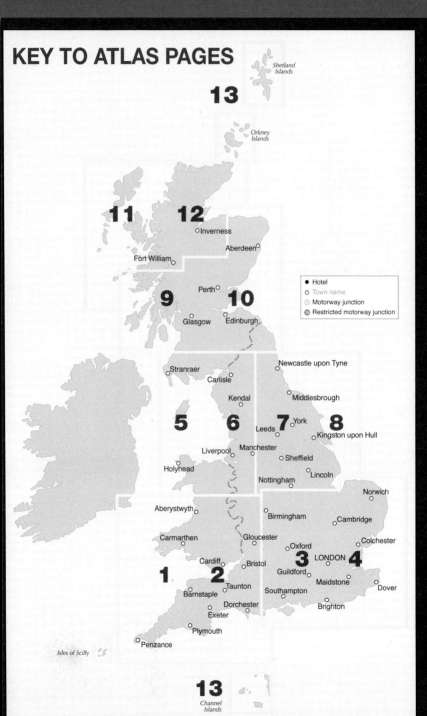

**KEY TO ATLAS PAGES**

Shetland Islands

**13**

Orkney Islands

**11**    **12**

○Inverness

Aberdeen○

Fort William○

| | |
|---|---|
| ● | Hotel |
| ○ | Town name |
| ⊕ | Motorway junction |
| ⊛ | Restricted motorway junction |

**9**    Perth○    **10**

Glasgow○    Edinburgh○

Stranraer○    Newcastle upon Tyne○

Carlisle○

Kendal○    Middlesbrough○

**5**    **6**    **7**    York○    **8**

Leeds○

Liverpool○    Manchester○    Kingston upon Hull○

Sheffield○

Holyhead○    Lincoln○

Nottingham○

Norwich○

Aberystwyth○    Birmingham○    Cambridge○

Carmarthen○    Gloucester○    Colchester○

Cardiff○    Oxford○    **3**    LONDON    **4**

**1**    **2**    Bristol○    Guildford○    Maidstone○

Barnstaple○    Taunton○    Southampton○    Dover○

Dorchester○    Brighton○

Exeter○

Plymouth○

Penzance○

*Isles of Scilly*

**13**

*Channel Islands*

© Automobile Association Developments Limited 2007

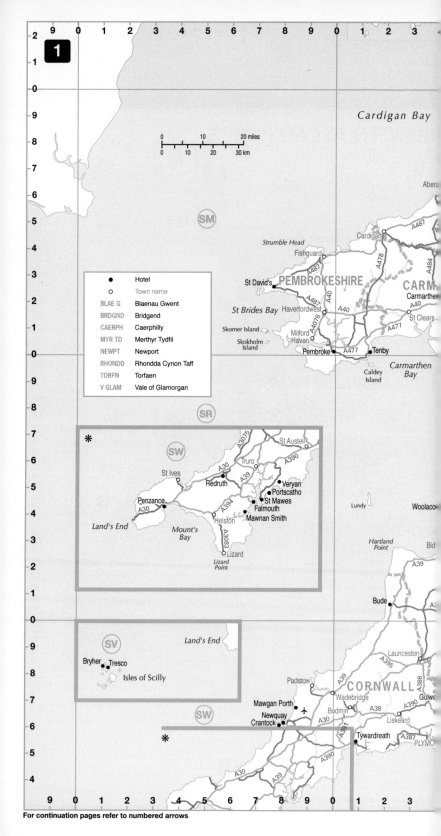

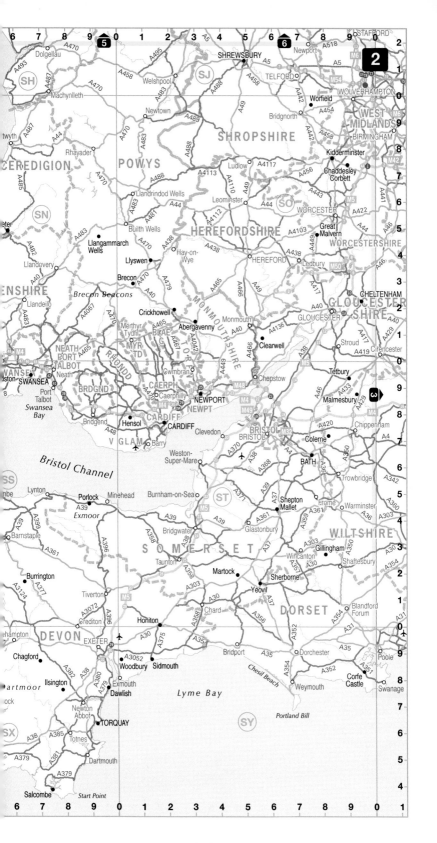

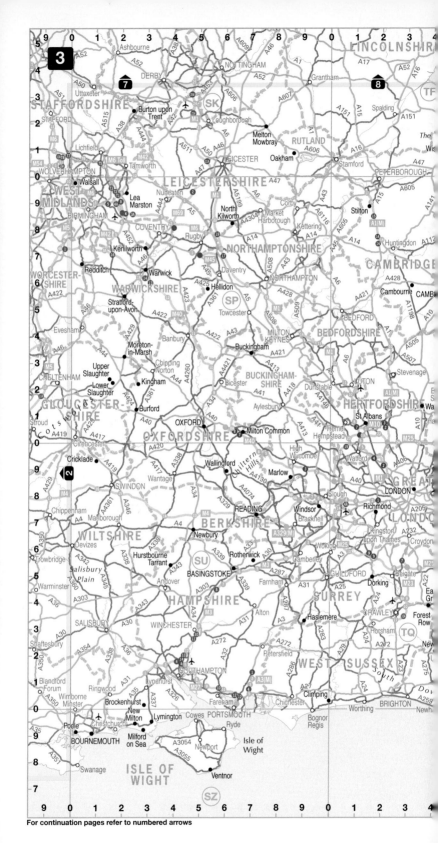

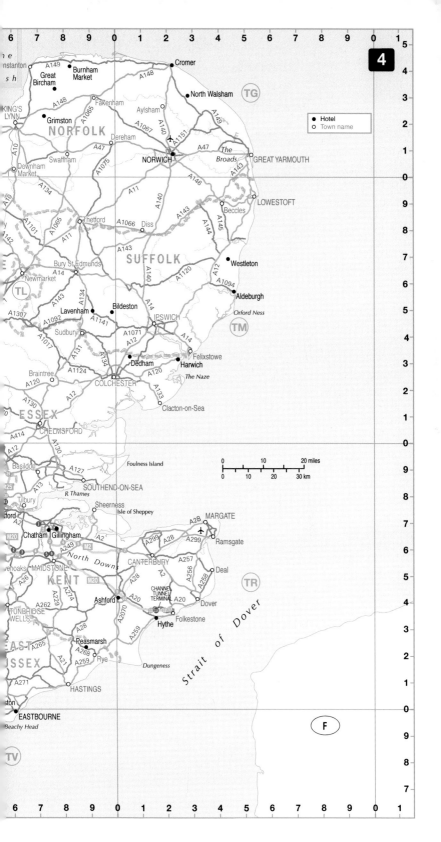

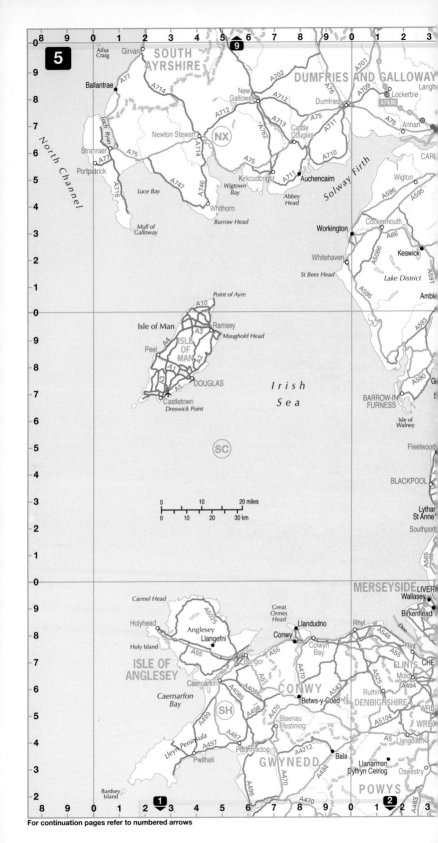

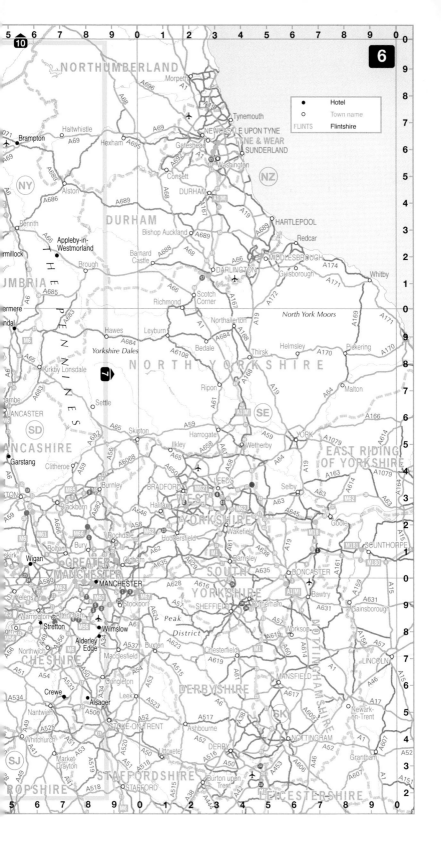

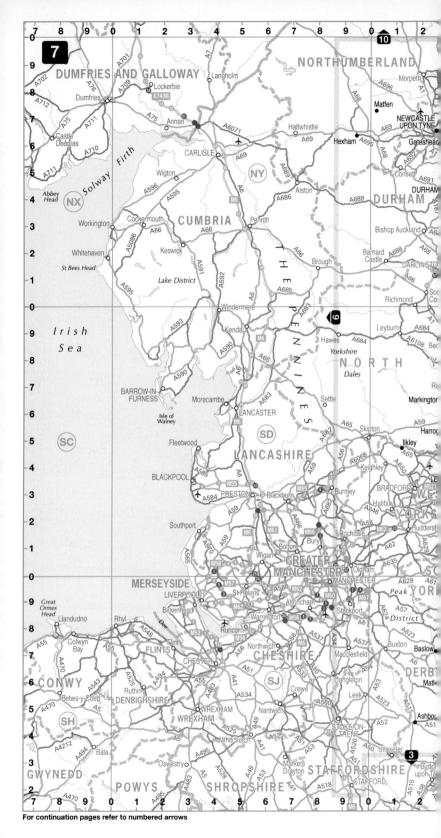

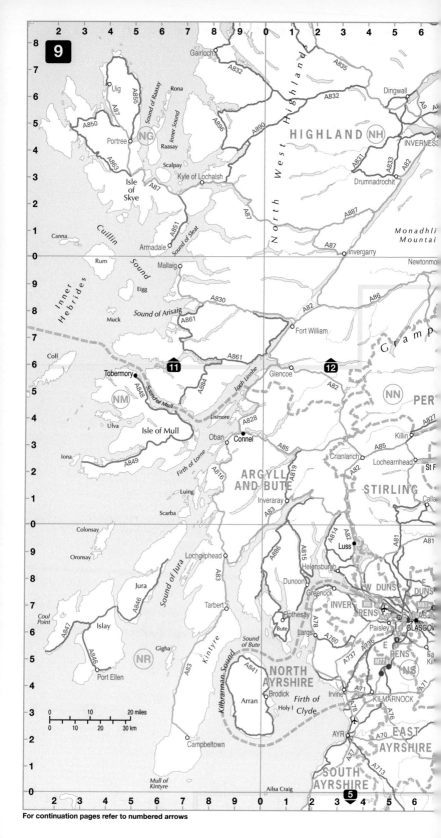

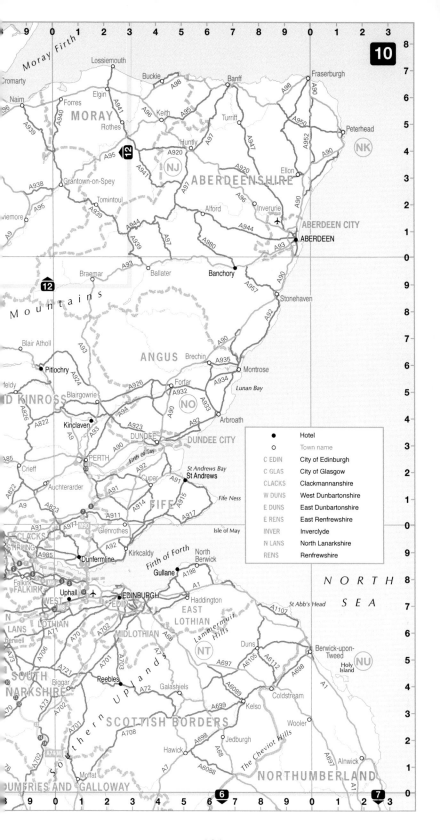

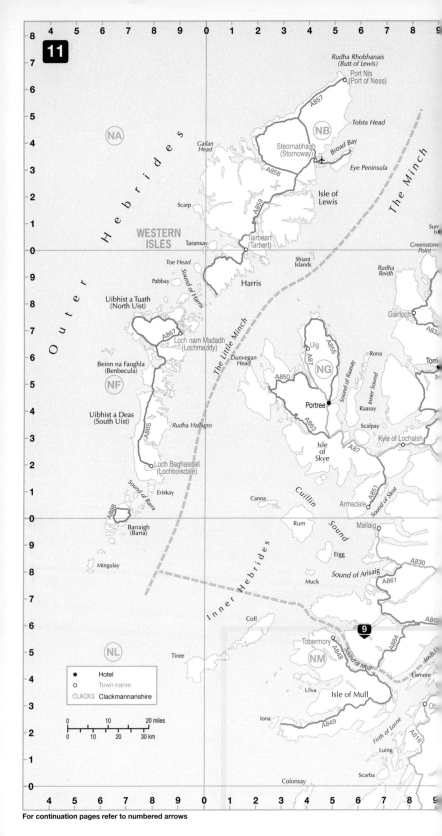

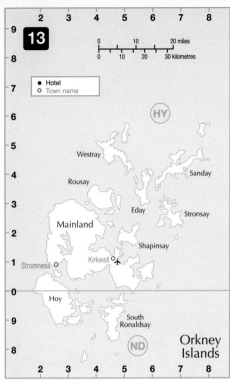

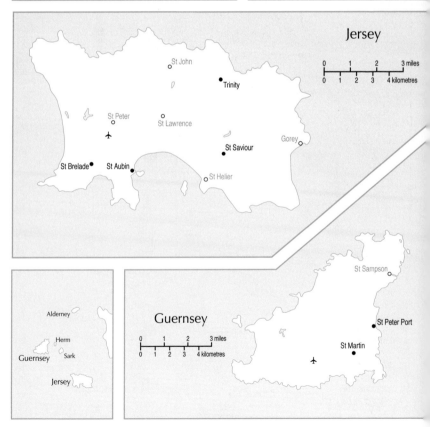

# County Map

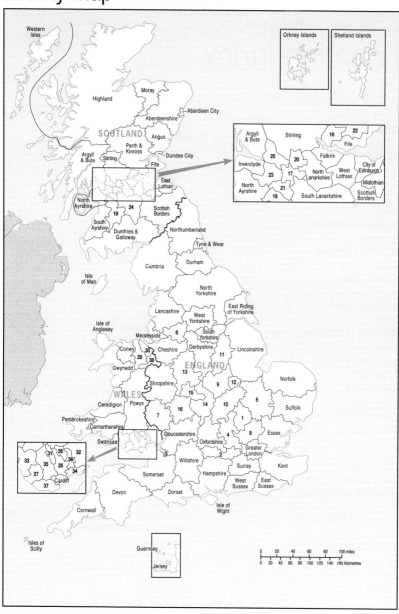

**England**

1 Bedfordshire
2 Berkshire
3 Bristol
4 Buckinghamshire
5 Cambridgeshire
6 Greater Manchester
7 Herefordshire
8 Hertfordshire
9 Leicestershire
10 Northamptonshire
11 Nottinghamshire
12 Rutland
13 Staffordshire
14 Warwickshire
15 West Midlands
16 Worcestershire

**Scotland**

17 City of Glasgow
18 Clackmannanshire
19 East Ayrshire
20 East Dunbartonshire
21 East Renfrewshire
22 Perth & Kinross
23 Renfrewshire
24 South Lanarkshire
25 West Dunbartonshire

**Wales**

26 Blaenau Gwent
27 Bridgend
28 Caerphilly
29 Denbighshire
30 Flintshire
31 Merthyr Tydfil
32 Monmouthshire
33 Neath Port Talbot
34 Newport
35 Rhondda Cynon Taff
36 Torfaen
37 Vale of Glamorgan
38 Wrexham

# Location Index

# Location Index

# Location Index

# Location Index

# Location Index

# Hotel Index

# Hotel Index

# Hotel Index

## Picture credits

# Notes